Software
Measurement
Guidebook

INTERNATIONAL THOMSON COMPUTER PRESS
I(T)P™ An International Thomson Publishing Company

London • Bonn • Boston • Johannesburg• Madrid • Melbourne • Mexico City • New York • Paris
Singapore • Tokyo • Toronto • Albany, NY • Belmont, CA • Cincinnati, OH • Detroit, MI

COPYRIGHT © 1995 International Thomson Computer Press

I(T)P· A division of International Thomson Publishing Inc.
The ITP logo is a trademark under license.

Printed in the United States of America
For more information, contact:

International Thomson Computer Press
20 Park Place, Suite 1001
Boston, MA 02116
USA

International Thomson Publishing Europe
Berkshire House 168-173
High Holborn
London, WC1V 7AA
England

Thomas Nelson Australia
102 Dodds Street
South Melbourne, 3205
Victoria, Australia

Nelson Canada
1120 Birchmont Road
Scarborough, Ontario
Canada, M1K 5G4

International Thomson Publishing France
1, rue st. Georges
75 009 Paris
France

International Thomson Publishing
Königswinterer Strasse 418
53227 Bonn
Germany

International Thomson Publishing Asia
221 Henderson Road #05-10
Henderson Building
Singapore 0315

International Publishing Japan
Hirakawacho Kyowa Building, 3F
2-2-1 Hirakawacho
Chiyoda-ku, 102 Tokyo
Japan

International Thomson Editores
Campos Eliseos 385, Piso 7
Col. Polanco
11560 Mexico D. F. Mexico

International Thomson Publishing
Southern Africa
Building 19, Constantia Park
239 Old Pretoria Road, P.O. Box 2459
Halfway House, 1685 South Africa

1 2 3 4 5 6 7 8 9 10   QEBFF 01 00 99 98 97 96 95

Library of Congress Cataloging-in-Publication Data (available upon request)

ISBN 1 850-32195 7

CONTENTS

ACKNOWLEDGMENTS

The authors of this guidebook are John Gaffney, Robert Cruickshank, Richard Werling, and Henry Felber. The Consortium wishes to thank Jerry Decker, James Marple, and Samuel Redwine for their helpful criticisms and suggestions in reviewing this material. George Bozoki, Paul Garnett, and Andy Rabinowitz of the Consortium member companies also provided insightful comments.

Thanks also go to the many member company personnel who attended the Software Measurement Course and whose comments contributed so much to this version of the guidebook.

The authors also wish to recognize Environment and Support Services for their many production services in making this guidebook happen.

1

INTRODUCTION

1.1 SCOPE

The *Software Measurement Guidebook* provides practical guidance for the measurement-driven management of software development and maintenance projects; it applies to software intended for both government and nongovernment users. Guidance is provided about the collection and validation of process and product metrics data and in the use of quantitative information to support project control and process improvement. This guidebook describes how to select quantifiable goals for a software project and metrics to support those goals. It presents practical methods for estimating software size, development and support cost, and development schedule. Also presented are measures of software quality and models for estimating and predicting software defects. The book describes an approach to software statistical quality control, a part of statistical process control. It also provides tracking and monitoring methods and the evaluation of project status. In addition, a description is provided of the impact of code reuse on software cost, schedule, and quality.

This guidebook describes the Software Engineering Institute (SEI) process maturity model and the role of software metrics in raising the maturity level of a software organization. It relates metrics to various levels of maturity. It also describes ways in which a measurement functional capability can be structured to support the operation of a software organization.

1.1.1 Guidebook Objectives

This guidebook is designed to:

- Present methods for the measurement-driven management of software development projects, including establishing goals for software process and product estimation, and tracking.

- Provide practical methods for the establishment, organization, and operation (including costs) of a software measurement program.

- Present methods for selecting metrics to support project goals. It defines practical metrics and describes how you can obtain and apply them during the software development cycle.

- Provide measurement models for estimating software development cost and schedule and software product size.

- Provide metrics and models to estimate the cost impact of software reuse on product cost, schedule, and quality.

- Provide techniques for estimating software development cost and schedule, software product size, and software quality.

- Show how to track and monitor software projects using metrics.

- Include lessons learned from experience.

1.2 AUDIENCE AND BENEFITS

The guidebook addresses the measurement needs of software managers and engineers, measurement analysts, finance personnel, program managers, and others involved in implementing and/or improving the software process. The others include systems and software line managers, project managers, business area managers, proposal managers, and senior financial analysts. This guidebook is useful to a broad spectrum of software development personnel, particularly those concerned with improving the predictability, control, and performance of the software process employed and the software it produces. The guidebook also explains what points in the software process are to be measured, the metrics that should be tracked for process and product control, and the relationship of the measures to management decisions that you need to make based on them. It will aid you in estimating the impact of software reuse and in gauging the viability of reuse in varied development environments.

The guidebook is designed to help those associated with software development to improve their control and improve the capability maturity level of their organization's software process by applying measurement-driven software management (MDSM) techniques. The guidebook was created to support the very important goals of helping software organizations attain the benefits of higher quality software at a lower net cost and of helping them to improve their software process and the software products generated. An aspect of both of these goals is to provide metrics models to estimate the cost, schedule, and quality impacts and benefits of software reuse. The guidebook presents methods for tracking and monitoring the software process and the software products it generates. These methods are consistent with the principles of the SEI capability maturity model (CMM) of software management. An important benefit of the measurement methodology presented here is that it is designed to aid a software organization in attaining higher SEI capability maturity levels and in producing higher quality and more usable software products.

The audience for this guidebook includes the following categories of people:

- *Senior Manager.* Area manager, division or corporate vice president, or equivalent responsible for improving the software development process and capable of authorizing a measurement program across all software projects. His responsibility includes authorizing both direct costs and the indirect (overhead) expense of the measurement program.

- *Hardware/Software System Manager.* The person responsible for managing a project containing both hardware and software.

- *Software Project Manager.* The person responsible for managing a software-based project.

- *Lead Software Engineer.* A technical supervisor responsible for developing or supporting a software-based system. He supervises the use of prescribed processes, methods, and standards to perform technical activities.

- *Software Engineer.* A person who works on developing or supporting a software-based system.

- *Cost Engineer, Measurement Analyst, or System Analyst.* A technical staff member responsible for collecting project cost and schedule status data and for analyzing this data.

- *Software Quality Engineer.* A technical staff member responsible for collecting data from reviews and inspections of requirements, design, code, and test and for analyzing this data.

- *Proposal Manager.* The person responsible for describing and supporting the estimated size, cost, schedule, and quality of a software product.

- *Financial Manager.* A person responsible for developing prices for software systems, consistency in tracking and monitoring procedures for software projects, the cost of software products, and comparing them to planned and budgeted figures.

- *Financial Analyst.* A person who works on financial matters such as tracking and monitoring the cost of software products.

1.3 GUIDEBOOK ORGANIZATION

The guidebook is composed of 13 chapters. They are:

- Chapter 1, "Introduction," describes the guidebook's objectives, benefits, and intended audience. This chapter includes a quick reference estimation guide listing various functions (such as size estimation) and related formulas and points to guidebook chapters having more detail.

- Chapter 2, "Measurement-Driven Software Management," relates software metrics to software management for project control and process improvement. It describes the MDSM model of the software management process, which includes setting goals, measuring the process and product, and taking action (as appropriate) based on those measurements. This model provides a closed loop control framework for project control and process improvement.

- Chapter 3, "Measurement and the Software Engineering Institute (SEI) Process Maturity Level Structure," describes the SEI process maturity/capability maturity level structure. It indicates the measurement requirements associated with achieving higher maturity levels. This chapter illustrates the central position of measurement in attaining higher capability maturity levels. It describes the measurement technology you must use as part of the software process to attain SEI process maturity Levels 2 through 5. This chapter defines the activities included in a software measurement function and relates them to the process maturity levels and describes alternative organizational strategies to implement the measurement function.

- Chapter 4, "How to Describe a Software Process," describes the entry-task-verification-exit (ETVX) paradigm for describing software process activities and related measurement requirement tasks.

- Chapter 5, "Setting Quantifiable Requirements and Goals and Managing to Them," shows how to establish quantifiable software process and product requirements and monitor the degree of their realization throughout the development process. It indicates the role of incremental verification during the development process in realizing process and product requirements.

- Chapter 6, "Mathematical Modeling and Metrics Selection," describes the nature (including limitations) of mathematical models as used in software metrics work. It describes the GQM paradigm and how to use it to select metrics for project control and for process improvement. This chapter presents a minimum set of metrics useful for project control and process improvement.

- Chapter 7, "How to Estimate Software System Size," shows various ways to estimate software size that can be applied throughout the development process.

- Chapter 8, "How to Estimate Software Cost," describes holistic and activity-based models for development cost estimation. It describes the effect of reuse on the cost of a software product and presents methods for estimating cost.

- Chapter 9, "How to Estimate Schedule," describes methods to estimate the software development schedule. It indicates the effect of reuse on product development schedules and describes how to do a schedule/development effort trade-off. It also describes how to determine if an estimated schedule, an estimated development effort, and an estimated product size are compatible.

- Chapter 10, "Software Quality Measurement," provides indicators of software quality including defect-based measures and others, such as "availability." This chapter relates quality considerations to the establishment of quantifiable requirements. It also shows the effect of software reuse on the (defect-related) quality of a software product and relates software defect estimates to software availability. This chapter describes an approach to statistical quality control involving the establishment and monitoring of software quality objectives during development.

- Chapter 11, "Management Indicators for Tracking and Monitoring," shows how to select management indicators (metrics) and how to use management indicators to track and monitor software development projects. It describes how to compute a measure of earned value (overall status) of a software development project, and it describes its relation to the estimated cost of completing a project.

- Chapter 12, "Experience Databases and Data Collection," shows how to collect, organize, validate, and archive software metrics data. It describes alternative work breakdown structures (WBSs) for collecting and analyzing cost metrics data. This chapter describes how to collect data for the purposes of product and process improvement and how to collect data to track and monitor software development to anticipate possible problems. Practical methods of validating data are given.

- Chapter 13, "Integrated Example," provides an integrated example of size, cost, schedule, and cost and schedule risk estimation for a software development project.

1.4 BENEFITS AND FEATURES OF THIS GUIDEBOOK

Feature	Benefit	Chapter
Quick reference guide	Provides a summary of important estimation formulas and measurement functions and points to chapter of book covering area	Chapter 1
Measurement-driven management approach	Shows role of metrics in software management. Provides a "closed loop" model of the process	Chapter 2
Measurement related to SEI process maturity levels structure	Illustrates the central role of measurement in attaining higher maturity levels	Chapter 3
The ETVX (Entry-Task-Verification-eXit) paradigm for describing a software process	Relates activities of a process and supportive measures	Chapter 4
Quantification of requirements and how to manage to them	Shows how to make verifiable requirements	Chapter 5
The GQM (Goal-Question-Metric) paradigm and mathematical models as used in metrics work	Shows how to select metrics to satisfy stated information needs	Chapter 6
Software size estimation methods	Shows how to estimate the size of a software unit	Chapter 7
Cost, reuse cost impact, and cost risk estimation methods	Shows how to estimate the effort and cost of, and the cost risk of developing a software unit; shows cost effect of reuse	Chapter 8
Schedule estimation	Shows how to estimate the amount of time required to develop a software unit	Chapter 9
Measurement of software quality	Presents methods for establishing software quality goals and measurement techniques	Chapter 10
Indicators for monitoring a software project	Shows how to monitor and track a software project	Chapter 11
The nature of software data collection and databases	Shows how to collect software data and how to construct a software database	Chapter 12
An integrated estimation example	Presents an integrated example of size, cost, schedule, and cost and schedule risk estimation. Helps to integrate material from various chapters of the book	Chapter 13

Table 1-1. *Guidebook Benefits and Features*

1.5 HOW TO USE THIS GUIDEBOOK

Your use of this guidebook will depend, to a large extent, on your specific interests in software metrics and their applications. It is not necessary to read this guidebook linearly, i.e., in the ascending order of chapters.

You can select chapters and read them for your specific interest at a specific time and then read the other chapters at a future time. Table 1-2 guides your reading relative to your interests.

You may find references to other texts useful when gaining an understanding of this material; relevant references are identified. You should be prepared to invest time in the study of the methods given in this book and in learning how to apply them.

1.6 QUICK REFERENCE ESTIMATION GUIDE

Table 1-3 is a quick reference estimation guide. It summarizes how to estimate certain key items such as development effort. It is designed to help guide you to chapters that show you how to estimate commonly used parameters such as the software size and development effort.

Interest-Specific View	Section
Measurement overview	1,2,3.7,12
Organizing for measurement	3.7,12
Deriving measurable requirements and determining their degree of attainment	5,10
Metrics selection for project control and process improvement	2,3,4,6
Metrics and database establishment	6,12
Quality metrics	10
Process maturity and metrics	3
Estimation of size, cost, and schedule	7,8,9
Monitoring a project	11
Reuse impacts	8.4,8.6,9.3,10.7
Statistical process control	2,10.8
Risk management	8.4,8.10

Table 1-2. *Interest-Specific Views of this Guidebook*

Estimate Of	Point in Process	Input Required	Formula	Output	Section
Software system size	Project initial stages	C_1 = Number of CSCIs	$S = 41.6C_1$	KSLOC	7.3
CSCI size	Project initial stages	C_2 = Number of CSCs	$S = 4.16C_2$	KSLOC	7.3
Software size	Project initial stages	A = Sum of 3 externals E = Sum of 4 externals + interfaces	$S = 13.94 + 0.034A$ $S = 12.28 + 0.030E$	KSLOC/ KSLOC	7.6
Development effort, COCOMO	Any (when size is known or estimated)	1,000 delivered source instructions (KDSI)	$LM = a(KDSI)^b$ for organic, semidetached, or embedded modes	LM	8.3.1
Schedule, COCOMO	Any	LM=labor months TDEV=development time in months	$TDEV = c(LM)^d$ for organic, semidetached, or embedded modes	months	8.3.1
Size, effort, or development time, given any two (devel. cycle model)	Any (when size is known or estimated)	C, technology constant S, size in SLOC K, effort, labor years t_d, development time in years	$S = CK^p t_d{}^q$	SLOC and/or labor years and/or years	8.3.2
Development effort, COPMO	Any (when size is known or estimated)	S=1,000 lines of source code (KSLOC) L=Ave. level in LM/month	$E = a + bS + cL^d$ for COPMO model	LM	8.3.3
Unit cost, development effort (activity-based)	Any (when size is known or estimated)	L/K; unit cost in LM/KSLOC for each activity, KSLOC	Total Cost = $\Sigma(L/K)_i \cdot$ KSLOC	LM	8.4
Reuse cost impacts	Any	Unit costs and sizes of new and reused code and domain (eng.) library	$Cs = CDEST/N + CVNSN + CVRSR$	LM	8.6
Document pages	Any	KSLOC estimate	$P = a(KSLOC) - b(KSLOC)^2$	pages	8.7
Documentation effort	Any	KP=thousand pages	$LM = uP/100$, $LH = vP/1000$	LM (or LH)	8.7
Top-down estimation of total project costs	Preproposal or proposal stages	Software development total unit costs in LM/KSLOC and size in KSLOC	Percent breakdown	LM	8.8
Costs of support to software development	Software development planning	Estimated software development costs	Cost for support in each area=$a_i \cdot$ (software development cost)	LM	8.9

Table 1-3. *Quick Reference Estimate Guide*

Estimate Of	Point in Process	Input Required	Formula	Output	Section
Risk estimate of cost	Any	Knowledge of distribution of size and cost estimates	Point and interval estimates of risk	Probability and LM	8.10
Software maintenance	Any	Size in KSLOC	Cost=(defects/KSLOC) x S KSLOC S (LM/defect)	LM	8.11
Schedule impact of reuse	Any	New & reused code unit costs, proportion of reuse	$t_{dr}/t_{dn} = P^{(1-p)/q}$ $P = C_{VR}/(C_{VN}(1-R) + C_{VR}(R))$	Relative schedule reduction	9.3
Schedule/effort trade-off	Any	K_0, estimated effort t_0, estimated schedule K_1, new estimated effort t_1, new estimated schedule		Labor years	9.4

Table 1-3. *Quick Reference Estimate Guide, continued*

1.7 SUMMARY OF RECOMMENDATIONS

You should adapt and implement, as appropriate, methods presented for predicting and monitoring your software process and the software products it generates. As shown in Table 1-4, the methods are consistent with the principles of the SEI process maturity concept. Implementing the methodology will aid you in achieving higher SEI process maturity levels allowing you to produce higher quality, more usable software products and simultaneously improving your software development process.

The primary benefit of having a sound measurement program is to increase the degree of predictability and control of software process and products. "Management by measurement" benefits both project control and process improvement by:

- Providing more and better information.

- Enabling management to make better decisions.

Level 2, Repeatable Process	Level 3, Defined	Levels 4 and 5
Estimate, plan, and measure: software size, resource usage, staffing levels, schedules, cost of development, and risk.	Level 2 data, plus:	Levels 2 and 3 data, plus:
Maintain profiles over time of actual versus plan for: software size; units designed, build/release content, units completing test, units integrated, and test progress; computer resource utilization; requirements status; and staffing.	Maintain formal records for progress of unit development.	Set quantitative quality goals and manage according to quality plan.
Maintain profiles over time of use of target system memory, throughput, and I/O channels.	In addition to Level 2 profiles, maintain profiles over time of ranges, variances, and comparisons with historical data.	In addition to Level 3 profiles, maintain control limit charts on size growth; costs; completions; and characteristics of peer reviews.
Collect statistics on trouble reports, on design errors, and on software code and test errors found in reviews and inspections.	Develop software measurement standards, and experience-based metrics for estimating size, cost, and schedule.	Collect process and product data, and analyze according to documented procedures, in systematic efforts to prevent defects, assess beneficial process innovations, and manage process change.
	Measurements of errors found and costs incurred by process activity. Pareto analysis of defects, and preliminary control charts.	Maintain managed and controlled process database for process metrics across all projects.
	Coordinate software process asset metrics database at organization level.	Maintain profiles over time for: ratios of rework time and cost of project totals; actual versus planned costs and benefits of process improvement and defect prevention activities.

Table 1-4. *Measurement-Related Activities by Process Maturity Level*

Chapter
2

MEASUREMENT-DRIVEN SOFTWARE MANAGEMENT

2.1 OVERVIEW

This chapter shows how you can integrate measurement with the software management process. The underlying concept is that effective management requires effective measurement. This chapter presents a model of the MDSM process as a closed loop feedback control system. It shows how project measurement data is generated and used in the software process. The MDSM process is also presented as a time-ordered sequence of the process activities and their descriptions.

2.2 MEASUREMENT-DRIVEN SOFTWARE MANAGEMENT

This chapter is concerned with the management of the software development process, not the structure of any particular process. Measurement that is required for effective management and improvement of the process is described.

2.2.1 What Is Measurement-Driven Software Management?

The MDSM process is a framework for software management that integrates the concepts of software measurement, management, process improvement, and statistical process and quality control. The main theme of MDSM is to drive the development process output toward quantified goals and to incrementally assess the degree to which these goals are likely to be attained.

Managing the size, cost, schedule, and quality of product development requires comprehensive measurement to provide the visibility needed for making both project and process management decisions. The following sections describe how measurement data originates and how it is collected and presented. To understand the MDSM process, you need to understand the terms *project control* and *process and product improvement.*

2.2.2 Project Control

Project control is the planned periodic assessment of the degree of realization of the software development project's preestablished goals. It includes taking the appropriate corrective action to mitigate the effects of anticipated or current problems indicated by the assessment. MDSM can help your organization achieve project control and process improvement. Guidelines for the identification of quantified goals and their resulting metrics are found in Chapters 5 and 6 of this guidebook.

2.2.3 Process and Product Improvement

Software process improvement is achieved through changes to the software creation and support process that result in improved products that exhibit higher quality and the same or lower cost than those created using the earlier process. Higher quality is associated with lower defect levels and higher functional content relative to cost. "Cost" relates to the consumption of all relevant resources, including labor, money, and time. The ultimate goal of MDSM is enhanced project control and measurable software process and product improvement. Process improvement, attained in part through the application of the MDSM process, leads toward reducing cost, time to market (schedule), and/or increasing quality, as well as raising an organization's process maturity level such as represented by the SEI CMM. More information about the SEI CMM is found in Chapter 3.

2.2.4 Software Management at Lower Maturity Levels

A software organization operating at the lower process maturity levels is probably doing very little measurement of its software process. Without measurement, there is no reliable way to assess the status of the product under development or to assess the effectiveness of the development process. A process in this state of maturity can be modeled as the open loop control system in Figure 2-1. An "open loop" control system is characterized by an "input" (the goals) to set the process objectives, the process, and an "output" product that may or may not meet the goals. The "noise" represents uncertainty in the requirements and estimates that are the bases of the process and product goals. Establishment of the process and product goals depends on the skill and experience of the project management. But any

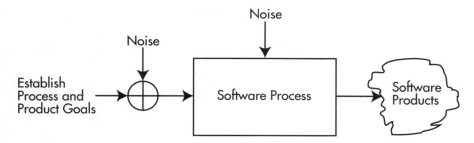

Figure 2-1. *Software Development at Early Software Engineering Institute Maturity Levels*

corrective action, required due to noncompliance of the product with the goals, will also depend upon the skill of management rather than actual information about the process and product. The lack of measurement data precludes the use, or feedback, of actual experience to compensate or adjust the process for performance variances from the goals.

2.2.5 Software Development Management at Intermediate Maturity Levels

A software development organization, operating at the intermediate process maturity levels, is likely to do at least some measurement of its software process; but it is not likely to derive full benefit from the data it obtains. Therefore, it is necessary to implement a well-planned measurement program that governs the collection and use of the measurements. The program should include development of software standards to define the metrics and procedures to collect and analyze them. Only then could meaningful benefit be expected from the measurement activity. Chapter 3 describes the nature of a software measurement program. A process in this state of maturity may be modeled as the open loop control system in Figure 2-2. The measurement activity has been initiated, but it has not yet developed to the point of applying the measurement data to improve the process. The application of the measurement data to adjust the process would "close the loop."

2.2.6 The Measurement-Driven Software Management Process Model at Advanced Maturity Levels

MDSM is a control model that represents:
- Setting process and product goals.

- Measuring the software development project performance at selected points in time throughout the development process.

- Analyzing the measurement data to discover any existing or anticipated problems.

- Determining risk.

- Feeding back the findings in the form of corrective action recommendations.

2.2.6.1 Analogy of the Software Development Process to a Closed Loop Feedback Control System

An example of a "closed loop" feedback control system is a thermostatically controlled heating system. The thermostat is set to a certain "set point" temperature, which is the input goal. The thermostat controls the process, which is the heater. The heat output is monitored by a temperature measuring device, which is continuously compared to the set-point goal. The thermostat uses the temperature measurement to determine if the heater should be on or off. The thermostat will turn the heater on for a temperature lower than the set point and off otherwise. Uncertainty can exist in the system in establishing the set point according to uncertain temperature requirements. Also, the temperature measuring device may be inaccurate. However, the system's operation can be improved by ascertaining the temperature requirements and servicing the thermometer so that the system will ultimately maintain an acceptable set-point goal temperature.

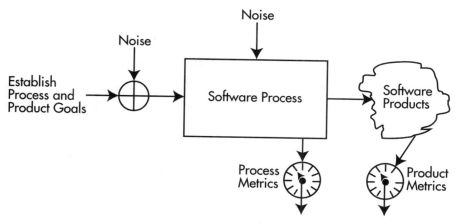

Figure 2-2. *Software Development at Intermediate Maturity Levels*

The software development process is represented by the closed loop feedback control system model shown in Figure 2-3. The model is characterized by "set-point" inputs for size, cost, schedule, and quality goals used to control a process. The process functions to achieve these process and product goals are measured at the output. The process output tends to undershoot or overshoot its goals, creating a variance in its attempt to achieve its set point. The amount and type of variance is used to determine the corrective action necessary to bring the process to its set point. The "outputs" of the process are measured at each activity that composes it, not just at the final activity, which provides the code for delivery to the customer.

2.2.6.2 The Measurement-Driven Software Management Process Closed Loop Feedback Control Model

The MDSM closed loop feedback control model represents the software process treated as a "black box" system with interest focused on the inputs and outputs at the interfaces to the system. Process and product goals are established based on the best estimates available. The process is initiated, and at the planned times, measurements are collected and analyzed and compared to measurement goals. The goals correspond to the set-point inputs and the measurements correspond to the outputs of the feedback control system. The measurements quantify the combined effect of the operation of the process and its uncertainties. These are

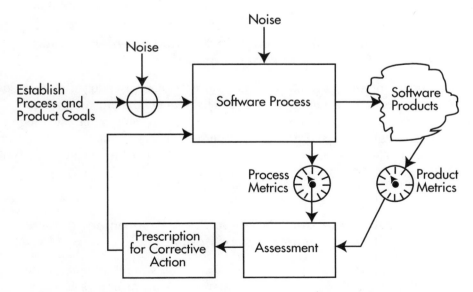

Figure 2-3. *Measurement-Driven Software Management Process at Advanced Maturity Levels*

the actual performance results. The difference between the goal and the measurements is the process variance that becomes the driver of the process correction.

2.2.6.3 Representation of Knowledge in the Measurement-Driven Software Management Process Model

The MDSM closed loop feedback control model represents the important aspects of software development. The model takes several important factors into consideration. First, the establishment of process and product goals is not an exact science. These goals are based, in part, on estimates of the expected performance of the involved people: the software engineers and the software development process managers. Also, the MDSM model considers the fact that the transformation of the product from its initial form of functional requirements through the various levels of design to the code level is not purely mechanical. People are required to apply their relevant knowledge to the process. At each activity of the process, "knowledge" is added to the product during its transformation of form. Knowledge is also added by the support a computer-aided software engineering (CASE) tool provides by constraining the developer to use standardized or approved methods and procedures. In most cases, the people involved will have to learn more about the application than they knew at the start of the project. They will also have to learn about the latest methods of accomplishing the process activities to maintain process competitiveness. The model represents the variability of education, experience, and the people's rate of accomplishment.

2.2.6.4 Representation of Technology in the Measurement-Driven Software Management Process Model

The MDSM model representation also includes the technology used to support the software and system engineers and the managers. The establishment of the process and product goals is based, in part, on estimates of the effectiveness of the information engineering methodology employed by the process, the CASE tool performance, and the supporting computer hardware capacity. The entire development environment is considered and represented by the model.

2.2.6.5 Representation of Uncertainty in the Measurement-Driven Software Management Process Model

"Noise," in the form of uncertainty, is introduced at several points in the process. Uncertainty in the process is evidenced in many ways. Some examples are:

- **Uncertainty in the product requirements**
  Software development projects are often initiated before all products requirements are known or established. In many cases, established requirements are subject to change as the product is developed due to increasing knowledge of the product and the product's operational environment.

- **Variability in the performance of the people assigned to the project**
  It is likely that some of the people available for project assignment do not possess the required skills or experience. A wide variety of abilities have to be integrated into a team to complete the project that require training and experience. An overall productivity of the team has to be estimated in setting project goals.

- **Inaccuracies in the measurement data**
  The noise also represents the inaccuracies in the measurement data that underlie the project and process status assessments each time they are performed. You must recognize that many people are recording the size, cost (effort), schedule, and quality measurement data; and not all of them interpret the standards for data collection and analysis in the same way. The measurement data may not be available to the analyst in a convenient form or organization, especially if it does not conform to the WBS of the project. If the data has to be reorganized before it is useful for estimating or assessing status, a certain amount of error may be introduced during reorganization.

- **Variation in the judgment of the project measurement analysts**
  Application of estimating models requires judgement on the part of the analyst who has to quantify the many parameters of the estimating models. These estimating models are truly the expression of the analyst's judgement. No matter how simple or intricate the model is, the result of its use depends, to a great extent, on the experience of the analyst in the field and his judgement in applying the experience.

2.2.7 Measurement-Driven Software Management Summarized

The MDSM closed loop control model concept must accommodate the activities of establishing goals, performing estimates, and collecting measurements, each with varying degrees of uncertainty. It deals with variations of the abilities among people and their application of methodologies and tools. The holistic approach of the closed loop feedback control model focuses on the input and output externals to the process. It combines and integrates all performance and uncertainties that provide this representational capability.

The model gives the project manager an assessment of the process performance and knowledge of the project's overall completion status compared to the projected goal. The holistic approach does not depend on knowledge of the exact cause of possible problems or uncertainties in the process or project. The technique is extremely useful in assessing the overall status of the project and pointing out the magnitude of a problem. The ETVX paradigm, a model of the software development process activities described in Chapter 4, then becomes useful in pinpointing the exact cause of the problems. Corrective action, then, is the feedback that compensates for the problems occurring in the process and acts to resolve them.

The major constituents of the MDSM process are:
- Set goals:
  - Estimate size, costs, schedule, and quality using past experience and expected impacts of process change
  - Set quantitative objectives for process and product
  - Determine approach for monitoring the project and verifying the goals

- Assess output:
  - Collect data
  - Monitor and track incrementally and compare with plan
  - Verify goals incrementally
  - Predict the development direction of process and product relative to goals and control limits
  - Determine whether the project is under control and whether the plan is still valid
  - Estimate the risks of proceeding to the next activity

- Take corrective action:
  - Modify process to achieve product and process goals
  - Prescribe and execute cost-effective management action

2.2.8 Goal Setting and Tracking

You can perceive a variety of top-level metrics-oriented goals for supporting the management of software project control and software process improvement. The sets of metrics-oriented goals suggested here are:
- Process Improvement:
  - Understand and quantify the software process (both short- and long-term)
  - Produce and update estimation algorithms
  - Support technology change impact analysis

- Control Project:
  - Assess process status (short-term)
  - Assess product status
  - Compare to goals
  - Support taking corrective action

Chapter 5 gives more detail on goal setting and metrics.

2.3 HOW TO USE MEASUREMENT DATA IN THE MEASUREMENT-DRIVEN MANAGEMENT PROCESS

Figure 2-3 shows the generation and flow of measurement data that occurs during the development process. While this is a useful model of the system and its components, it would be beneficial to supplement it with another view that shows the time-ordered sequence of the events taking place during the process of software development. Figure 2-4 is a flow chart view of the MDSM process. A description of the MDSM process actions, with emphasis on the measurement events, follows.

2.3.1 Store Proposal Data in the Experience Database

Any proposal for new or follow-on software development is based on estimates of the expected product size, cost (effort), schedule, and quality. These estimates are measurement data that should be captured and stored in the organization experience database before it is distorted or lost. The data exists in one document and is easily entered into storage to become a valuable resource for future reference. Chapter 12 contains more information about the experience database.

Aside from the fact that project plans are based on these estimates, the focus here is on the estimating models and how they were applied. Continuous improvement in the accuracy of the models and their application should be an organization measurement goal. It is possible to benefit from lessons learned during product development by comparing the original estimate with the outcome of the project, allowing for all the changes that were made to the original requirements. The estimating models and their application may then be adjusted to more closely resemble actual performance and other results that are experienced.

2.3.2 Establish Process, Project, and Product Goals

Establishment of the technical project goals is based on the requirements specified for the product and process. Chapter 5 describes the selection of project goals. The project and

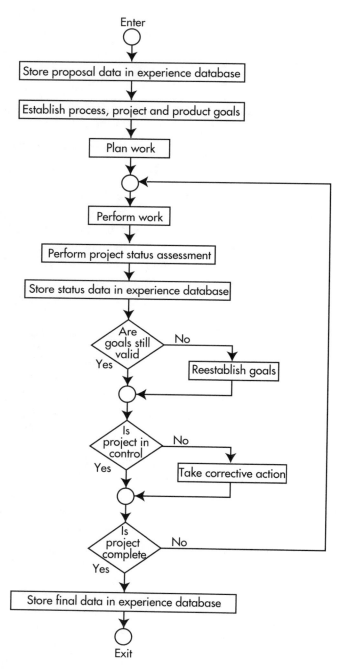

Figure 2-4. *Measurement-Driven Software Management Process*

process goals are concerned with variations in the product size, cost, schedule, and quality. The process of goal establishment includes estimating size, cost, and schedule.

2.3.3 Plan the Work

Much of the high-level planning of the work has probably been done during the proposal activity. If, by some oversight, a measurement plan was omitted or was not prepared in sufficient detail, this is the time to rectify any deficiencies. As the project manager develops the project technical work plan details, the metrics analyst should be coordinating the measurement plan. The measurement plan should be based on an organization's standard for measurements. The standard should define, in detail, all the possible metrics of interest and the procedures for their collection and analysis. The project measurement plan can then reference the standard and enumerate the applicable chapters. The most important feature of the project measurement plan is the schedule for the project status assessments. These may be at major milestone dates or at other specific points in the development schedule; for example, at the projected 1/3, 2/3, and completion points. The budget for the status assessments should be allocated at about 2 percent of the software development costs. The project manager should expect to receive and use the results of the assessment analyses.

2.3.4 Perform the Work

This guidebook focuses on collecting, analyzing, and monitoring status data on product, project, and process. How to perform the planned product development technical work is not discussed here. That is subject to the requirements of the particular product and development procedures of a particular organization.

2.3.5 Perform Project Status Assessment

The project status assessment is essential to the project's success. It is just as crucial to the project as the proposal. It provides the project manager with snapshot visibility into the project in terms of its size, cost, schedule, and quality. He receives an assessment of the project's earned value or overall proportion complete. He also receives a projection of how the project development will proceed until its completion. This projection is an estimate to complete (ETC) that includes a statistical evaluation of the risks of not attaining any project goals and the associated exposures. Additional management indicators, such as productivity and various work rates, should be calculated. Chapter 11 contains more detail on the management indicators, project status assessment, and the analysis report format used to convey the resulting information to project and development management.

2.3.6 Store Status Data in the Experience Database

The activity of the project status assessment is another generator of measurement data. This snapshot of project size, cost, schedule, and quality status can easily be preserved by entering the data from the project assessment analysis report into the experience database. The data will have to be identified as assessment data to keep it separate from the proposal data.

2.3.7 Validate the Goals

It is inevitable that the product functional requirements will change during the course of a product's development. The customer increases his understanding of his requirements and the product as it approaches maturity and completion. This increased familiarity suggests additional uses for the product, some of which will lead to requirements changes. Therefore, project management periodically reviews project goals to determine whether any of the project goals change in product functional requirements. It is likely that if a goal is changed, the associated targets and limits for the statistical process controls will need to be correspondingly changed. These changes should be made prior to any attempt to compare the results of the project status assessment with the goals and limits.

2.3.8 Control the Project

The project status assessment results may be compared to the project targets and limits after you have determined that the project goals are still valid. If the measurement analysis indicates that the targets were hit or the measurements fell within a certain range, it can be said that the project is in control. If the measurements fall outside their prescribed range, then you can call for corrective action. Project management can judge the severity of problems discovered during the project status assessment by utilizing the risk assessment provided in the analysis report. The report should also contain the recommended corrective actions.

2.3.9 Complete the Project

If it has been formally verified that all the product functional requirements have been met and the product is delivered to the customer, then the project is complete for measurement purposes. If the project is not complete, then work continues to advance toward the next project status assessment.

2.3.10 Store Final Data in Experience Database

The measurement data for the project performance, i.e., the "actuals" of the project, should be collected immediately upon completion of the project. (In many cases, this data will not remain available for long.) This data represents the actual size, cost, schedule, and quality of the product and is the most important measurement information generated by the project. You should prepare an analysis that is similar in format to the project status assessment to provide an organized summary of the project measurements. It is highly recommended that you use the final data to derive the unit costs of the individual process activities, using the activity-based model view of the software process. Chapter 8 contains further information about calculating unit costs.

This is the data that will be bridged (adjusted for requirements changes) back to the initiation of the project and compared to the proposal data. This is the time for making corrections and further enhancements to the estimating models and their application. After the final project data has been stored in the organization database, it may be retrieved in combination with the final data from other projects. This combined data may be analyzed to discover long-term trends and averages.

2.4 SUMMARY

The closed loop feedback control system is a model of the MDSM process. This model provides an overview (see Figure 2-3) of the MDSM process showing the generation and flow of measurement data that occurs during the development process. It is a useful representation of the system that provides important measurements of process performance, product size, cost, schedule, quality, and earned value. It is also valuable in assessing the magnitude of problems with product development and associated risks and exposures. This chapter provides you with a second, time-ordered, sequential view of the MDSM process and each of the activities are described from a measurement point of view. The close association of measurement and management is demonstrated in these representations.

Chapter

3

MEASUREMENT AND THE SOFTWARE ENGINEERING INSTITUTE PROCESS MATURITY LEVEL STRUCTURE

3.1 INTRODUCTION

This chapter describes the key role that software measurement plays in reaching higher maturity levels defined by the SEI. A measurement-based strategy to reach higher maturity levels is defined. This chapter also describes the measurement activities that should be provided for any software organization, and it presents several alternative organizational approaches for implementing these activities.

It is impossible for an organization to progress to higher process maturity levels without having institutionalized a software measurement program. The measurement-based approach to improving maturity levels stems from observing that an effective measurement activity, which is necessary for maturity Level 2, is an essential underpinning for all activities needed to manage software projects at SEI Level 3 and above. However, while an effective measurement program is necessary, it is not sufficient to achieve higher capability maturity levels. When your organization successfully has attained Level 2, it has simultaneously built the foundation for its future progress to Levels 3, 4, and 5.

3.2 PROCESS/CAPABILITY MATURITY LEVELS

SEI published two versions of its process/CMM: one in 1987 and one in 1991. The first model (Humphrey and Sweet 1987) described the process maturity framework and gave the 1987 version of the process maturity assessment questionnaire. The 1987 questionnaire, which was intended to be "a simple tool for identifying areas where an organization's software process needed improvement," served as the starting point for nearly all assessments performed through 1992. In assessment practice, it has recently been supplemented extensively by the more definitive CMM.

By 1991, SEI had evolved the framework into a fully defined product, the CMM for Software, which "...provides organizations with more effective guidance for establishing process improvement programs than was offered by the (preliminary process) maturity questionnaire" (Paulk, Curtis, and Chrissis 1991, vii). In developing the CMM, SEI used knowledge acquired during many software process assessments and information gathered by extensive feedback from industry and government. In assessment practice, the more definitive CMM has been used to supplement the 1987 model. When revised assessment questionnaires are available, perhaps in early 1993, the CMM will likely supersede the earlier version.

The SEI models rest on the premise that software process maturity is a credible indicator of capability. The concept (1) implies that the productivity and quality resulting from an organization's software process can be improved over time and (2) presumes that improvement comes through consistent gains in the discipline achieved by applying the capability model. The implication is that as an organization gains in software process maturity it institutionalizes its software process both by means of policies, standards, and organizational structures and by building a corporate culture that supports the methods, practices, and procedures of the business. In this way, the software process (with its methods, practices, and procedures) endures after those who originally defined it have gone.

Finally, each higher level of process maturity is taken as indicating both greater control of an organization's software process and greater consistency with which the process is applied in projects throughout the organization. Hence, the results of applying the process are expected to be more predictable at successively higher levels.

Both versions of the SEI model were developed by applying conventional tools of process management and quality improvement to the field of software development and maintenance. The result provides a consistent and robust maturity model of the software process (null), which allows comparison of process maturities for software development organizations.

The SEI model serves three important needs of software development organizations:

- An underlying structure for reliable and consistent assessments.

- A framework designed to help software organizations to:
  - Characterize in consistent terms the state of their current software practice;
  - Set goals for improving their software process;
  - Set priorities for instituting their process changes;

- A guide to organizations planning their evolution toward a culture of engineering excellence.

3.2.1 Five Levels of Software Capability Maturity

Table 3-1 characterizes the five levels of SEI process maturity. The third column summarizes actions required to reach the next higher level. These levels of process maturity form the stable skeleton, the "process maturity framework," on which software process assessments and evaluations have been conducted since 1987.

Process	Typical Characteristics	Required Actions to Reach Next Level
1. Initial	Professionals driven from crisis to crisis by unplanned priorities and unmanaged change. Surprises cause unpredictable schedule, cost, and quality performance. Few processes are defined, and success depends on individuals' heroic efforts.	**NEED:** Process must become stabilized and repeatable. **REQUIRES:** Estimation, measurement, and planning (for requirements, size, costs, risks, and schedules); performance tracking; requirements management; configuration control; quality assurance; and ability to manage subcontracts.
2. Repeatable	Basic project management processes are in place to track cost, schedule, and functionality. Necessary process discipline is in place to repeat earlier successes on projects with similar applications. Product quality is variable.	**NEED:** An organization standard process for developing and maintaining software. **REQUIRES:** Developing and documenting process standards and definitions, assigning process resources, and establishing methods for managing requirements, design, test, and inspection. Also requires measures of intergroup coordination and of training programs.
3. Defined	Defined software process for both management and engineering activities is documented, standardized, and integrated into an organizationwide software process. All projects use a documented and approved (tailored) version of the organization's process to develop and maintain software. Costs and schedules are reliable, although quality performance is still unpredictable.	**NEED:** Quantitative quality goals for software products. **REQUIRES:** Establishing and tracking over time process measurements and quantitative quality goals, plans, and process cost and performance. Calculate cost of poor quality and compare to costs of achieving quality goals.
4. Managed	Detailed measures of the software process and product quality are collected. Both the software process and products are quantitatively understood and controlled using detailed measures. There is reasonable statistical control over process, and thus over costs, schedules, and product quality. Organizationwide process database is in place.	**NEED:** Process must become optimizing; first by narrowing variation in performance to within acceptable quantitative boundaries, then by continuous process improvement. **REQUIRES:** Quantitative productivity plans and tracking, instrumented process environment, and economically justified technology investments.
5. Optimizing	Continuous process improvement is enabled by quantitative feedback from the process and from testing innovative ideas and technologies. Quantitative basis is used for continuous process improvement and for continued capital investment in process improvement and automation.	**NEED:** Continuous process improvement. **REQUIRES:** Continued emphasis on process measurement and process methods for error prevention.

Table 3-1. *Levels of Software Capability Maturity*

3.2.2 How Activities Evolve from Levels 2 through 5

The nature of project activities evolves as an organization performs at higher levels on the CMM. It is important to realize that a capability maturity level is one number that represents a multidimensional assessment. Thus, an organization could be at some level, say 2, but have elements of its practice that are associated with higher levels. You should not hold back progress in instituting more advanced degrees of measurement practice just because they may be associated with a higher level than that at which your organization is currently assessable. Indeed, assessing your organization at a specific CMM level is somewhat analogous to trying to represent a vector as one number, instead of N numbers, one for each of its dimensions.

3.2.2.1 Measurement-Related Activities

Table 3-2 shows how measurement-related activities evolve in both the process and CMMs for Levels 2 through 5. Level 2 functions use a minimum set of data (described in Chapter 6) needed to control and manage a software project. Level 3 functions add to Level 2's by

Level 2, Repeatable Process	Level 3, Defined (Customizable "standard" process)	Levels 4 and 5 (Measured, analyzed process)
Estimate, plan, and measure: software size, resource usage, staffing levels, schedules, cost of development, and risk.	Level 2 data, plus: Maintain formal records for progress of unit development.	Levels 2 and 3 data, plus: Set quantitative quality goals and manage according to quality plan.
Maintain profiles over time of actual versus plan for: software size; units designed, build/release content, units completing test, units integrated, and test progress; computer resource utilization; requirements status; and staffing.	In addition to Level 2 profiles, maintain profiles over time of ranges, variances, and comparisons with historical data. Develop software measurement standards, and experience-based metrics for estimating size, cost, and schedule.	In addition to Level 3 profiles, maintain control limit charts on size growth; costs; completions; and characteristics of peer reviews. Collect process and product data, and analyze according to documented procedures, in systematic efforts to prevent defects, assess beneficial process innovations, and manage process change.
Maintain profiles over time of use of target system memory, throughput, and I/O channels.	Measurements of errors found and costs incurred by process activity. Pareto analysis of defects, and application of statistical control charts.	Maintain managed and controlled process database for process metrics across all projects.
Collect statistics on trouble reports, and on design errors, and software code and test errors found in reviews and inspections.	Coordinate software experience database at organization level.	Maintain profiles over time for: ratios of rework time and cost of project totals; actual versus planned costs and benefits of process improvement and defect prevention activities.

Table 3-2. *Evolution of Measurement-Related Activities by Maturity Level*

defining and institutionalizing the organization's software development process and on estimating for a project's defined software process (obtained by tailoring the organization's standard process). Level 4 then focuses on further identifying and quantifying the organization's software development processes; selecting process and product data to be collected, analyses to be performed, process and product metrics to be used in managing a project; and defining quantitative goals for product and process quality. The software product quality goals are flowed down to subcontractors. Level 5 focuses on the "optimizing" process by incorporating the lessons learned from continuing process measurements and development experience. Table 3-2 is adapted from Humphrey and Sweet (1987), Weber et al. (1991), and Baumert and McWhinney (1992).

The progression for definition of methods and standards follows a similar path. Level 2 organizations provide training for newly appointed managers of software projects and for conducting reviews, inspections, and audits; estimating, planning, and scheduling resources; managing risk for technical, schedule, and cost issues; quality assurance; configuration management of changes to requirements, designs, and code; and management of subcontracts.

3.3 BENEFITS OF MATURE SOFTWARE MANAGEMENT

This chapter illustrates the benefits organizations gain by raising their software process maturity levels. Benefits include (1) enhanced ability to predict accurately software size, cost, quality, and schedule by reducing statistical variability of the process; (2) improved results from greater control of the software process and from changing the shape of the process distribution curves; and (3) greater technical and managerial visibility into the software process.

3.3.1 Enhanced Ability to Predict Accurately

Greater predictability stems from two major activities: (1) decreasing the process variability (variance) and (2) process improvement work that changes the shape of the process distribution curve. You first discuss the effects of decreasing process variability.

3.3.1.1 Reducing Variability around Process Mean

Figure 3-1 shows how predictability improves at higher maturity levels as the actual results of the software process around the process mean become more controlled and less variable. The chart represents predictability of effort or cost of a software construction process. All five levels have the same mean (indicated by the solid vertical line) but different variance around the mean. The narrowing pattern of the shaded areas is typical of higher maturity level organizations, which maintain their software process under statistical control. For a Level 5 process, actual results diverge only a little from the estimated mean; however, for lower maturity levels, process dispersion is much greater. At Level 1, actual results may bear little resemblance to the estimated effort or cost.

The dashed vertical lines, within which about 95 percent of the Level 5 process results fall, show how relatively unpredictable results are at lower levels.

3.3.1.2 Improving Shape of Process Distribution

Figure 3-2 illustrates changes to the shape of the process distribution curve resulting from process improvement work.

At Level 1, the distribution curve has a long thick "tail" representing the many projects with effort or costs higher than predicted. The actual results for a high proportion of projects are far above average.

At higher levels the processes are measured, analyzed, and steps taken to correct the difficulties. One by one, in sequence of priority, causes for the most frequent delays and bottlenecks are identified, systematically studied, and resolved. These efforts pay off with the marked reductions in size of the tail at the right of the distributions at higher levels. This is illustrated by the steadily decreasing size of the results shown in the tails of the effort distributions.

The smaller area in the tail shows that fewer projects require higher than

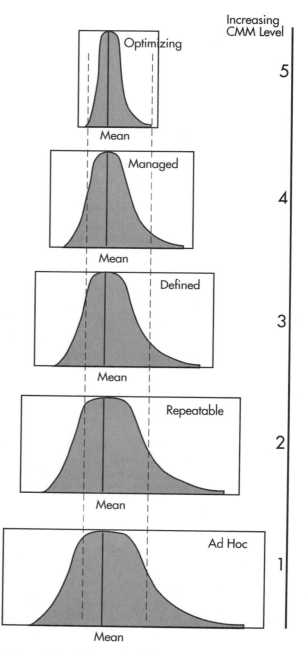

Figure 3-1. *Enhanced Ability to Predict Accurately for Processes under Statistical Control*

predicted effort or cost. This leads to a lower average effort for all projects.

3.3.2 Improved Results From Greater Control of the Process

When the effects are combined, as in Figure 3-3, you can see how higher process maturity levels are characterized by a combination of reduced variability around the process mean performance and by improved process results, which combine to yield greater accuracy of prediction. The figure represents the effect on schedule predictability.

Greater predictive accuracy is shown by the closer match of target delivery date with distributions of schedule performance. At Level 1, the dashed line denoting the mean delivery date is noticeably later than the target date; scheduled delivery commitment is met for only a minority of projects, while the vast majority are late. By Level 3, the mean delivery date is much closer to the target, and the distribution of dates is nearly "normal." About half the projects are earlier and half are later than the scheduled target date. The improved predictability results from a better selection of target delivery dates using the factual knowledge of process capabilities instead of naive optimism or wishful thinking.

Targeted results improve as maturity increases. As an organization's

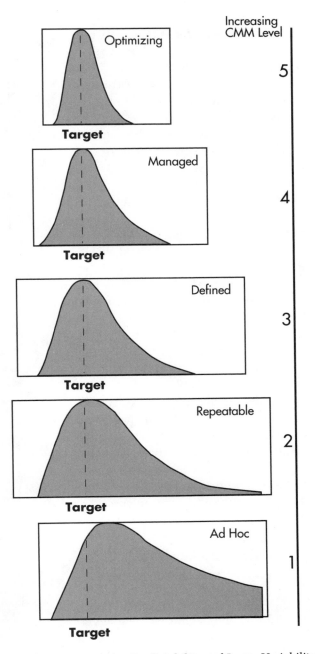

Figure 3-2. *Increasing Predictability and Lower Variability with Increasing Capability Maturity Model Levels*

process matures, development time and cost decrease as quality and productivity increase. In the Level 1 organization, for example, development time can be excessive because of the extensive rework needed to correct errors. At higher maturity levels, defect prevention techniques (inspections and peer reviews) eliminate rework and increase process efficiency.

Decreased variability of actual results around the target is shown by the narrower distributions at higher maturity levels. The widest curve, with the greatest variability, is at Level 1; this contrasts with the tighter distributions achieved at higher levels, where the process is operating within controlled parameters.

Sections 3.3.1 and 3.3.2 illustrate the benefits that organizations gain by raising their software process maturity levels. Benefits described here enhance the ability to accurately predict software product size, cost, and quality and to schedule and improved process results. Section 3.3.3 illustrates how higher maturity levels provide greater technical and managerial visibility into the software development process.

3.3.3 Visibility into the Software Development Process

The following diagrams show how visibility into the nature of the software process increases with higher maturity levels.

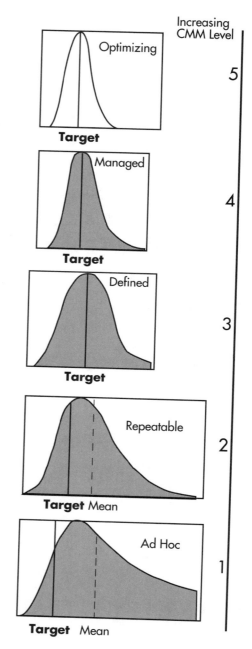

Figure 3-3. *Increasing Predictability and Lower Variability with Increasing Capability Maturity Model Levels*

3.3.3.1 Level 1, Initial

The initial level, Figure 3-4, is typical of organizations and projects that function at the initial level of software process maturity. The process is essentially a "black box." It provides virtually no visibility into the nature of the process being used. The Level 1 process can be described as:

> ...an amorphous entity, and visibility into project processes is difficult. Since the staging of activities is ambiguous, managers have an extremely difficult time establishing the status of project progress and activities. Requirements flow into the software process in an uncontrolled manner, and a product results. Software development is frequently viewed as black magic, especially by managers who are unfamiliar with software. (Paulk, Curtis, and Chrissis 1991, 16)

At this maturity level, the software process is constantly changing as project work progresses. It is virtually impossible to accurately predict product size, schedule, functionality, quality, or budget. If performance can be predicted at all, it is only by individual rather than organizational capability. Level 1 successes are largely due to the inspiration and heroic efforts of gifted software professionals. Thus, managers often complain that the process is a "black box" that consumes large amounts of resources and ejects products of questionable quality at irregular intervals.

3.3.3.2 Level 2, Repeatable

At Level 2, the software process becomes more visible and controlled. While the internal process activities have become visible, they are not well defined. Figure 3-5 shows how increased detail at completion of activities such as requirements, design, code and unit test, and integration is available at Level 2.

Level 2 process activities (such as requirements, design, code and unit test, and integration) are known and stabilized, especially for estimating, planning, and monitoring progress of a software project. At this level, organizations can repeat and apply practices that they have found to be successful, especially on similar projects. Realistic project commitments are made based on a record of estimates and results from previous projects. Software

Figure 3-4. Level 1, Initial Process

requirements and the configuration of interim products developed to satisfy requirements are baselined and controlled. Project standards are defined and followed. Projects track software size, schedules, functionality, and costs (perhaps using little more than minimum data). Implementation may still use ad hoc methods and may still rely on heroic efforts by the project people.

3.3.3.3 Level 3, Defined

The Level 3, defined, process illustrated in Figure 3-6 extends the degree of visibility to activities within the "white box" process. The nature of the process activities is better known than in the Level 2 process. Process performance is no longer dependent entirely on the capability of the individual performers. The "organization standard" process is institutionalized and embedded in the organization's policies, standards, and procedures for both software engineering and management processes. Consequently, process performance becomes considerably more repeatable and variability is reduced substantially. Each project's defined process is a tailored, documented, and approved version of the "organization standard" process for developing and maintaining software.

To maintain and improve the visibility into the process activities, there is a permanent, active software engineering process group (SEPG). Organizationwide training ensures that all software managers and practitioners have the knowledge and the skills needed to perform the tasks assigned to them. Although much improved, the process contains some degree of unpredictability, especially with regard to product quality.

3.3.3.4 Level 4, Managed

The Level 4, managed, process in Figure 3-7 adds still more visibility into the white box process (sharpening the image with measurements symbolized by meter dials) at key points in the process. This process instrumentation, providing well-defined and consistent measures, yields enhanced levels of predictability into process quality and precision in estimating and controlling size, cost, and schedule.

The Level 4 process capability is measured and operates within stated limits. The organization can predict and track trends of process and product quality within the known (statistical) limits of its process capabilities. The organization sets quantitative goals for the quality of its software products. It measures quantity and quality for important software process activities across all projects in the organization. It uses an organizationwide process database to collect and analyze process data from many projects.

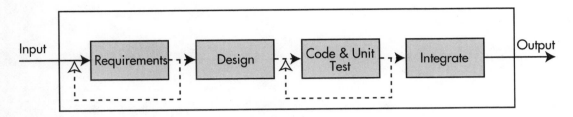

Figure 3-5. *Level 2, Repeatable Process*

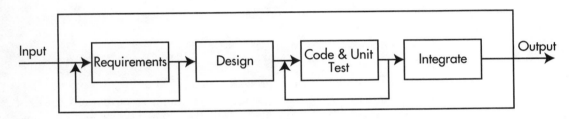

Figure 3-6. *Level 3, Defined Process*

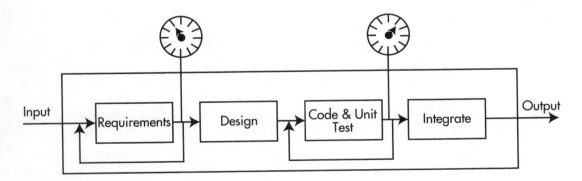

Figure 3-7. *Level 4, Managed Process*

3.3.3.5 Level 5, Optimizing

Finally, at the Level 5, optimizing, the measurements made at key points in the process lead to process modifications designed to improve process performance as illustrated in Figure 3-8. Measurements are used both as input into process optimization activities and as feedback to confirm the results of process changes. At the optimizing level, the software organization has a primary focus on continuous improvement of its process. It continuously works to enhance

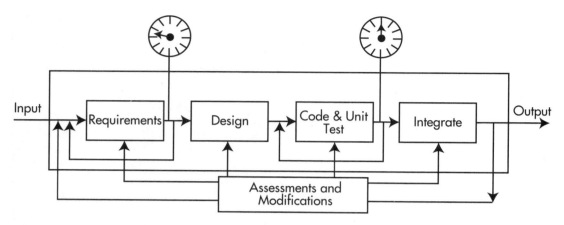

Figure 3-8. Level 5, Optimizing Process

predictability and to raise the upper bound of its process capability. It maintains and uses statistical evidence for effectiveness of its process activities for planning to exploit the best software engineering practices available in its business domains. Project teams routinely analyze defects, with the purpose of eliminating defects caused by the process itself.

3.3.4 Summary

Section 3.3 has illustrated key benefits that organizations gain by raising their process maturity levels. They are:

- More accurate predictions for software product size, cost, quality, and schedule;
- Reduced variability;
- Improved software process results.

In addition, organizations benefit from better technical and management visibility into their software development process. More accurate predictions are most useful for controlling the process and producing products on time and within cost projections. Improved process visibility, control, and product quality are critical to success in software projects.

3.4 MEASUREMENT ACTIVITIES REQUIRED FOR LEVELS 2 AND 3

The goal of this chapter is to help organizations systematically use measurement technology to more quickly achieve process maturity Levels 2 and 3 than might otherwise be possible. It shows how to use minimum data and minimal levels of software measurement practices to improve an organization's software capability maturity level to Level 2, and later to Level 3.

Raising process maturity level is not an easy or trivial accomplishment. Only one in six software development organizations now function at Level 2 or higher and have repeatable or defined processes. In late 1992, the industry "state-of-practice" software processes are at Level 1, the initial or "ad hoc" level.

Many items in the CMM and in the SEI assessment questionnaire imply the use of measurements and metrics, even when they are not explicitly prescribed. Activities required at higher levels often involve measuring properties of the software process and products, deriving metrics from those measurements, and taking effective action based on the results. To ensure credibility, recommended procedures and a suggested minimum set of project data are traced to individual assessment items and to key practices in the CMM (Humphrey and Sweet 1987, App. B; Paulk, Curtis, and Chrissis 1991).

Tables 3-1 and 3-2 were originally derived from the above 1987 publication. They represent a basic and still accurate description of observable process activities. An SEI assessment addresses each characteristic shown in these tables, with at least one question. Responses to these questions are reviewed, then followed by detailed questions to verify the extent to which the questionnaire responses are typical of the organization's standard processes. For an organization to be assessable as having attained a particular level of software process maturity, investigation of responses to questions on the 1987 SEI assessment questionnaire (still in use in 1992) must show that from 80 to 90 percent of the indicated characteristics are present at each level of process maturity.

3.4.1 Measurement Foundation

Your hard-earned experience and the CMM both teach that managing a project effectively requires countless actions, many involving measurements. From the project beginning, you must, as a minimum:

- Estimate the characteristics of your end products, including functional capability, quality, and size. Specify how the delivered product was tested to ensure that it meets the requirements imposed on it.

- Estimate resource requirements and schedule for developing the product (including any known risks that might impede the effort) and prepare the software development plan. You know the need for intermediate milestones and review points to verify progress on project tasks: both internal reviews and those done by subcontractors.

- Change the development plan, as needed, to reflect changes in requirements throughout the development effort.

- Provide adequate tools for developers, testers, configuration management, and quality assurance staff to avoid impairing effectiveness of your project team.

- Rely on a continuing process of measurement to track and monitor project status and to evaluate product and process quality during development (while it is still possible to benefit from feedback and build in features that will delight users or to correct deficiencies).

- Periodically compare actual project progress to projections, analyze reasons for discrepancies, and develop corrective actions as needed.

3.4.2 Measurement Activities Required at Maturity Level 2

The list of essential project management actions (in Section 3.4.1) corresponds to the measurement-related activities required to be in place to demonstrate that your organization has a maturity Level 2 process. To reach maturity Level 2 you should follow formal procedures to:

- Estimate, plan, and measure software size, resource usage, staffing levels, development cost, schedules, and risks (software technical risks and risks for resources, schedule, and costs) from proposal throughout project life.

- Maintain profiles over time, compared to plan for (a) status of each requirement allocated to software, and staffing; (b) units designed, build/release content, units completing test, units integrated, test progress, and trouble reports; (c) achievement of schedule milestones (e.g., units designed, build/release content, units completing test, units integrated, and test progress); (d) computer software configuration item (CSCI) size, work completed, effort and funds expended per computer software component (CSC) and CSCI; (e) critical target computer resources (utilization of target system memory, I/O channels, and throughput); (f) cost and schedule status of software subcontracts; and (g) numbers of product reviews, process reviews, and audits.

- Collect statistics on design errors and on code and test errors found in reviews and inspections.

Figure 3-14, at the end of the chapter, is a "fishbone" chart graphically depicting the CMM requirements for reaching maturity Level 2. The major "bones" on the chart generally correspond to the critical measurement activities shown in Figure 3-9.

- Process analysis and optimization SEI Levels 4 and 5

- Error analysis SEI Levels 4 and 5

- Project tracking SEI Levels 3 through 5

- Project estimating and tracking SEI Levels 1 through 5

Project tracking activities are shown because there are so many at Level 2 with none for process tracking. The largest number of activities fall into the more general category of organizational activities. Figures 3-15 to 3-17 are similar depictions leading to Levels 3, 4, and 5. In Figure 3-15 the shaded boxes indicate the location of the six CMM key process activities.

In summary, to reach Level 2, your organization needs to have defined documents and institutionalized methods. Defined methods are required for:

- Software design, code, and tests.

- Estimating software size.

- Projecting, planning, and scheduling resources.

- Making changes to requirements, designs, and code.

- Conducting reviews, inspections, and audits.

3.4.3 Measurement Activities Required at Maturity Level 3

The measurement activities required to reach maturity Level 3 deal with the process and product in more detail than do the methods and activities associated with Level 2. For example, the methods provide more detail for estimating resources for each key activity by the defined software process and in managing risk for technical, schedule, and cost issues. The measurement activities to help you reach the process maturity of Level 3 consist of the required Level 2 data and activities plus:

- Maintaining formal records for progress of unit development.

- Developing software measurement standards.

- Maintaining formal records for test coverage.

- Developing experience-based metrics for estimating size, schedule, and cost.

Figure 3-15 is a "fishbone" chart graphically depicting the CMM requirements for reaching maturity Level 3. The major bones generally correspond to the critical measurement

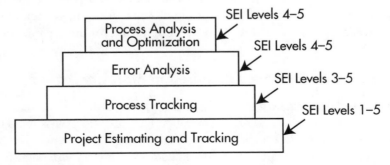

Figure 3-9. *Measurement Foundation for Maturity Levels 2-5*

activities in Figure 3-9: project estimating and tracking; process tracking; error analysis; and process analysis and optimization. Measurement and project tracking activities are each shown separately because there are so many at Level 3 with none for process tracking. A large number of activities fall into the more general organizational category with training and project management specialties. In Figure 3-15, the shaded boxes indicate the locations of activities devoted to estimating, planning, and measurement; to reviews and audits; and to process definition and control.

3.4.4 Measurement Activities at Maturity Levels 4 and 5

Measurement plays a more significant role in the management of software organizations at Levels 4 and 5 than in ones at lower levels. At these higher levels, measurement-driven software management becomes integral to the management process. Quantitative information is used for quality management, and for organizations at Level 5, for process optimization as well. Some organizations at Level 3 will find that it is appropriate for them to perform cost-benefit analyses of possible changes to their processes which would be necessary in order that it could be assessable at a higher level. They would use such analyses as part of their consideration whether they can justify the investment to do all of the things required to attain a higher level of process maturity. Upon careful evaluation, they might decide that it is more appropriate for them to adopt a key practice area associated with a higher level, but not do everything required to become assessable at that higher level.

Sections 3.4.4.1 and 3.4.4.2 describe the nature of measurement activities at Levels 4 and 5, respectively.

3.4.4.1 Measurement Activities Required at Maturity Level 4

Figure 3-16 is a "fishbone" chart graphically depicting the CMM requirements for reaching maturity Level 4. The major bones correspond to the critical measurement activities in Figure 3-9: measurement, project tracking, error analysis, and process analysis and optimization. The largest number of activities at Level 4 are in the measurement and process analysis and optimization areas. A few activities are located in the organizational category.

3.4.4.2 Measurement Activities Required at Maturity Level 5

Figure 3-17 is a "fishbone" chart graphically depicting the CMM requirements for reaching maturity Level 3. The major bones generally correspond to the critical measurement activities in Figure 3-9: measurement, project tracking, error analysis, and process analysis and optimization. At Level 5, most activities fall into the organizational category with significant measurement activities only in the error analysis and the process analysis and optimization areas.

3.5 MEASUREMENT FOUNDATIONS FOR RAISING PROCESS MATURITY LEVEL

The CMM has expanded the detail of coverage in the 1987 SEI process maturity model. This is highlighted next.

3.5.1 Capability Maturity Model Key Process Areas

The process maturity framework shown in Table 3-1 was expanded in the SEI's CMM (Paulk, Curtis, and Chrissis, 1991 28,40). Table 3-3 shows the 18 "key process areas" (KPA) that organizations must have in place to qualify at each level of process maturity. Process areas in **bold** type are related to, or rely heavily on, measurement techniques. The six key process areas at Level 2 are shown in **bold** type to indicate that they have significant measurement-related components. Acronyms, shown at the right edge of the table, are used in this chapter as shorthand for the full name of a key process area. Key Process Areas in bold type are measurement-related. For example, "**CM**" represents "software configuration management."

Process Level	Key Process Areas	Acronym
5. Optimizing	**Prevent defects**	**(DP)**
	Manage process change	(PC)
	Manage technology innovation	(TI)
4. Managed	**Process measurement and analysis**	**(PA)**
	Management of quality	(QM)
3. Defined	Focus on organization process	(PF)
	Define organization process	(PD)
	Training programs	(TP)
	Integrated software management	(IM)
	Software product engineering	(PE)
	Intergroup coordination	(IC)
	Peer reviews	**(PR)**
2. Repeatable	**Manage requirements**	**(RM)**
	Plan software projects	**(PP)**
	Track and oversee software projects	**(PT)**
	Manage software subcontracts	**(SM)**
	Software quality assurance (SQA)	**(QA)**
	Software configuration management (SCM)	**(CM)**

Table 3-3. Key Process Areas (KPA) of the Software Engineering Institute Capability Maturity Model

3.5.2 Measurement Foundations

Figure 3-9 graphically characterizes the critical measurement activities of each maturity level. The specific SEI maturity levels at which the activity is required are shown. For example, the activity "project estimating and tracking" emphasizes that tracking project size, schedule, and cost must begin at the initial process level. It is required at Level 2 and at all higher maturity levels. By Level 3, emphasis of measurement functions shifts from project to process, where it remains through Level 5. Systematic process change begins at Level 3, and organizations check for potential reuse of their existing designs and code. By Level 4, an expanded, managed, and controlled process metrics database is in place for process improvement across all projects.

To reach Level 2, begin measuring. Your organization cannot wait until it has been assessed at Level 2 process to begin estimating, tracking, and collecting data on errors found in reviews and inspections. These must be in place for an organization to be considered Level 2. Do not wait; start as soon as you can to put your measurement program into action.

Figure 3-9 shows how an effective measurement program begins with project estimating and tracking. A necessary foundation for Level 2, it is also the essential foundation for all activities needed to manage software projects at SEI Levels 3 and above. For clarity, the descriptions begin at the bottom function, project estimating and tracking, and extend upward.

- **Project estimating and tracking.** These activities must be formally documented and in place at Level 2 to ensure that the process is repeatable. The activities initially focus on estimates and measurements for project planning, managing requirements, tracking, and oversight. The amount and nature of data collected will evolve at higher levels to include process measures as well. Included here are the Table 3-3 key process areas RM, PP, PT, and SM.

- **Process tracking.** In order for your project to be assessable at Level 3 as having a documented organization-standard process, you follow documented procedures to measure, track, and maintain profiles by key tasks of the project's defined software process. Included are key process areas IM, IC, PF, PD, TP, PR, and PE.

- **Error analysis.** At Level 4, the **managed** level, this function routinely uses the organization's standard software process as a basis for determining data to be collected, analyses to be performed, process and product metrics to be used in managing a project, and for defining quantitative goals for product quality. Establish, measure, and track quantitative quality goals for software errors found in reviews and inspections of requirements, design, code, and formal software tests. Compare projections to actuals, and analyze the design errors and the code and test errors. The emphasis is on measuring to verify that operations remain within measurable process limits and to continuously narrow the variations in process performance. Use results from analyses of process data to bring an organization's standard process under statistical control. Flow the software product quality goals down to subcontractors. Monitor the performance baseline for the organization's standard software process on a regular basis to identify areas that could benefit from new technology. Included are key process areas PA and QM.

- **Process analysis and optimization (at Levels 4 and 5).** At Level 5, the optimizing level, continuing process improvement is institutionalized. Detailed quantitative process performance and trend data is relied on for analyses of benefits, costs, and risks. The organization maintains a process database for process metrics across all projects and for coordinating defect prevention actions across the organization. Over time, it tracks the overall productivity and quality trends for each project, reporting the results to the project managers and senior management. The organization analyzes its standard software process to identify areas that need or could benefit from new technology and incorporates appropriate new technologies into the organization's standard software process and the projects' defined software processes. It follows up by comparing effects of implementing each process improvement to its defined goals; the organization uses results to identify needed changes to the process improvement process. Included are key process areas DP, TI, and PC.

3.6 MEASUREMENT SUPPORT

You should collect as much useful data as possible, but begin with at least the minimum data set described in Chapters 6 and 12. The minimum data set represents the smallest number of data items you need to manage your software project and to characterize your process. Your minimum data set will include the actual values of software size, cost (mainly effort, in labor hours), defect counts, and schedule. The minimum data set, adequate at the lower process maturity levels, is augmented progressively as required for the higher process maturity levels. At Levels 3 and 4, your organization can add detailed process data elements developed using the GQM paradigm described in Section 6.3.

3.6.1 Experience Databases

Your measurement program should collect data from software projects and organize that data into an experience database. The establishment and maintenance of an organization software experience database should be an activity conducted at the highest levels of the organization since many projects and organizations will contribute information to it, and many organizations will want to use data from it. Software development, systems engineering, system test, quality engineering, configuration management, product support (logistics), and project management are among the organizations that will contribute to the database and will benefit from the software information it contains. Chapter 12 describes the nature of the creation of a software experience database.

3.6.2 Feedback of Metrics Data

Metrics should be fed back as quickly as possible to serve as input to those persons having the authority to take appropriate actions to improve the process and the product. This feedback process is the essence of closed loop software process control (see Chapter 2) and, as shown in Figures 3-5 through 3-8, this process is required at SEI Levels 3 to 5. The metrics data, indicating past performance in the organization's software experience database, should be fed back to improve present and future project performance. The measurements from the database can be used to develop metrics that in turn can be used not only to evaluate the software development performance of the project from which they came but also to establish estimation standards and project control methods for better plans and proposals.

An essential element of closed loop software process control is to track and monitor ongoing software development projects. This feedback process is really a continuous quantitative management process of measuring the product and process, comparing those measurements and metrics with the goals and limits set by the project plans, and taking corrective action when the performance falls outside the preset limits or falls short of the preset and/or project goals. See Chapter 2 for a detailed description of the quantitative management process.

3.6.3 Software Management Indicators and Metrics for Maturity Levels 2 and 3

Table 3-4 brings together in one place the measurement activities and metrics you need to reach higher maturity levels. To increase its usefulness, the primary key for the table is the question number of the 1987 assessment questionnaire.

- The measurement-related SEI assessment questions on pages 23 to 28 of Humphrey and Sweet (1987).

- Process maturity level, where required.

- CMM key process area from Paulk, Curtis, and Chrissis (1991).

- Guidebook chapter in which it is described.

- Management indicators and related metrics in this guidebook.

Table 3-4 includes only the requirements needed at Levels 2 and 3 (with the exceptions of four requirements related to the corporate experience database, which is required at Level 4). Ninety percent of the requirements marked with asterisks on the 1987 questionnaire must be met.

3.7 HOW TO ORGANIZE FOR MEASUREMENT

This chapter describes measurement functions and several alternative organizational arrangements for implementing those functions. Rifkin and Cox (1991) give additional detail on the characteristics of successful metrics programs and organizations.

The organizational measurement program grows from the CMM requirement for a defined organization-standard software process. A written policy is required to define both the organization's standard software process and the use of tailored versions by software projects.

3.7.1 Benefits to the Organization

A measurement program, regardless of size and form, exists to support management (both senior and project management) and to aid in improving the organization's software process. The major software development functions supported by the measurement program include

SEI Requirement				Metrics and Description		
1987	Process Maturity Level	CMM KPA	Chapter	Indicator Category	Metrics	Units
2.1.4	2	PT	11	N/A	N/A	Formal procedure ensures periodic management review
2.1.7	2	QA	11	N/A	N/A	Independent audits for each step of the software development process
2.1.14	2	PP	6	Size	Current estimate or count	New, reused, and total KSLOC (or function points)
2.1.15	2	PP	8	Schedule	Elapsed development time	Elapsed months
2.1.16	2	PP	7	Cost	Cost to date Percent budget spent to date	LM or LH Dollars ($) Percent LM or Percent LH

Table 3-4. *Process Maturity Level and Associated Metrics*

SEI Requirement				Metrics and Description		
1987	Process Maturity Level	CMM KPA	Chapter	Indicator Category	Metrics	Units
2.2.1	2	PT	7	Cost	Cost to date Percent budget spent to date	LM or LH Dollars ($) , Percent LM, or Percent LH
2.2.1	2	PT	11	Stability	Authorized positions staffed Percent planned positions staffed to date	Count people (Staffed/planned) 100
2.2.2	2	PT	6	Size	Current estimate or count Percent current estimate of original estimate	New, reused, and total KSLOC (or function points) KESLOC(Current/initial)100
2.2.3	3	PD	10	Quality	Number of defects per KSLOC in preliminary design reviews Number of defects per KSLOC in detailed design reviews	Defects or errors in preliminary design reviews/KSLOC (actual or estimated KSLOC) Defects or errors in detailed design reviews/KSLOC (actual or estimated KSLOC)
2.2.4	2	PT	10	Quality	Number of defects per KSLOC in code inspections	Defects or errors in code inspections/ KSLOC (actual or estimated KSLOC)
2.2.4	2	PT	10	Quality	Predicted defects/KSLOC at delivery	Predicted defects/KSLOC at delivery
2.2.5	4	PA	10	Quality	Number of defects per KSLOC (preliminary, detailed)	Defects or errors projected and compared to actuals
2.2.6	4	PA	10	Quality	Number of defects per KSLOC in code inspections	Defects or errors projected and compared to actuals

Table 3-4. *Process Maturity Level and Associated Metrics, continued*

SEI Requirement				Metrics and Description		
1987	Process Maturity Level	CMM KPA	Chapter	Indicator Category	Metrics	Units
2.2.7	2	PT	11	Status	Percent requirements designed	(Requirements designed/total requirements) 100
				Status	Percent requirements coded	(Requirements coded/total requirements) 100
				Status	Percent measurement units (KSLOC, function points, CSUs, or CSCs) designed to date	(Units designed/total units) 100
				Status	Percent measurement units (KSLOC, function points, CSUs, or CSCs) coded (including CSU test) to date	(Units coded/total units) 100
2.2.8	2	PT	11	Status	Percent requirements tested	(Requirements tested/ total requirements) 100
				Status	Percent tests passed	(Tests passed/total tests)100
				Status	Percent measurement units (KSLOC, function points, CSUs, or CSCs) tested (including CSC test) to date	(Units tested/total units) 100
2.2.9	2	PT	11	Status	Percent measurement units (KSLOC, function points, CSUs, CSCs, or CSCIs) integrated (including CSCI test)	(Units integrated/total units) 100
2.2.10	2	PT	11	Computer resources	Proportion of memory utilization (words, bytes, characters, or bits)	CPU used/CPU available or mass storage used/mass storage available
2.2.11	2	PT	11	Computer resources	Target CPU processing speed (for standard functions)	(Target mips/host mips) x (function size in mips/host processing second) = estimated target mips for standard function
2.2.12	2	PT	11	Computer resources	Proportion of software I/O capacity used	(Message length)(arrival rate)/(processing speed)

Table 3-4. Process Maturity Level and Associated Metrics, continued

SEI Requirement				Metrics and Description		
1987	**Process Maturity Level**	**CMM KPA**	**Chapter**	**Indicator Category**	**Metrics**	**Units**
2.2.12	2	PT	11	Computer resources	Proportion of software I/O capacity used	(Message length)(arrival rate)/(processing speed)
2.2.13	4	QM	10	Quality	Number of defects per KSLOC in PDRs Number of defects per KSLOC in detailed design reviews	Defects or errors in PDRs/KSLOC (actual or estimated KSLOC) Defects or errors in detailed design reviews/KSLOC (use actual or estimated KSLOC)
2.2.14	4	QM	10	Quality	N/A	Test coverage is measured and recorded for each phase of functional testing
2.2.15	3	PR	10	Quality	Number of defects per KSLOC in PDRs Number of defects per KSLOC in detailed design reviews	Defects or errors in PDRs/KSLOC (actual or estimated KSLOC) Defects or errors in detailed design reviews/KSLOC (use actual or estimated KSLOC)
2.2.16	2	PT	11	Stability Stability	Number of SAIs Percent SAIs closed to date	Count SAIs (SAIs closed/total SAIs) 100
2.2.16	2	PT	11	Quality Quality	Number (valid) PTRs to date Percent PTRs closed to date	Count (PTRs closed/total PTRs) 100
2.2.16	2	PT	11	Quality	PTRs/KSLOC in CSC test	PTRs/KSLOC
2.2.16	2	PT	11	Quality	PTRs/KSLOC in system test	PTRs/KSLOC
2.2.17	3	PR	11	Quality	Percent SAIs closed to date	Action items resulting from code reviews are tracked to closure
2.2.17	3	PR	11	Quality	Number of defects per KSLOC in code inspections	Defects or errors in code inspections/KSLOC (actual or estimated KSLOC)

Table 3-4. *Process Maturity Level and Associated Metrics, continued*

SEI Requirement				Metrics and Description		
1987	**Process Maturity Level**	**CMM KPA**	**Chapter**	**Indicator Category**	**Metrics**	**Units**
2.2.18	2	PT	11	Status	Percent measurement units (KSLOC, function points, CSUs, CSCs, or CSCIs) tested (including CSCI test) to date	(Units tested/total units) 100
					Percent measurement units (KSLOC, function points, CSUs, CSCs, or CSCIs) integrated (including CSCI test) to date	(Units integrated/total units) 100
2.3.1	4	PA	12	Experience database	N/A	A managed and controlled process database is established for process metrics data across all projects
2.3.2	4	QM	12	Experience database	N/A	Review data gathered during preliminary and detailed design reviews is analyzed Review data gathered during code inspection is analyzed
2.3.3	4	PA	12	Experience database	N/A	Error data from code reviews and tests is analyzed to determine likely distribution and characteristics of errors remaining in the product
2.3.9	4	PA	12	N/A	N/A	Software productivity is analyzed for major process steps
2.4.1	2	PT	7	Cost	Cost to date Percent budget spent to date	Dollars ($) Percent $
2.4.1	2	PT	8	Schedule Schedule	Percent of schedule elapsed Elapsed development time	(Elapsed months/schedule months) 100 Elapsed months
2.4.1	2	PT	11	Product completion	Overall proportion of software (in KSLOC, function points, etc.) complete	Product completion

Table 3-4. *Process Maturity Level and Associated Metrics, continued*

SEI Requirement				Metrics and Description		
1987	Process Maturity Level	CMM KPA	Chapter	Indicator Category	Metrics	Units
2.4.7	2	PP	8,11	Schedule	Elapsed development time	Elapsed months
2.4.7	2	PP	7,11	Cost	Cost to date Percent budget spent to date	Dollars ($) Percent $
2.4.7	2	PP	11	Product completion	Overall proportion of software (in KSLOC, function points, etc.) complete	Product completion See Chapter 11
2.4.8	3	PE	11	Status	Percent tests passed	(Tests passed/total tests) 100
2.4.9	2	CM	11	Stability	ECPs	Count ECPs
2.4.9	2	CM	11	Stability	Percent requirements undefined	(Requirements to be defined/ total requirements) 100
2.4.11	—	PE	11	Status	Percent tests passed	(Tests passed/total tests) 100
2.4.12	3	PR	10,11	Quality	Number of defects per KSLOC in PDRs Number of defects per KSLOC in detailed design reviews	Defects or errors in PDRs/KSLOC (actual or estimated KSLOC) Defects or errors in detailed design reviews/KSLOC (actual or estimated KSLOC)
2.4.12	3	PR	10,11	Quality	Number of defects per KSLOC in PDRs	Defects or errors in PDRs/KSLOC (actual or estimated KSLOC)
2.4.12	3	PR	10	N/A	N/A	Internal software design reviews are conducted
2.4.15	3	PD	11	N/A	N/A	Formal records are maintained of unit (module) development progress
2.4.16	3	PR	10	N/A	N/A	Software code reviews are conducted
2.4.16	3	PR	10	Quality	Number of defects per KSLOC in code inspections	Defects or errors in code inspections/ KSLOC (actual or estimated KSLOC)

Table 3-4. *Process Maturity Level and Associated Metrics, continued*

proposal development and analysis, project management and control, management of the software experience database, and software process and product improvement. Benefits to the organization of a formal measurement activity include:

- Improved ability to meet software commitments for costs, quality, and schedule.

- Demonstrated ability to stabilize and then to systematically improve the organization's standard software development process. The standard process is tailored to fit the needs of individual projects, customers, and end users.

- More effective use of the organization's software experience.

A vital activity of the measurement function is to establish and maintain an organization-standard software project database. Software projects produce software experience data of great potential value to the organization when data elements are defined in organization-standard terms and stored in consistent formats. That data, the essence of an organization's software development experience, is a valuable corporate asset, usable to great advantage by subsequent software development projects.

3.7.2 Functions of an Organization-Standard Measurement Program

Establishing a systematic measurement program in an organization requires coordinating activities performed by several functions: labor accounting, finance, configuration management, quality assurance, and software project management. This coordination may need to be implemented on several levels: site, division, and corporate. The measurement program begins by providing a minimum set of project control information. The program evolves, both as the organization's SEI process maturity level rises and in response to increasing demands for information, by projects and by the maturing development organization.

The measurement program objective is to support the development organization in:

- Proposal development and analysis.

- Project control (planning, tracking and monitoring).

- Process improvement (greater predictability, lower cost, and higher quality).

- Development of experience data for future use in estimating.

At any level of maturity, a measurement program is a set of activities that:

- Quantitatively characterizes the software project and process.

- Supports project control and process improvement.

3.7.2.1 Support for Proposal Development

Software development projects typically begin with proposals, which must include cost and schedule estimates. The measurement function assists the program office in developing proposals by providing consistent organization-standard estimates of most probable software size, cost, and schedule and by providing risk estimates for technical, cost, and schedule.

The measurement function may develop estimates in parallel with the software development organization or be the sole estimating agency. The objectives of an estimate made by the measurement function are to show the most probable actual cost, not to dictate proposal price, and to indicate the risk of the organization's exceeding a proposed cost. Many techniques for estimating these critical system characteristics are described in Chapters 7, 8, and 9.

3.7.2.2 Support for Setting Quantified Goals

The measurement function can assist project management in setting quantifiable, measurable and testable goals for the development process. Some of these goals become the targets or "plan" against which actual accomplishment will be compared. See Chapter 5 on setting quantifiable, testable goals.

3.7.2.3 Support for Analyzing Subcontractor Proposals

Subcontractor proposal analysis is closely related to proposal development. The same models and techniques are used to verify subcontractor estimates that would be used if the development organization were performing the work itself. These "should cost" estimates can then be compared to subcontractor proposals to determine their credibility. The measurement organization can then support the program office during negotiation of subcontracts by indicating questionable items in the proposal.

3.7.2.4 Support for Tracking and Monitoring Ongoing Projects

Measurement support of ongoing projects mainly involves tracking and monitoring. The status of a project is measured at planned points and is compared with project goals for product size, cost, schedule, quality, and earned value.

Organizing and analyzing measurement data involves calculating derived metrics and comparing those metrics to those planned. By using the cost and schedule models developed for the proposal plus a model to predict and control software product quality, the analyst can determine the proportion of the project work that has been completed and forecast the size, cost, schedule, and quality at project completion. This ETC, and many other management indicators, can be derived from analysis of measurement data. Chapter 11 discusses tracking and monitoring in detail and provides examples of management indicators.

3.7.2.5 Support for Taking Corrective Action

A measurement analyst will be deeply involved in collecting and analyzing measurement data to provide management indicators during the performance of a project assessment. As a result, the analyst is often in an ideal position to recommend actions to avoid or correct problems that can potentially throw the project out of control. The measurement data provides quantifiable information to use as a basis for management decision making.

3.7.2.6 Support for Improving the Software Development Process

As a software development organization progresses from the initial toward the more advanced SEI process maturity levels, the focus widens beyond assessment of the software products yielded by the process to include analysis of the functioning of the process itself. The software process itself becomes the subject of systematic improvement efforts that will lower cost and shorten the schedule while achieving higher quality.

3.7.3 Implementing a Project Measurement Program

The following actions are needed to implement an organizationwide measurement program.

3.7.3.1 Getting Started on a Systematic Measurement Program

First, demonstrate to management that improving maturity levels and continual process improvement make good business sense in today's business climate. The benefits of a formal measurement activity, as a key practice for improving the software development process, will then be evident. The development environment must support a goal-oriented measurement program, and the measurement function must provide project tracking and monitoring methods to support management's need to know project status, i.e., to control the project. When these conditions are present, management will support the need to invest in a measurement program. It will be clear that the investment costs for the measurement program will be recouped through the cost savings effected by the improved process.

You should identify a "champion" of measurement, a person convinced of the business and technical benefits the organization will obtain from a measurement and metrics program. This person will sell those benefits to the organization. Widespread recognition of benefits to all levels of management is necessary, as is a risk aversion plan to ensure that the benefits are realized. Managers must first be convinced of the net benefits of the software measurement program. Management support is obtained most easily when the need to attain higher CMM levels has been recognized, and in environments that already have an institutionalized belief in quantitative management.

3.7.3.2 Setting Objectives for a Measurement Program

The following excellent advice about organizing a measurement program is found in Fenton (1991, 112–113). This guidebook endorses and uses these organizational principles for measurement.

> Every measurement program, no matter what scale is envisaged, must have very clearly stated objectives and goals.

> No matter how humble or grand the objectives for a measurement program, it will only be taken seriously if the right people are given responsibility for it.

> The ideal way of implementing a measurement program is to establish a small independent team of highly motivated personnel. This metrics team should have responsibility for all measurement activities.

You should begin by developing your measurement program plan. This plan must define objectives for the program, considering the strategic needs of the organization as well as the known needs of customers and end users. Begin with the minimum data set in Chapter 6, to identify measures and metrics that meet the needs of the organization, customers, and end users. Then, use the GQM paradigm (Chapter 6) to expand the set of data to be collected, as required by your organization's business and technical needs. A representative set of metrics that you may use to capture project size, cost, schedule, quality, and environmental factors is given in the same chapter. Metrics chosen to meet goals for a project are often included in the organization's standard metrics. When nonstandard metrics are required, define and add them to the standards.

3.7.3.3 Essentials for Early Action

You should quickly take several essential actions:
- Specify, describe, and document every organization-standard measure and metric to avoid ambiguity of interpretation among various projects and users. People will use the metrics as the bases for project tracking and control, and for development and analysis of proposals.

- Document procedures for collecting measurement data and for using the data. Procedures should identify where and when to acquire the data, how to validate and analyze it, and how to use the data. Illustrate with models and formats of the spreadsheets to be used. Describe procedures for calculating average unit size, cost and quality by project phase, and update frequency, for use in customizing estimation models. Later, document all additional functions of the measurement program as they are identified. Include how and when to make an independent assessment of a project, with the format of the report to present the findings.

- Develop a basic tool set for the measurement program. It facilitates collection of measurement data, conversion to metrics, and presentation of the results in ways that help take corrective actions. The tool set may include:
  - Estimate models (such as COCOMO, calibrated for the organization's process). Over time, as they estimate more accurately the actual performance of the development process, these become the most significant tools in the set.
  - Analysis spreadsheets and report formats, to use measurement data easily and consistently.
  - Computer programs that implement standard code counting rules.
  - CASE tools, which provide a wealth of measurement data on the requirements, design and code for both the data and the process sides of the software system. Other software tools, for use where manual data collection is impractical or impossible, can be built to automatically collect data such as computer time used during development; number of pages of documentation; or number of test procedure steps implemented.
  - Organization-specific estimating ratios and rules of thumb.

- Establish procedures for data entry, validation, deletion, modification, and retrieval to prevent corruption of the data. The more standardized the data, the less it will have to be adjusted for analysis.

3.7.4 Beginning to Measure a Project

The measurement program will have obtained from organization management the business objectives to be met by all projects and will have verified the likelihood that the program will yield benefits in measurable business terms. Once a measurement program has been established and is operating in an organization, it is only necessary to define the set of measurement activities required by management for a particular project. The following steps are guidelines for doing this:

- **Develop a plan for implementing all measurement related activities.**
  The first action is always to document a plan that specifies the measurement support to be provided for the project. For the simplest case, the measurement plan may be simply a memorandum of understanding. The purpose of the document is to communicate to the project management details of the support to be provided by the measurement function. The plan contains the information obtained through the next three steps.

- **Identify the metrics to be used for the project.**
  Identification of project metrics should begin with the minimum data set in Chapter 6, which covers project size, cost, schedule, quality and environmental factors. In adding to this minimum data set, the GQM paradigm helps guide the project management in identifying those key factors that are most critical to the success of the project. These factors, which need to be tracked closely, may be both technical and process-oriented. The resulting project goals will lead to a set of subgoals, which include project-specific and facility-wide goals. Metrics chosen to indicate satisfaction of the goals will usually, but not necessarily, be among the facility's standard metrics. If nonstandard metrics are required, they should be defined and added to the standards.

- **Identify measurement support needed for proposal, subcontract, and negotiations.**
  The plan should include all support to software development during the proposal phase. Measurement can provide estimates of size, cost, and schedule. Project management may elect to subcontract parts of the project or team with another contractor. Measurement can provide "should cost" analysis of the resulting proposals. Measurement can also support negotiations by indicating questionable proposal items and providing dynamic recalculation of costs reflecting alternative proposals occurring during negotiations.

- **Identify the support that measurement will provide to the project.**
  Deriving management indicators several times during the project development cycle constitutes tracking and monitoring or, stated in another way, project assessments. A project assessment typically provides size, cost, schedule, and quality information at a point in time, plus earned value and an ETC. The assessment can also provide early warning of potential problems indicated by the values of the project indicators and, in many instances, recommend a course of action to avoid or mitigate the effect of the problem. When a project assessment is performed during development, it is an effective tool for project control.

  Some development organizations will want to save the data collected at each project assessment, but, at a minimum, the final data from a project should be saved. The saved data should compare the management indicators to the planned values and indicate variances. This is the beginning of statistical process control. Measurement can also provide early warning of potential problems indicated by the statistical controls and in many instances, recommend a course of action to avoid or mitigate the effect of the problem.

- **Develop a final report.**
  A final report should be developed at the completion of each software project. The final report is oriented toward both the project and the facility measurement program. Effectively, it is another assessment of the project "actuals" without the necessity for estimation. It is used as the basis of the final project experience data collection. The final data is the most critical data from the project. It must be carefully organized and stored in the measurement program database. The measurement analyst can "bridge" back to the original project proposal estimate and, allowing for all changes to the original requirements, assess the accuracy of the original proposal estimates.

3.7.5 Measurement Organizational Models

A single person can comprise the entire measurement function when first established. Later, it can be a distinct group, depending on the needs of the enterprise. Alternatively, measurement activities can be performed by a number of groups and/or individuals in different parts of the development organization. However, the measurement function must be budgeted separately to ensure that resources will be focused on this important area and so that the measurement costs themselves can be measured. The measurement function should also have the responsibility for training the software organization in measurement techniques.

The effectiveness of the measurement function depends to some extent on its organizational position. The resources that measurement can use and the constraints under which it operates are closely related to the organizational unit of which it is a part and to the organizational units it deals with. This chapter shows four of the many possible organizational alternatives. For your organization, you should choose or invent a model that is compatible with the mission of its measurement function.

SEPG does not appear as a named organization in Figures 3-10 through 3-13 because this organization is mostly a consumer and not a generator of measurement and metrics information. Many organizations and functions use or "consume" measurement information, and they all play vital roles in software development. But the organizational diagrams shown here were intended to show the active role of generating measurement and metrics data. The contribution of the SEPG is primary to improving the software process and advancing the organization's maturity level. But its measurement activities are, in most cases, limited.

Measurement, finance, configuration measurement, quality assurance, and software development are generators as well as consumers of measurement data and metrics.

3.7.5.1 Measurement Function under Project Control in a Project Environment

Figure 3-10 shows a software organization in which each software development project is an independent organization unto itself, in which the measurement function is confined to that project only, and in which each project maintains its own measurement database. This is a typical measurement function in a Level 1 organization. In this organization model, it is very difficult to share measurement data among projects or to establish overall software standards. There is no common software database shared by the projects in the organization. It is difficult for new projects to profit from the experience of concurrent or previous projects.

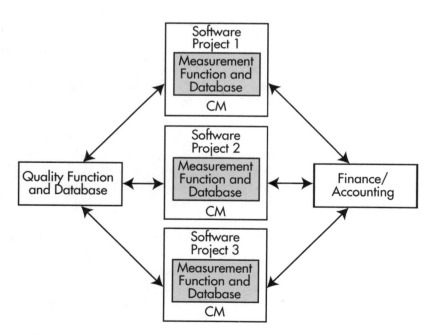

Figure 3-10. *Measurement Function under Project Control in a Project Environment*

3.7.5.2 Measurement Function as a Part of Software Development

Figure 3-11 shows the measurement function as a part of software development, typical of a Level 2 organization. The measurement function communicates with the software development organizations to collect software development data and to provide process and product information. When the measurement function is a part of software development, and is under control of software development, relations with organizations outside of software development may be more constrained. Data from outside organizations will be inconsistent and may be more difficult to collect and use.

Quality assurance (QA) needs a reporting channel to senior management that is independent of software development. It may in this organizational model maintain its own database. The measurement and quality databases may exchange data with more encompassing databases at a higher organizational level. This is shown by a dashed line in Figure 3-11.

Configuration management (CM) serves the software development organizations and contributes data to the measurement database. The finance organization also contributes data to the measurement database and may maintain its own database.

The organizational model for measurement may change as the software development organization's process maturity level rises. For example, the measurement function may be part of the software development organization when that organization is at the lower maturity levels. As a software organization raises its maturity level, and as measurement concentrates more intensively on process performance, the measurement function may become organizationally independent. Similarly, a central measurement function may be set up as the organization reaches the higher maturity levels.

In Figures 3-10 and 3-11, measurement is part of the same organization as that for the software development projects. The next two figures show measurement organizationally independent of software development projects. The alternatives within these categories

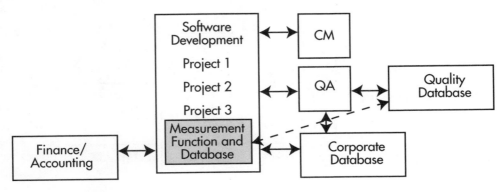

Figure 3-11. *The Measurement Function as a Part of Software Development*

show different ways that the measurement function can relate effectively to other functions in the organization.

Figure 3-12 shows an organization in which the measurement function is organizationally independent of the software development organization. This is typical of Level 3 organizations. The measurement function communicates with the software development projects, providing them with quantitative information about the process and product and collecting their data for the measurement database. QA is also independent, communicating with both the software development organization and the measurement function, which is shown receiving and validating the quality data to be stored in the measurement database. The measurement database contains cost, size, schedule, and quality information, which can be used in proposal efforts and by software projects.

The CM function shares data with both the development projects and with the measurement function. CM data, as well as QA data, is stored in the measurement database in this model (shown by dashed lines). The finance organization also contributes data to the measurement database.

When an organization, such as a division or major business area of a large corporation, maintains a separate measurement database, often it is necessary to contribute selected data from that database to a higher level corporate database and to exchange information with that database. The corporate database in turn gives overall corporate performance data to the lower level organizations so that they can compare their performance with other organizations in the corporation. The possible modes and methods for data collection and of information exchange are not discussed in this guidebook.

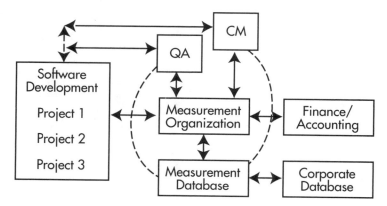

Figure 3-12. *The Independent Measurement Function*

3.7.5.3 The Measurement Function Shared in a Project Environment

Figure 3-13 shows an organization in which software development projects are independent of each other, i.e., perhaps reporting to a single software organization, but under different managers. This is typical of a Level 4 organization. The measurement function deals separately with each software project to coordinate collection, validation, and dissemination of experience data. The measurement function in this model maintains the measurement database. Through the database, the measurement function becomes the unifying measurement force for the enterprise, communicating data and methods to all of the projects and making significant contributions to establishment of software standards and to improvement of process and product.

Both measurement and quality assurance communicate with each project independently and each group maintains its own database. The model in Figure 3-13 shows quality and measurement maintaining separate databases. Alternatively, there can be one common measurement database containing size, cost, schedule, and quality data. These databases could communicate with a corporate database (not shown here).

3.8 SUMMARY

This chapter is intended to help your organization to improve its internal process for developing software. It describes the SEI CMM, demonstrates that effective measurement is essential in successful implementation of a maturity growth program, shows how to practice software measurement so as to improve the level of both process and capability maturity, and gives organizational guidelines for an effective measurement program.

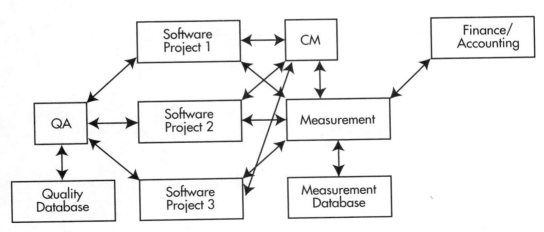

Figure 3-13. *Measurement in a Project Environment*

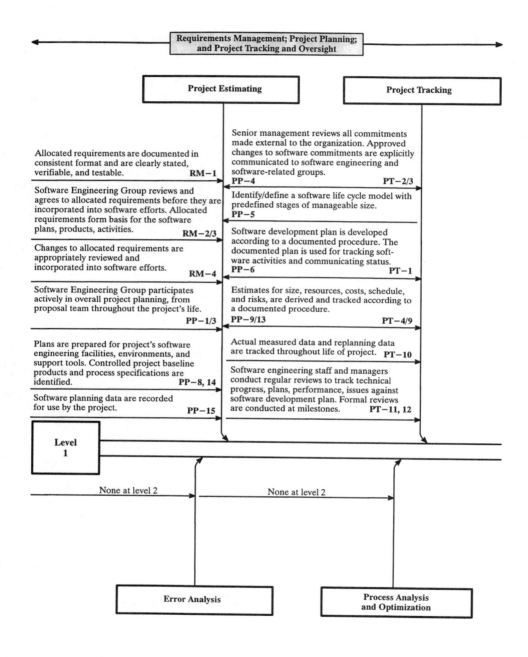

Figure 3-14. *Fishbone Chart for Attaining Process Maturity Level 2*

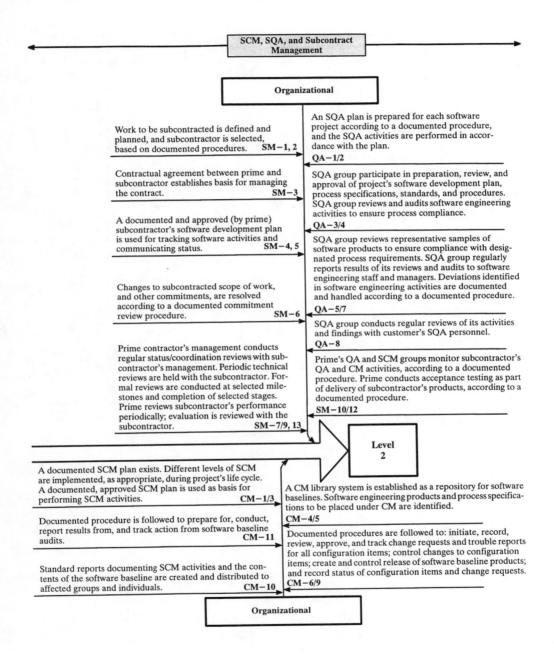

SCM, SQA, and Subcontract Management

Organizational

Work to be subcontracted is defined and planned, and subcontractor is selected, based on documented procedures.   SM–1, 2

An SQA plan is prepared for each software project according to a documented procedure, and the SQA activities are performed in accordance with the plan.
QA–1/2

Contractual agreement between prime and subcontractor establishes basis for managing the contract.   SM–3

SQA group participate in preparation, review, and approval of project's software development plan, process specifications, standards, and procedures. SQA group reviews and audits software engineering activities to ensure process compliance.
QA–3/4

A documented and approved (by prime) subcontractor's software development plan is used for tracking software activities and communicating status.   SM–4, 5

SQA group reviews representative samples of software products to ensure compliance with designated process requirements. SQA group regularly reports results of its reviews and audits to software engineering staff and managers. Deviations identified in software engineering activities are documented and handled according to a documented procedure.
QA–5/7

Changes to subcontracted scope of work, and other commitments, are resolved according to a documented commitment review procedure.   SM–6

SQA group conducts regular reviews of its activities and findings with customer's SQA personnel.
QA–8

Prime contractor's management conducts regular status/coordination reviews with subcontractor's management. Periodic technical reviews are held with the subcontractor. Formal reviews are conducted at selected milestones and completion of selected stages. Prime reviews subcontractor's performance periodically; evaluation is reviewed with the subcontractor.   SM–7/9, 13

Prime's QA and SCM groups monitor subcontractor's QA and CM activities, according to a documented procedure. Prime conducts acceptance testing as part of delivery of subcontractor's products, according to a documented procedure.
SM–10/12

Level 2

A documented SCM plan exists. Different levels of SCM are implemented, as appropriate, during project's life cycle. A documented, approved SCM plan is used as basis for performing SCM activities.   CM–1/3

A CM library system is established as a repository for software baselines. Software engineering products and process specifications to be placed under CM are identified.
CM–4/5

Documented procedure is followed to prepare for, conduct, report results from, and track action from software baseline audits.   CM–11

Documented procedures are followed to: initiate, record, review, approve, and track change requests and trouble reports for all configuration items; control changes to configuration items; create and control release of software baseline products; and record status of configuration items and change requests.
CM–6/9

Standard reports documenting SCM activities and the contents of the software baseline are created and distributed to affected groups and individuals.   CM–10

Organizational

Figure 3-14. *Fishbone Chart for Attaining Process Maturity Level 2, continued*

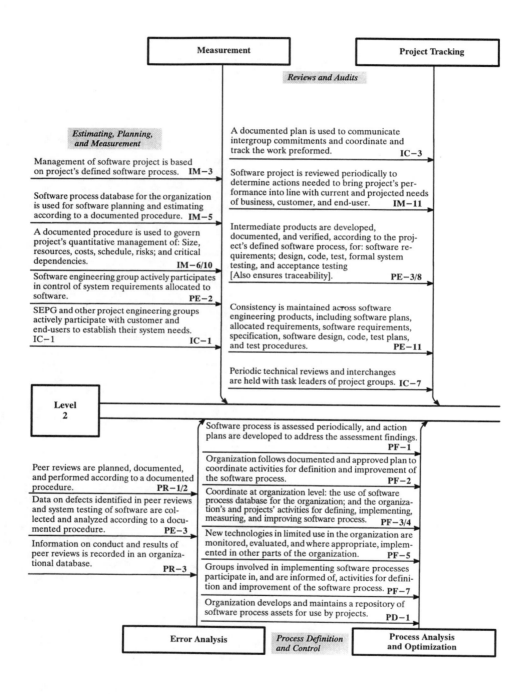

Figure 3-15. *Fishbone Chart for Attaining Process Maturity Level 3*

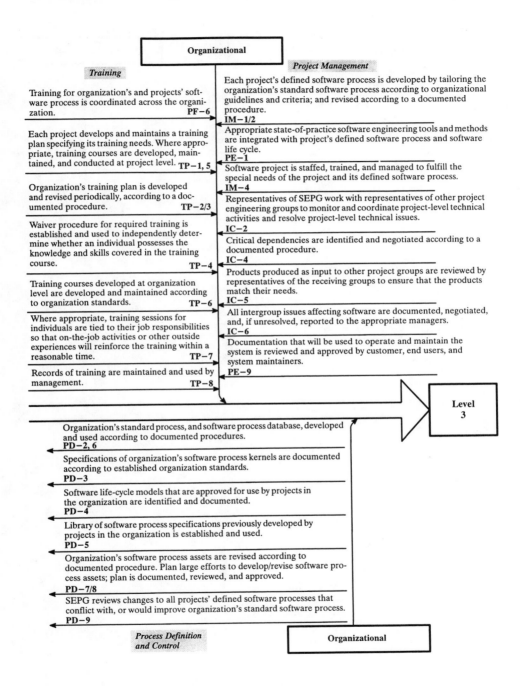

Figure 3-15. *Fishbone Chart for Attaining Process Maturity Level 3, continued*

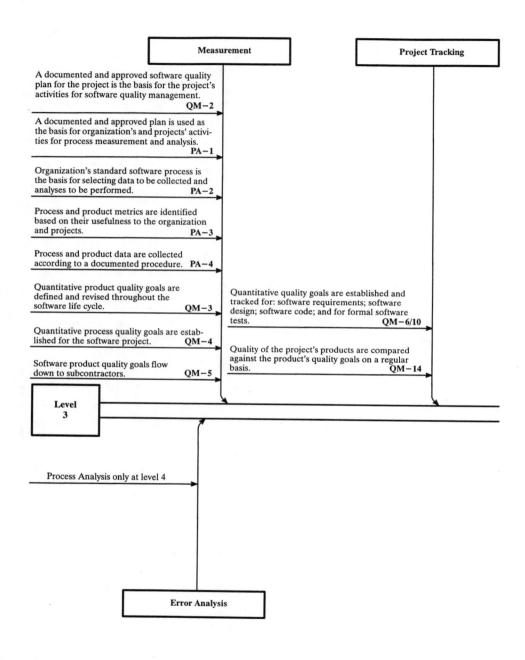

| Measurement | Project Tracking |

A documented and approved software quality plan for the project is the basis for the project's activities for software quality management.
QM−2

A documented and approved plan is used as the basis for organization's and projects' activities for process measurement and analysis.
PA−1

Organization's standard software process is the basis for selecting data to be collected and analyses to be performed.
PA−2

Process and product metrics are identified based on their usefulness to the organization and projects.
PA−3

Process and product data are collected according to a documented procedure. **PA−4**

Quantitative product quality goals are defined and revised throughout the software life cycle.
QM−3

Quantitative process quality goals are established for the software project.
QM−4

Software product quality goals flow down to subcontractors.
QM−5

Quantitative quality goals are established and tracked for: software requirements; software design; software code; and for formal software tests.
QM−6/10

Quality of the project's products are compared against the product's quality goals on a regular basis.
QM−14

Level 3

Process Analysis only at level 4

Error Analysis

Figure 3-16. *Fishbone Chart for Attaining Process Maturity Level 4*

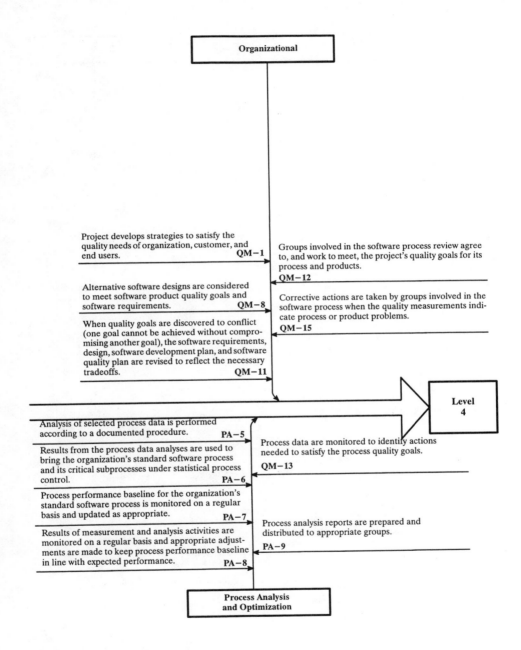

Organizational

Project develops strategies to satisfy the quality needs of organization, customer, and end users.   QM—1

Alternative software designs are considered to meet software product quality goals and software requirements.   QM—8

When quality goals are discovered to conflict (one goal cannot be achieved without compromising another goal), the software requirements, design, software development plan, and software quality plan are revised to reflect the necessary tradeoffs.   QM—11

Groups involved in the software process review agree to, and work to meet, the project's quality goals for its process and products.   QM—12

Corrective actions are taken by groups involved in the software process when the quality measurements indicate process or product problems.   QM—15

Level 4

Analysis of selected process data is performed according to a documented procedure.   PA—5

Results from the process data analyses are used to bring the organization's standard software process and its critical subprocesses under statistical process control.   PA—6

Process performance baseline for the organization's standard software process is monitored on a regular basis and updated as appropriate.   PA—7

Results of measurement and analysis activities are monitored on a regular basis and appropriate adjustments are made to keep process performance baseline in line with expected performance.   PA—8

Process data are monitored to identify actions needed to satisfy the process quality goals.   QM—13

Process analysis reports are prepared and distributed to appropriate groups.   PA—9

Process Analysis and Optimization

Figure 3-16. *Fishbone Chart for Attaining Process Maturity Level 4, continued*

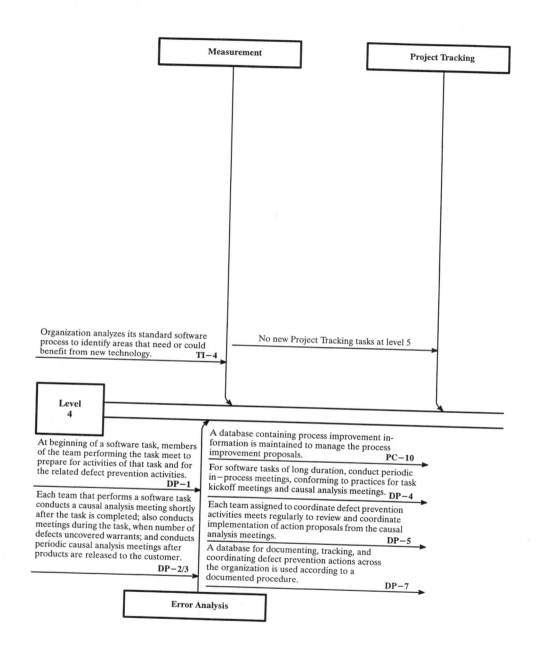

Measurement	Project Tracking

Organization analyzes its standard software process to identify areas that need or could benefit from new technology. **TI–4**

No new Project Tracking tasks at level 5

Level 4

At beginning of a software task, members of the team performing the task meet to prepare for activities of that task and for the related defect prevention activities. **DP–1**

Each team that performs a software task conducts a causal analysis meeting shortly after the task is completed; also conducts meetings during the task, when number of defects uncovered warrants; and conducts periodic causal analysis meetings after products are released to the customer. **DP–2/3**

A database containing process improvement information is maintained to manage the process improvement proposals. **PC–10**

For software tasks of long duration, conduct periodic in–process meetings, conforming to practices for task kickoff meetings and causal analysis meetings. **DP–4**

Each team assigned to coordinate defect prevention activities meets regularly to review and coordinate implementation of action proposals from the causal analysis meetings. **DP–5**

A database for documenting, tracking, and coordinating defect prevention actions across the organization is used according to a documented procedure. **DP–7**

Error Analysis

Figure 3-17. Fishbone Chart for Attaining Process Maturity Level 5

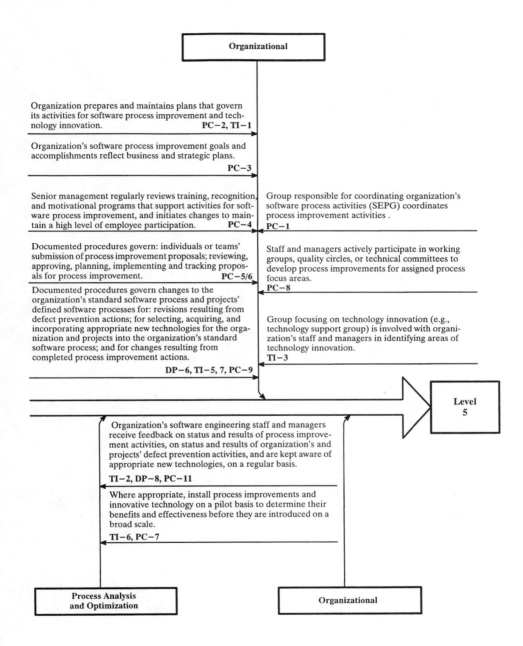

Figure 3-17. *Fishbone Chart for Attaining Process Maturity Level 5, continued*

4

HOW TO DESCRIBE
A SOFTWARE PROCESS

4.1 OVERVIEW

This chapter shows you how to describe a software process in terms of the activities that compose it and the communications among them. Each activity is presented in terms of the Entry-Task-Verification-eXit (ETVX) paradigm as defined by Radice and Phillips (1988). The paradigm may be used to characterize the overall process or any part of the process. Several key questions are posed as a basis for developing the model and a set of metrics is provided for quantitative characterization of the process and indication of process improvement.

4.2 THE ACTIVITY-BASED PROCESS MODEL

A process is a way of accomplishing an objective. The objective of a software development process is to transform a set of requirements into a software system. The software development process that is ultimately created is composed of a set of activities that occur, in some order, to produce software. A software process can be described in terms of the activities that compose it and the interconnections among them. Indeed, as indicated in Selby and Basili (1991), "One central feature of the structure of a software system is the nature of the interconnections among its components (e.g., subsystems, modules)." Clearly, this same view can be applied to the process of creating software systems where the interconnections are among the process activities.

Although there are differences in structure, most software development processes contain such activities as requirements analysis, design, implementation, and test. (This is a natural order of presentation but not necessarily the expected order of development.) The order of execution of the activities may change from project to project. For example, the design activity may have to be repeated because too many defects were discovered during the inspection.

Also, the overall design activity may contain other activities such as preliminary design and detailed design. Thus, a process is the selective combining and ordering of activities appropriately suited to a particular development project.

The ordering of the process activities can be described as a network that represents the sequence of the activities to be implemented during development. The sequence of activities may vary during the course of the project. This network of activities can be assembled from experience with a particular process, or it can be a selected subset of a larger set or "menu" of possible process activities. For example, a certain project may be established to upgrade the computer hardware for a system, which only requires a rehosting of the software. In this case, it is probable that no requirements analysis or preliminary design would be necessary and a reduced detailed design would be sufficient. In another example, a project may be initiated with the objective of producing a major new software system through the preliminary design of the system, with a strategy in place for a separate procurement for the system's production. In this case, the process is complete after the preliminary design is complete.

The interconnections among the activities must be defined for each specific project with the flexibility to change during the course of the project. This ordered set of process activities is the basis of a flexible, activity-based model of software development.

You can also think of the development process for a software product as consisting of a set of minor activities within the major process activities. Both the minor process activities and the major process activities can be represented by the ETVX paradigm. Design is an example of a major process activity. Examples of minor activities within that major activity are preliminary design and detailed design. The minor activities must be ordered, just as the major process activities must be ordered. Also, the interconnections among the major process activities and minor activities must be defined.

Each of the ordered set of major process activities (and minor activities) must be quantitatively characterized in a manner appropriate to the generation of a specific software system. This defined, ordered, and quantized set is then an activity-based model of software development for a specific software product. Chapter 8 discusses several specific activity-based cost models.

4.3 THE ENTRY-TASK-VERIFICATION-EXIT (ETVX) PARADIGM

Process activities have certain characteristics in common. The ETVX paradigm, discussed below, is a general paradigm for describing four common characteristics of software process activities: Entry criteria, Task to be accomplished, Verification of task accomplishment, and eXit criteria.

4.3.1 Entry-Task-Verification-Exit Paradigm Description

The ETVX paradigm is shown schematically in Figure 4-1. The ETVX paradigm, as defined by Radice and Phillips (1988), used the term validation rather than verification. Verification refers to conformance to a documented specification while validation is conformance to a perceived requirement.

Each software development activity can be defined to answer the following questions.

4.3.1.1 What Is the Nature of the Input to the Activity?

The entry criteria identifies exactly what information, i.e., inputs, must be available for initiation of this activity. For example, in the case of the detailed design activity, the preliminary design specification must have completed development and inspection and be ready for use before the detailed design task can begin. The preliminary design specification document must be available along with the inspection result metrics, indicating that the observed defect rate was within the predefined project tolerance. The size of the document should be in the range indicated for like-sized projects to provide an indication of completeness and adequacy. The delivery of the document should be according to the project schedule to assure that the process will not encounter an unanticipated delay. The effort at this point can be captured in terms of engineering effort expended in design to serve as cost data for the experience database and also to be compared with other like development efforts to discover any excess costs or cost savings and their reasons.

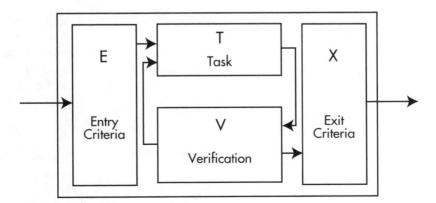

Figure 4-1. *Entry-Task-Verification-Exit Activity Paradigm*

4.3.1.2 What Is the Nature of the Output from the Activity?

The exit criteria identifies exactly what information, i.e., outputs, is produced as a result of this activity. For example, the detailed design is complete when the software detailed design document is complete and has passed inspection. Important metric data similar to that from the input criteria should be captured at this point. The exit criteria may call for capturing the size, cost, schedule, and quality data so it is available to input the next process activity. There are no hard and fast rules for what data should be selected or whether the data is captured at the input or output stage of an activity. Each development organization should derive a method appropriate to its particular needs.

4.3.1.3 What Is the Nature of the Transformation from Input to Output?

The transformation from input to output, i.e., the task, specifies exactly what action is performed by this activity. There is no intent to specify how the transformation is accomplished. To continue with the above example, you can state that the detailed design activity shall advance the design of the system from the CSC level to the computer software unit (CSU) level. While there may be metrics associated with this activity, they would be technical in nature rather than the managerial metrics of size, cost, schedule, and quality. The techniques for identifying and selecting quantifiable goals and their resulting metrics are the same (see Chapter 6 for the GQM paradigm) for the technical and managerial data.

4.3.1.4 How Do You Know When the Activity Is Completed?

The verification criteria are defined for each activity. Early in a project, most verification is achieved by requiring the product, at each defined level of completion, to pass an inspection and later in the project to pass various levels of product testing. This process, known as incremental (periodic) verification, provides continuous assurance of acceptable product quality during development. The inspection and test criteria become the verification criteria for each process activity. Defects discovered during the design and implementation inspections and program operational test failures must be documented and completely resolved or at least resolved to a specified level before declaring an activity to be complete.

4.3.1.5 How Well Did the Activity Do What It Was Supposed to Do?

How well the activity was accomplished can be determined by the quality of the product produced by the activity. Quality data, captured during the verification portion of an activity, can be analyzed to determine the level of product quality, and the data can be used as the basis of a prediction of the defects that will be discovered during future process activities. Inspection and test efforts find many errors but not all of them. Statistical process control may be used to determine a level of confidence in the degree of the activity completion. If the number of defects discovered is not within some predicted range, as determined by statistics (see Chapter 10), this may suggest that product development is not proceeding according to standard or that the inspection process itself is not performing properly. Other metrics, such as the length of time and cost of the activity, can also be controlled statistically in the same way by using control charts.

4.3.1.6 What Activity Is to Be Performed Next?

The activity to be performed next will usually be determined by the predefined sequence (network) of activities and the flexibility of the process. The flexibility of the process can accommodate the cases of failed inspection or test criteria that would cause an unplanned recycle back through the current activity or back through prior activities to maintain product quality. Figure 4-2 is an example of a process that illustrates these feedback loop conditions.

Figure 4-2 shows two instances of information feedback (recycling) to prior activities. In the first instance, the developer doing the design found that the requirements were inconsistent and had to be changed. He used the existing design product as input to that change process. In the second instance, the developer found a discrepancy in the design when writing the code. He used the code product as an input to the design change process. Note that Figure 4-2 does not illustrate rework effort within an activity.

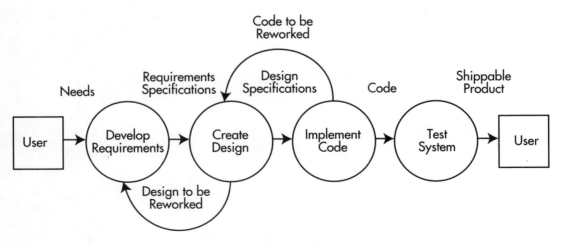

Figure 4-2. *Example Process Network Instances*

4.3.2 Further Description of Process Activities

In the development of large software systems, several activities necessarily progress in parallel. Various parts of the system may not have any direct development dependence on each other. This allows the system development to be subdivided into segments so that equivalent activities, such as design and implementation of the segments may take place simultaneously with the coded and unit tested segments coming together as needed for integration and system test.

A process can also be composed of activities that overlap in time. Most large software development projects are examples of this situation. The project is subdivided into segments and planned so that work on the segments begins in a time-overlapped sequence of activities. This compresses the overall project schedule by more uniformly distributing effort among the staff. Figure 4-3 shows notional time profiles of the effort expenditure versus time for each of the overlapping activities.

In addition to the process activity questions posed in Section 4.3.1, you can ask other questions that address process activity implementation issues, such as those addressed in the following sections.

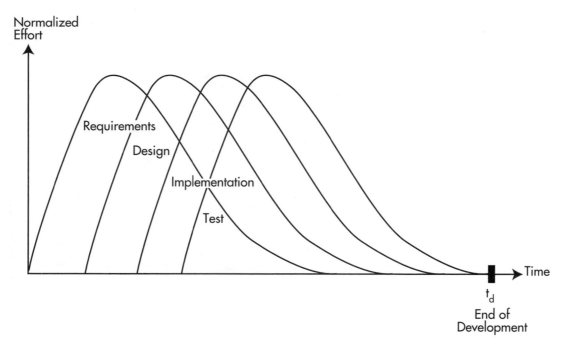

Figure 4-3. *Resource Profiles for Each Principal Development Activity*

4.3.2.1 What Method Should Be Used to Implement the Transformation from Input to Output?

A commercially available or a locally developed methodology may be specified for an activity or to include several activities. Software development methodologies that are implementation-supported by CASE tools exist, and may be part of the specified transformation activity.

4.3.2.2 What Verification Methods Should Be Used to Determine the Degree of Success of the Process Modification?

The degree of success can be determined by statistical methods of quantitatively assessing a project to determine the size, unit costs, schedule status, and quality and then by comparing the results to past projects or accepted industry norms if known. If the product quality is lower, costs are higher, or development lagged behind schedule, then process improvement may be beneficial. Other production factors must also be considered such as the capability of the technical staff and CASE tools used. An improvement in the expertise of the technical staff can produce an improvement in the process: for example, a process improvement that occurs without any change in the process activity structure.

4.3.3 Example of Quantifying Aspects of a Process Activity

A set of metrics can be derived using the GQM paradigm to quantify the main aspects of each of the four principal components of the ETVX paradigm as applied to a software process activity. As an example, the detailed design activity could suggest the following questions and metrics for use in answering the questions:

- Entry:
  - How much input? Metric: Number of process "Bubbles" from a high-level design representation of a program to be developed.

- Task:
  - How much effort does it take and how long does it take to perform the transformation? Metric: Number of labor hours per source line of design produced by the detailed design activity, and clock hours (provide this information for each transit of the process).
  - How many times was this process activity transited during the given development? Metric: Number of times.

- Verification:
  - How good is the output? Metric: Number of defects per thousand source statements found in inspections of the output compared with established criteria to determine if the quality is at an acceptable level.

- EXit:
  - How much output? Metric: Number of source lines of design.

4.3.4 Entry-Task-Verification-Exit Paradigm Flexibility Issues

As discussed above, the ETVX paradigm describes process activities of any level, from the entire process through the major process activities to the individual minor activities. At the major activity level, the ETVX criteria should be documented as a standard describing the official process. This fundamental principle also holds at the minor activity level. The flexibility of the ETVX paradigm is illustrated in the following situations:

- *Activity Decomposition.* The process may contain the design activity depending on the project requirements and the type of process selected. The design activity may be decomposed into the activities of preliminary design and detailed design. The preliminary design activity can, in turn, be decomposed into the activities of preliminary design document, preliminary interface design document, software test plan and CSC test requirements. The ETVX paradigm is implemented for the four lower level activities with documented descriptions of their initiation and completion criteria. The completion of these activities becomes part of the completion criteria for the higher level (inclusive) preliminary design activity.

- *Prototyping.* Prototyping can be considered as working ahead for a selected part of the project. For example, it may be felt that the design of a complex algorithm could possibly subject the project to great risk if not successful. It could, therefore, be decided to advance this algorithm through the process activities of code and unit test preceding the normal project schedule. The ETVX paradigm can accommodate this prototype situation by defining all the special completion criteria for the prototyping sequence.

- *Single Activity Iteration.* Within one activity, it may become necessary to repeat the task due to failure to satisfy the verification criteria. If the design or code inspection reveals an unacceptably high defect rate, the ETVX paradigm of the single activity will have to be "repeated" through the task and verification requirements until their criteria are met. This task (verification iteration path) is shown in Figure 4-1.

- ***Multiactivity Iteration (Rework).*** It may become necessary to repeat several activities of the process. For example, if a change to the software requirements occurs and it affects a portion of the software that has already progressed to the integration test activity, that portion of the software will have to be recycled back to the design activity. In this case, the ETVX paradigm accommodates the rework by applying the original completion criteria to the reworked portion of the software.

4.4 PROCESS IMPROVEMENT

The ETVX paradigm represents the software development process during product development and for process improvement. This chapter describes how the ETVX paradigm represents process improvement.

4.4.1 Impacts of Process Modification

The interconnections among the activities may change during development of a specific software product. For example, an analysis of errors may show that it is advisable to recycle the product development sequence back through the design activity to lower the error rate. Or, a large number of test errors may indicate an unacceptably high level of risk if the product is delivered in that condition. Therefore, testing is continued past the planned time. These are examples of short-term process modification.

The interconnections among the activities or the activities themselves may change over time and over the development of several products due to the introduction of new technology (e.g., CASE tools). This is an example of long-term process modification.

The effect of process modification is measured by the effect of the modification on each of the activities in the process. The effect on each activity should be measured in terms of:

4.4.1.1 Changes in Unit Cost of Doing the Activity

An improvement in the software process usually results in a lower overall cost to develop software. However, it is not necessarily true that every activity in the process decreases in cost. You may decide that it is more cost-effective to invest increased effort in the design activity and find development errors early in the process rather than later during the test activity. This causes a corresponding increase in the cost of the design activity, but that increase is more than offset by savings in rework to correct errors discovered later during the test activities. The cost of each activity should be monitored using the metrics developed for project tracking and control to quantify the effects of the process modification. You can then determine whether the modification is producing the desired improvement.

4.4.1.2 The Impacts on the Inputs and Outputs

It is quite likely that an improvement in the process will result in changes in the inputs required for one or more activities in the process and/or the outputs of these activities. Indeed, you would expect that often a process change will result in a quantifiable change in the output of a given process activity. For example, an improvement in an activity could result in there being a reduction in the number of defects expected to be experienced. When characterizing the effects expected from a process improvement initiative, be sure to consider the likely effects of such change on the inputs required by the activities in the process as well as in the the outputs that they generate. Ultimately, process improvement should result in quantifiable improvement in the principal final output of the process, the code and/or in a characteristic of the transformation from input to output (such as unit cost, time required, etc.).

4.4.1.3 Changes in the Transformation from Input to Output

The results of applying a software development process depends, to a great extent, on the level of its supporting technology, or software development environment. While software development is a labor-intensive, intellectual process, its efficiency can be increased by improvements in the automation of selected parts of it. Steady improvement in computer hardware technology has made cost-effective software CASE tool applications possible. CASE tools allow the implementation of automated graphical techniques of design and automatic code generation, and CASE provides extensive repository facilities. It is almost inevitable that CASE tools will be adopted by most software development facilities. The potential cost reductions are significant enough to provide a competitive advantage. In this case, upon adoption of a CASE tool, the ETVX description of process activities will have to be revised to reflect the changes in the methods of accomplishing the tasks of all affected activities. Careful monitoring of costs is absolutely necessary at this point to accumulate the experience data on which to base decreases in proposed cost of new work.

4.4.1.4 Impacts on the Determination Method of How and When the Activity Is Completed

Verifying the completion of the process activities' tasks is one of the most significant cost drivers of the process. As the process becomes more automated, the verification task becomes more orderly and less time consuming due to the traceability of design and code provided by CASE tools. Such things as consistency and completeness of design are greatly improved by process automation through adoption of CASE tools. The manner of the inspection process can be changed toward reduction of effort as familiarity with the tool is gained. Automatic code generation might eliminate the need for all coding effort. However, some code inspection should be retained to verify that the proper code was generated. The ETVX descriptions will need to reflect the changes in inspection procedures. Also, it is important that the activity be monitored to ensure that the reduction in inspection effort is not having a detrimental effect on the process.

4.4.1.5 The Impact on the Quality of the Activity

You may decide that sufficient experience in a specific domain (business area) permits the quality limits to be tightened somewhat, causing an increase in the quality of the software product: for example, the effect of the experience level of the people staffing the project. A change in the statistical process control limits (see Chapter 10) standards may be required to solidify the improvement in the product quality. The ETVX activity descriptions will need to be changed accordingly. This is an example of a process improvement that is subject to some variability from project to project. It is highly dependent on continuity of staff which is not always possible to maintain. This being the case, it becomes important to have good quality tracking and monitoring mechanisms in place to determine whether quality levels are being maintained.

4.4.1.6 Changes in What Activity Is Done Next

The requirements, design, implementation, and test order of precedence are generic to any development effort. Greater emphases on such things as software reuse and formal risk analysis may change the emphases placed on various process activities. It is in activity iteration or temporary deviation from the normal process activities, in the short term, where process order modification occurs. This can be due to such things as rework or prototyping. These activities should also be tracked to determine their effect on costs and quality.

4.4.2 Metrics for Process Modification

You accomplish process improvement when lower cost and/or a shorter schedule result in a higher or at least the same level of quality. Process improvement is also accomplished when higher quality is achieved at no increase in cost and/or schedule. You achieve process improvement when small increments of increase in cost and/or schedule result in large increments of increase in quality. Metrics that can be used to indicate the effects of the above impacts should be specified at the initiation of the project. You should derive and apply metrics that can measure the direction (improvement or deterioration) and the amount of change in process performance resulting from every process modification action.

You should also derive and apply metrics to measure the impact of new technology. New technology often influences process performance changes over the course of several projects. You should measure the long-term effects of new technology. While process improvement can take place without process modification, as in the case of increasing skills of the staff, it often occurs with some modification to the process.

Table 4-1 presents a summary of metrics that can be used to evaluate the impact of process changes and the amount of process improvement. You should apply the indicated metrics before and after a process modification action to evaluate the impacts. See Chapter 6 for additional information about metrics selection.

Metric	Apply Metric To
LM/KSLOC or LH/KSLOC	Each Activity, Overall Process
Estimated defects/KSLOC	Overall Process
Discovered defects/KSLOC	Each Activity
Estimated schedule—time to complete	Overall Process

Table 4-1. Metrics for Process Changes and Improvement Evaluation

4.5 SUMMARY

A software development process may be modeled in terms of the appropriate set of activities and their interconnections that will accomplish the project objectives. The ETVX paradigm provides a discipline for use in describing the software development process, by rigorously defining the Entry, Task, Verification and eXit criteria of the individual activities that compose the process. Process modification for improvement has impacts on the process ETVX activity definitions. Examples of these impacts on the process and their effects are given and related to the ETVX descriptions of the process activities. You are provided with a set of metrics to evaluate the effectiveness of process performance and modifications to the process.

Chapter
5

SETTING QUANTIFIABLE
REQUIREMENTS AND GOALS
AND MANAGING TO THEM

Developing quantitative requirements is an important part of MDSM. This chapter describes how to express requirements in quantitative terms and how to associate them with testable/measurable targets. This will enable you to objectively verify performance. Users' operational requirements dictate a project's goals, which in turn determine the minimum set of management data required to effectively manage the project. This chapter also shows you how to establish quantitative product requirements and process goals.

Other chapters in this guidebook relate to the material covered in this chapter. Chapter 2 describes MDSM, how to apply the MDSM process, and how to use measurement as part of the software process. Chapter 6 shows you how to derive a minimum set of measurements needed to effectively manage a software project by using the GQM paradigm. Chapter 10 presents statistical quality control methods to help you determine the degree of satisfaction of the quantified requirements imposed on the product and the process used to create it.

5.1 QUANTITATIVE PRODUCT REQUIREMENTS AND PROCESS OBJECTIVES

This section describes how to identify the most critical software project requirements, how to quantify requirements, and how to express them in measurable/testable terms. Clearly identified and quantified requirements, quality objectives, and resource limitations are essential to project success.

5.1.1 Identifying Critical Requirements

This section describes how to identify the critical attributes (the highest priority attributes) so essential in defining how, and how well, the end user needs to have the software product work in its intended operational environment. You should not expect software to be accepted by your customer if its performance level for a measurable/testable critical attribute is less than the minimum acceptable level specified. For mission-critical software such as for use in aircraft control systems, power plant systems, etc., you expect the critical requirements to include system attributes of performance, reliability, user satisfaction, and maintainability. Examples of these and other attributes of requirements are given in Chapter 10. You will need to define what is meant by each attribute with respect to your particular customer's needs. You will then need to define quantitative measures for these attributes.

In identifying the critical requirements for software, you may also need to consider critical characteristics of the system of which software is a part (example as cited in Department of Defense [1991a]). Such critical system characteristics may include compatibility with other forces and systems including postdeployment support organizations, survivability, transportability, electronic countermeasures, energy efficiency, interoperability, and standardization.

Requirements evolve, and refinements and clarifications are often negotiated during projects in discussions between the system's developer and its customer (or a surrogate for the customer, such as the development organization's marketing people). The first sets of requirements are often "wish lists." They are nearly always much too long and imprecisely stated to use as practical requirements, and they often fail to identify the relative importance of the individual requirement statements. It may be literally impossible to meet all requirements posed at project start, particularly for systems that push the state of the art. Even in a routine project, there might be some detailed requirements changes later on. Also, during the course of development effort, new requirements may be imposed.

To cope with this situation, a development manager may begin by identifying the small number of "critical" requirements—those few that the software must meet (within ranges prespecified with users) for the system to satisfy users' minimum needs. The development effort can then be concentrated on meeting those few needs to the degree that they satisfy the users. The much larger proportion usually consists of features that would be "nice to have" but are not essential for system performance. Usually, the less critical requirements are met with a little extra effort when the critical requirements are satisfied. Many "requirements" may not be measurable, for example, "usable" and "maintainable" (see Chapter 10).

Figure 5-1 is a notional representation of the distribution of the requirements for a software system in terms of the proportion of satisfaction that they provide to the user. In this example, there are 100 requirements. They are subdivided into 5 groups of 20. The degree of satisfaction provided by each of them to the user is depicted in the graph. Depending upon the threshold that you might set, you might say that the first 20 requirements are the critical

Proportion of User Satisfaction

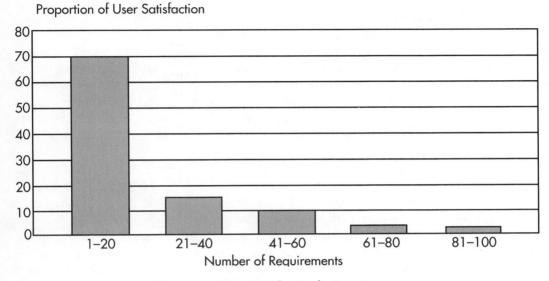

Figure 5-1. *User Satisfaction by Requirement*

ones, since, if satisfied, they will capture 70 percent of the user's satisfaction with the system, on average. The distribution shown is a Pareto distribution. Such a distribution characterizes many natural phenomena. For example, it characterizes the distribution of defects in some software systems, in which a few modules contain a majority of the defects in the system.

5.1.2 How to Quantify Attributes of Software Requirements

Attributes are measurable characteristics, or indicators, of software structure or performance. Attributes can describe performance of system functions or capabilities (what the system/software must do) of nonfunctional attributes (such as usability, maintainability, etc.), and resource/schedule requirements (what the system will cost, and when the customer or user will be able to use it). Attributes can be true/false or multivalued.

5.1.2.1 True/False Attributes

Begin by recognizing that requirement attributes can be described in two ways: as true/false and as multiple value. True/false attributes have only one future state: true or untrue. For example, a project will use Ada for all new code, or it will not.

5.1.2.2 Multiple Value Attributes

Cost, schedule, and other space and time objectives are normally expressed and measured in quantitative terms (e.g., dollars, labor months, calendar months). You can describe, in equally measurable/testable terms, performance for user-required capabilities such as work capacity and adaptability. For example, you can describe a measurable testable requirement in this way: "At the specified workload, in 99.9 percent of transactions, response time will be less than 1.3 milliseconds." As the project progresses, you can incrementally verify the likely satisfaction of the objective at each stage (e.g., low-level design) by static analysis and/or by using simulation and modeling tools.

An example may help to make these distinctions clear. The project requirements might include performance objectives such as those in the first column of Table 5.1. You should quantify functional objectives using metrics such as those shown in the second column of Table 5.1. Quantifying a requirement begins by identifying the functional objectives needed for success. The "critical" requirements for project success are those that the user considers essential. In this example, the critical requirements include execution/workload processing rates and quality. You can quantify each of these so that its attainment becomes measurable and testable (Gilb 1988).

Functional Objectives (**What** must be done by the system:)	Quantified Attributes of Objective (**How well** it must be done)
Execution rates	Under prespecified conditions and using the specified data sample, the CSCI executes at rates no less than 1,300 transactions/second.
Workload processed	Within specified conditions, the system processes at least 130 transactions/second. At specified degraded capability, it processes at least 72 transactions/second.
Quality	Transaction accuracy is no less than 99.5 percent under all conditions.

Table 5.1. Example of Quantifying Functional Objectives

5.1.2.3 Identifying Requirements

Quantifying requirements enables you to establish clear, complete, and measurable/testable objectives for software products and processes that are agreed upon by the developer and the intended users (or surrogates for them). To be useful, quantified requirements must describe the results users really want, the goodness of those results, and statements on the costs they are willing to incur for those benefits. Figure 5-2 is an overview of quantifiable

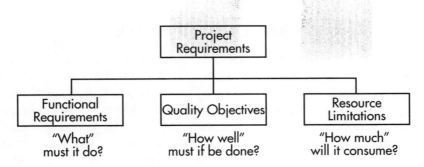

Figure 5-2. *Requirements Hierarchy*

requirements. You can help users select requirements by conducting cost-effectiveness trade-offs (see Section 5.2.1).

The three categories of requirements are:

- *Functional Requirements.* These represent the functions to be performed by the software: what the software is to do for the end user. The extent and nature of functions the software must perform for the system drive the size of the software product.

- *Quality Objectives.* Quality may be defined as conformance to requirements (Crosby 1979). Chapter 10 describes quality further. You can and should unambiguously state all quality requirements. Ease of use, reliability, maintainability, portability, and usability are typical requirements that you should try to quantify (Gilb 1988). Chapter 10 shows you an example of a methodology for doing so. "Usability" is an example of a quality objective that can be quantified. (See Chapter 10 for an example of how to do so.)

- *Resource Limitations.* Resource limitations identify such constraints as dollar cost, labor hours, computer time, and calendar months available until delivery. The development effort depends on the size of the software system and is the primary driver of cost. To a lesser extent, the software size also drives other expenses incurred in development (such as computer support).

The greatest difficulty in establishing quantitative requirements is in getting a "clear, complete, unambiguous statement of our quality requirements" (Gilb 1988). Gilb (1988) points out that there is "a certain art to finding the necessary metrics concepts and measuring tools. Often they have no traditional written form, and it is essential that they are tailored to the case in hand."

The quantitative objectives you establish for each product goal (especially for software quality characteristics) permit you to make meaningful assessments of project risk based on probabilistic analysis at each stage of the software development project.

5.1.3 How to Specify Attributes of Requirements

Decisions made at the beginning of a software project are the most vital one and therefore hardest to change. Base your subsequent project plans and budgets on the few critical performance requirements that you formalize in this early work. Typically, the plans and budgets change throughout the development process. This is not a random or careless process. A baseline is essential for evaluating the effects of changes on schedule and cost.

Table 5-2 provides several examples of how you can express requirements in quantitative terms. The critical performance requirements columns list what the product must do and how well it must do it; the Method of Measurement column identifies the method for measuring the degree to which those requirements are satisfied.

Examples: Critical Performance Requirements		
What it Must Do	**How Well**	**Method of Measurement**
Pass acceptance tests for critical abilities (by physical test or simulation)	Specified in terms that you can measure and test	Specify agreed-on test or measuring tool
Transaction rate at given volume levels	Transactions/second	Transactions/second, under simulated field operating conditions
Response time for given transaction loads	Less than 0.3 seconds from receipt of incoming signal	Simulation prior to FQT
Availability, etc.	More than 99.8 percent	FQT
Pass design review	Fewer than 10 major faults to be corrected before proceeding	Pass review, with no open major faults from CDR

Table 5-2. *Examples of Critical Requirements*

You must state how each performance requirement can be measured on some scale and how it can be verified. You will find it helpful to make comparisons among the current level of performance, the minimum acceptable levels (at delivery) and performance objective level (at delivery), and the "best ever" or current state of the art. Reference the authority that quantitatively specifies the minimum acceptable and performance objective levels. In the past, the minimum acceptable level and the performance objective level have often been assumed to be the same. You can continue with this simplifying assumption, if you wish. However, in a competitive market, as your process capabilities improve at higher maturity levels, you may benefit by differentiating your performance objective from the minimum acceptable level.

Table 5-3, shows an example in which four levels of performance need to be quantified for each of two typical requirements: response time and availability. The critical performance requirements columns list what the product must do and how well it must do it. The performance objective and minimum acceptable levels are those on which the users and software developers have agreed. The best ever (record, state of the art, or best performance known) puts these levels into perspective by comparing the performance objective and minimum acceptable levels with the state of the practice and/or the art. The current level shows performance of whatever current system is in use, whether the technology is manual or automated.

	Critical Performance Requirements			
Performance Level	**What it Must Do**	**How Well**	**What it Must Do**	**How Well**
Performance objective level (at delivery)	Response time	0.10 second	Be available	99.8%
Minimum acceptable	Response time	0.50 second	Be available	99.2%
"Best ever" level	Response time	0.01 second	Be available	99.9%
Current level	Response time	1.10 second	Be available	98.5%

Table 5-3. Example of Performance Objective, Minimum Acceptable, and Current Levels of Requirements

5.1.4 Unstated Critical Product Attributes

Be alert to the possibility that your customers may not (at least initially) explicitly be able to express the requirement attributes that are critical to them. You cannot leave "obvious" things that "everybody knows" to take care of themselves. When you read a statement of product objectives, you should assume that several of the most important attributes have not been stated. This, paradoxically, is often because these objectives are so essential that the customer takes them for granted. Work with your customer to assure yourself that you have identified these possibly hidden critical requirements and stated them clearly.

5.2 HOW TO BENEFIT FROM NEGOTIATING REQUIREMENTS

Experienced developers have learned that all other project activities depend on getting agreement on the final end-user needs the system must fulfill and how well those needs are to be fulfilled (the quality). Because requirements (at least initially) are normally incomplete and involve trade-offs, setting measurable/testable targets involves negotiation. It is worthwhile to do so.

Quantitative terms permit agreement to be better communicated so that both the user and developer can measure product performance. Recognizing that requirements changes are not free, you should also refine the corresponding size estimates, resource projections, and schedule each time you refine the requirements and communicate them to the customer who is buying your system (see Chapters 6, 7, and 8).

5.2.1 Level of Flexibility in a Requirement

The user/customer may be willing to trade exact adherence to a requirement in order to obtain (or retain) a more critical requirement, to save money, and/or to reduce the development schedule (for example, reusing existing functionality—while possibly giving less functionality than the customer desires—may give functionality that is "good enough").

Figure 5-3 shows a simple example of utility, or usefulness, to the user. The performance requirement is shown as a curve of performance level versus utility to the user. The maximum utility to the user (1.00) occurs when the maximum required performance—1,300 transactions per second—is met. The minimum acceptable level of utility to the user (0.50) corresponds to the minimum acceptable performance or 1,000 transactions per second. This would also be the critical attribute for a performance level that, if not attained, would make the entire system worthless to the prospective user.

The utility curve rises more sharply in the range of 1,100 to 1,300 transactions per second. If everything else is equal, of course, the user would like to have performance corresponding to maximum utility. However, when cost-performance trade-offs need to be made, the user would get maximum operational utility with a transaction performance rate of 1,250 transactions per second, different from that in the formal requirement. Clearly, such situations offer opportunities for negotiation. You should recognize such situations and negotiate these requirements with the customer.

5.2.2 How to Negotiate Product Requirements

The term "negotiating" is useful for describing the process frequently observed during the course of a project. Negotiating is a search for "win-win" alternatives where no one loses. Negotiating is an interactive process that converges upon a cost-effective set of requirements. The negotiation process is cyclical and continuous throughout a project. In the case of DoD projects, initial requirements are negotiated prior to—and during—the System Requirements Review (SRR) milestone. Changes occur after preliminary design review (PDR) as users make trade-offs among costs and desired product functionality.

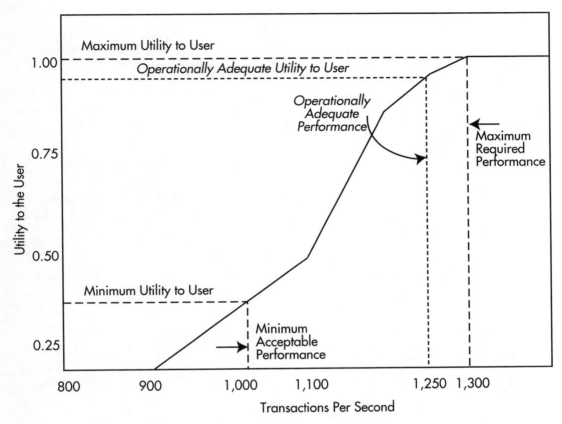

Figure 5-3. *Example of Utility of a Product Capability to a User*

You should follow these steps when working with your customers to solidify requirements:

- Identify the subset of critical product attributes that the software product must meet to survive and be successful. These attributes are the means for determining project success, and you need to control them throughout the project. Other product attributes, those in the "like to have" category, would not cause catastrophic system failure if they were not met. Obviously, a continuing close relationship with the customer is necessary to maintain awareness of the customer's current priorities and to ensure that the documented requirements are met. When possible, use customer language in describing critical product attributes.

- Differentiate critical attributes of requirements from feasible solution(s), which are alternative ways of obtaining the results you want. Often solutions are confused with objectives, particularly in the early stages. Try to avoid developing solutions to meet end-user needs before you have broken down those needs into product "attributes" and have quantified those attributes by negotiating with your customer, and you have agreed to them. You must differentiate between customer requirements and feasible solutions. You can easily mistake a feasible solution for a requirement.

- Quantify the minimum acceptable level for each critical attribute, e.g., "usability." This is a crucial step.

- Find and describe critical attributes that may seem so obvious that they are not written down. When you read a statement of customer objectives, it is wise to assume that the customer has not stated several of the most important attributes. This, paradoxically, is often because these objectives are so critical that the customer takes them for granted (Gilb 1988).

- Identify all product attributes in terms of measurable/testable results needed by the final end user. Determine the limits within which each attribute can vary, such that the system will still be acceptable to the user.

5.3 HOW TO MOTIVATE THE CUSTOMER TO QUANTIFY REQUIREMENTS

Although there are many reasons to quantify requirements now, it is a substantial change in culture for both customers and developers. You need to motivate both your colleagues and your customers to quantify requirements. The following approaches have succeeded in allaying concerns and fears (Gilb 1988):

- Recognize that your organization may need to educate your customers with regard to allocated software requirements. In the next few years, few acquisitions are likely to include fully quantified requirements. This situation represents an opportunity for your organization to gain competitive advantages.

- Appeal to your customers' need for clarity. Quantifying requirements reduces the risk of a proposal failing because of misunderstood requirements. It stimulates an earlier, more intense discussion among customer personnel about what they really want. As a result, you can prepare better estimates based on a firmer understanding of the real requirements. Your company may use "design by objectives" to systematically engineer and cost a solution to the customer's requirements.

- Relate or trace quantified software requirements to customer and management requirements. By doing so, the customer is much more certain of getting what he wants. At the same time, the customer cannot surprise you later with more demanding results requirements than you expected to have to deliver without being willing to pay for the changes.

- Show that quantified requirements do not require exact knowledge. Rough estimates (that you can refine as data becomes available) are more useful than none at all. Often, you must express estimates for controversial or especially significant values as uncertainty estimates, expected values, or ranges of possible values. For further protection against misinterpretation, attach a short description of the assumed conditions under which the estimate is valid.

- Show your colleagues that quantified requirements are not set in stone. As user needs change (they always do), your company can more easily show that those needs are different from earlier approved statements and justify a cost change.

5.4 SUMMARY OF RECOMMENDATIONS

By using the recommendations presented in this chapter as a foundation, you can fully benefit from the detailed measurement techniques presented in the following chapters. You can:

- Reduce the amount of unnecessary rework by assessing the completeness of your team's understanding of user needs/requirements and plan the work. Knowledge of how much user need for each requirement is to be met is indispensable in delivering software products that meet user performance requirements and are delivered on time and within budget. Select the measures based on user concerns and with the benefits they anticipate from a completed system. Future agreement is aided when you describe requirements in quantitative terms and associate them with testable/measurable targets that enable you to verify performance.

- Avoid contention at project end by agreeing on how the customer will recognize success. You and the customer need to agree on how he will recognize success (including responsibility for acceptance testing), the criteria to be used, and any warranties or other consequences of failure. You should clearly establish links with customers who know the application well (to stay aware of approaching changes in requirements).

- Select measurements of software process and product according to the GQM paradigm. Using this paradigm helps you identify what measures you should use based on a rationale for their selection. The paradigm provides a systematic approach to metrics selection.

- Identify and monitor with special care the handful of critical requirements that the software must meet (within ranges prespecified by users) for the system to satisfy minimum user needs. The critical attributes typically include measures describing how well the end user wants the software product to work, such as performance, reliability, user satisfaction, maintainability, and extendability. No user will accept software if its performance level for a critical attribute is less than the worst acceptable level he specified. This action is essential for setting priorities and assigning staff and resources to the requirements of most value to the customer.

- Have measurements relate to requirements, and express requirements in quantitative terms.

Chapter

6

MATHEMATICAL MODELING AND METRICS SELECTION

6.1 OVERVIEW

This chapter discusses mathematical modeling and its use in the context of software metrics. It presents the benefits and limitations of mathematical models together with the rules of application for project control and process improvement. It presents the GQM paradigm for the selection of software metrics. You should apply this paradigm when establishing project goals and software metrics for process improvement and project control. Project goals are stated as numerical values or as simple mathematical models called software metrics. This chapter presents a set of software process and product metrics for size, cost, productivity, quality, and schedule. You can adopt this set for your development environment to define, control, and improve your software development process.

You should use the measurements and metrics discussed in this chapter, representing actual software development experience, not only for controlling project performance but also for helping to set future software development planning and control standards and for process improvement.

6.2 MEASUREMENTS AND METRICS

This section provides some definitions, defines categories of metrics, and defines categories of code.

6.2.1 Definitions

- ***Software measurables.*** They are directly observable quantities that you can count, such as source statements (source lines of design [SLOD], source lines of code [SLOC], thousand of source lines of code [KSLOC]), or that you can otherwise measure, such as labor hours (LH) and labor months (LM). A measurable is a primitive.

- ***A software measurement.*** It is a number assigned to an observable aspect (i.e., a quantitative assessment) of a software process or product (DeMarco 1982).

- ***A software metric.*** It is a number assigned to a quantifiable concept that relates to a software product or to the process that created it. A metric is not always directly observable. A metric may be a single measurable as defined above, or it may be a function of one or more measurables. For example, a SLOC is a measurable that is an indicator of software system size; therefore, it is also a metric. SLOC/LM is a productivity metric that is composed of the two measurables, SLOC and LM.

6.2.2 Metrics Categories

The main categories of metrics are:
- Product size (Section 6.7)

- Product cost (effort) (Section 6.8)

- Schedule (Section 6.9)

- Quality (Section 6.10)

- Product application environment (Section 6.11)

- Development environment characterization (Section 6.12)

- Development constraints (Section 6.13)

- Development personnel characterization (Section 6.14)

The metrics in each of these categories are discussed later in this chapter as indicated.

6.2.3 Basic Measurement Set

Your software organization should implement the collection of a basic measurement set, if it has not already done so. A recommended basic set is given in Table 6-1. This set corresponds to the basic set presented by the Software Engineering Institute (Carleton et al. 1992) with one exception: this guidebook recommends logical source statement counts (see Section 6.2.4) rather than physical source statement counts as the prime measure of size. Logical source statements are recommended because their count is subject to less variability. In addition to logical source statements (LSSs), you may want to count physical source statements (PSSs) in order to compare with others who count physical statements (Carleton et al. 1992). You can derive these metrics in terms of the GQM paradigm described in Section 6.4.

Metric Category	Metric (Measurement)	Definition
Size	SLOC or KSLOC	Logical source statements without comments. (PSSs for comparison purposes.) Identify language and separate new and reused code counts.
Effort	Labor hours (LH)	Effort for each activity, at least to the level of requirements, design, etc. Prefer LH to LM.
Schedule	Calendar time (months, weeks)	Total development time. Completion times for principal milestones such as CDR, etc.
Quality	Defects	Normalize to KSLOC (defect/KSLOC). Collect at each stage of development.

Table 6-1. Recommended Basic Measurement Set

In addition to the above recommended basic measurement set, you should always identify and record the development and target computers by type and model.

Table 6-2 shows the application of the GQM paradigm to the basic measurement set.

Goal	Question	Metric Category	Metric
Manage and control the project	How much have we made? How much is left to be made (progress)?	Size	SLOC (or KSLOC)
	How much effort has been expended?	Effort	Labor hours
	When will the product be completed?	Schedule	Calendar time (months, weeks)
	How good is the product?	Quality	Defects (or Defects/KSLOC)

Table 6-2. Goal-Question-Metric Paradigm Applied to the Basic Measurement Set

6.2.4 Code Counting

A "new" software system results from a combination of adding, modifying, removing, and reusing code. The counts of these categories of code are related as follows:

$$
\begin{aligned}
\text{new} &= \text{added} + \text{modified} \\
\text{deleted} &= \text{modified} + \text{removed} \\
\text{reused} &= \text{original} - \text{deleted}
\end{aligned}
$$

(Gaffney and Cruickshank 1991a and 1991b; IEEE 1992)

This new software system can be composed of new and reused code. New code can be a mixture of newly developed code and modified code from another system or from a reuse library. (The original system can be one or more reuse libraries and/or one or more software systems that are not in a library.) When you add newly created code and/or modified code to the reused code, you create a "new" software system. The new product consists of a new set of code plus a reused set that you obtain intact from the original product. A "new" system may be a "new" version of an existing system.

The definitions for "new" and "reused," etc., do not imply that you must estimate or count any of the code types in any particular way. These are general rules for categorizing the types of code you use in composing a new system. Furthermore, these definitions do not imply what level of code you must count. A software metrics standard may require that you count several levels of code, such as source statements and object statements. This guidebook strongly recommends counting source statements.

This guidebook recommends that you count LSSs, but you may build rules for counting both LSSs and PSSs into your code-counting facility. A source statement is anything that a programmer writes except comments. You should count all source statements (i.e., executables, data declarations, and compiler directives). If you count comments, you should count them separately. Also, you should have separate counts of source statements for each development language used.

You should always make separate code counts for each computer program unit and for each development language with an identification of the function or program unit, the level, the code type, the count type (LSS or PSS), and the language. You should make separate counts for source statements and comments. It is optional to count a blank comment line; however, do not count noncomment blank lines used as separators. You should also maintain separate counts for each CSCI or software product in the software system.

6.3 MATHEMATICAL MODELING

The creation and use of mathematical models are integral parts of software measurement practice. Software measurements are quantified observable aspects of software processes and products, and software metrics are mathematical functions of these measurements. These functions are called mathematical models, and they provide a framework for relating various software measures to make predictions of size, cost, schedule, and quality. Mathematical models also provide procedures for relating one set of metrics to another, such as generating productivity metrics from size and effort metrics or generating a resource profile from effort and schedule metrics. This guidebook presents and shows the application of various types of mathematical models that can be used in process improvement and project control.

A mathematical model is an idealized representation of a real-world situation, such as a problem. This representation is actually an abstraction, a simplified representation of reality, to which mathematics can be applied to yield information about the problem. You can employ mathematical models as aids in analyzing and in problem solving to answer a question, to help in decision making, and/or to make a prediction. In employing mathematical models you, in effect, reduce the level of complexity with which you must deal. This reduction enables you to focus on the aspects of the situation that the modes provide, which interests the information users. This user might be the person who has asked a question, a person who must make a decision, or a person who wishes to make a prediction.

A mathematical model should be in a form amenable to using mathematical manipulations and techniques, and the model and its application should be understandable, at least on an elementary level, to the user of the model outputs and results. The results of applying the model must be credible to the information user; he should be comfortable with the idea that the model results apply to his (perhaps) larger problem. The model must be of practical use in decision making.

Finally, a mathematical model must be verifiable in the sense that real-world inputs to the model produce outputs that both the modeler and the user know correlate with established real-world conditions. This verification can be intuitive in the sense that the model results "make sense," or it can be analytical based on information gathered from experience or from other models, both objective and subjective.

Both the modeler and the user of a mathematical model must understand its limitations. They must understand that the model represents a simplified view of reality, and it does so in an approximate fashion. Then, being cognizant of these characteristics, both user and modeler must recognize that the model can only be applied to a limited set of situations. They must recognize that mathematical modeling reduces complexity and thus may limit the generality of the results of applying the model. The user must tailor his expectations to the limited environment that is being modeled and to the specific problem addressed.

6.4 SELECTION OF METRICS USING THE GOAL-QUESTION-METRIC PARADIGM

The GQM paradigm is a framework for the systematic specification of metrics appropriate for an identified need for an information consumer (such as a project manager, a software manager, or a software quality assurance group). The paradigm indicates who needs to know what and why this person or group needs to know it (Weiss 1981; Basili and Weiss 1984). You select software process and product measurements according to the GQM paradigm. Using the paradigm helps you to avoid picking measures "out of the air." Following it aids you in identifying what measures you should use based on a rationale for their selection. The four principal steps of the GQM paradigm are:

1. State the goal(s). This answers the questions, "Who is the information consumer and what does he need to know?"

2. State the item(s) of information that the consumer wants to know. This answers the question, "What question(s) is the consumer going to ask to satisfy the goal?"

3. State the specific metric that you need and the things that are to be measured to answer each of the questions posed in step 2. This step answers the question, "What metric do you need and what must you measure to obtain it?"

4. Apply the metrics selected, evaluate their usefulness, and go back to step 1, 2, or 3, if indicated.

For example, a **goal** of this guidebook is to help a project team get higher quality software at lower net cost and net elapsed time by improving its project management methods. The **question** follows from the goal, e.g., how do you use quantitative management technology in the planning, organization, control, and technical leadership activities? The relevant metrics, then, are those needed to answer that question. For example, a project goal might be to deliver a product (meeting requirements) that costs no more than 500 labor months of effort. The questions then asked at several points during development is, "how much have we spent?" and "how much more is development going to cost?" The metric associated with this goal is the estimated total cost, which at any point in time is the sum of effort (cost) expended to date and the ETC.

The power of the GQM paradigm is that it is a systematic method for selecting metrics appropriate to your needs. Also, GQM may help you reduce the costs of data collection by helping you concentrate on the metrics that you need. Each metric has been clearly shown to support project goals such as assessing the likelihood of attaining a product development objective of staying within a maximum cost bound. The metrics resulting from the application of the GQM paradigm quantify the characteristics of software products, processes, and development progress that are most useful to project management (Gilb 1988).

6.5 ORGANIZATION AND GOALS

This section identifies various consumers of metric data, their goals, and the questions of interest to them.

6.5.1 User Groups

The first step of applying the GQM paradigm is to identify who is a measurement information consumer (user) and identify his goals (relative to measurement). There is a considerable variety of such consumers. The majority of them belong to one or more of the following (user) groups:

- Measurement (including Software Cost Engineering and/or other groups that collect and analyze software data)

- Software Engineering Process Group (SEPG)

- Software Quality Assurance (SQA)

- Configuration Management (CM)

- Systems Engineering (SE)

- Project or Program Management

- Software Management (various levels, each of which may have different information needs; one may want to know about design, but another may want to know about testing, for example)

- Finance/Accounting

- Software Engineering (both development and test groups, each of which may have different information needs)

Table 6-3 provides an association of the top-level process improvement goals discussed later in this chapter with the involved groups. An "X" indicates that the indicated group is actively involved in the indicated process improvement goal.

Tables 6-3 and 6-4 are not intended to suggest that the indicated groups are associated with the goals on every software development project. While each group of consumers has the goal of product assessment, this does not mean that each group would be interested in precisely the same data set. One group may be interested in a view at a higher level than another. For example, a program manager would probably not be interested in the detailed status of a CSCI design, code, and test. Instead, he would most likely want to know only one measure indicative of the CSCI's degree of completion one that covers all of the activities that comprise the development process. Such a top-level measure is "earned value" and is discussed in Chapter 11.

Table 6-5 presents the management goals for project control. The goals are cross-referenced to the project control questions presented in Table 6-8. Management goals for process improvement are not given because they are closely tied to the organization's specific development process, and this guidebook does not discuss organization-specific process detail.

Involved Group	Understand and Quantify Software Process	Produce/Update Estimation Algorithms	Support Technology Change Impact Analysis
Project/Program Management	X	—	X
Software Management	X	—	X
Measurement	X	—	X
Software Engineering	X	—	—
SEPG	X	X	X
SQA	X	X	X
CM	X	—	—
SE	X	—	X
Finance/Accounting	—	X	—

Table 6-3. *Top-Level Process Improvement Goals and Involved Groups/Users*

Involved Group	Assess Process Status	Assess Product Status	Compare To Goals	Support Taking Corrective Action
Project/Program Management	X	X	X	X
Software Management	X	X	X	X
Measurement	X	X	X	X
Software Engineering	—	X	X	X
SEPG	X	X	X	X
SQA	—	X	X	—
CM	—	X	—	—
SE	—	X	X	X
Finance/Accounting	—	X	X	—

Table 6-4. *Top-Level Project Control Goals and Involved Groups*

Table 6-6 presents some typical goals of each of the involved groups. The list is not exhaustive, but it shows how goals and their associated activities differ among the involved groups.

Table 6-7 shows some typical information systems items that are required to support the project control goals of each of the involved groups of users. In some cases, the individual

General Management Goals	Measurement Activities	Questions
1. Stay on schedule.	1.1 Determine schedule.	1, 2, 3.7, 11.3
2. Stay within budget.	2.1 Do cost estimate. 2.2 Do size estimate.	2, 3.4, 3.5, 3.6, 6, 7, 8, 11.2 3.1, 3.2, 4, 6, 11.1
3. Maximize requirements stability.	2.2 Do size estimate.	3.1, 3.2, 4, 6, 11.1
4. Maximize staff stability.	5.1 Develop staffing profile for each development activity and for project overall.	2
5. Meet product quality requirements.	6.1 Determine defect content at each process stage. 6.2 Estimate defect content at delivery. 6.3 Estimate defect discovery rate during operation.	3.3 3.3, 11.4 3.3
6. Keep product development consistent with resource expenditure.	7.1 Determine status of each unit of the software product. 7.2 Determine overall software product status and earned value.	2, 3.4, 4, 5, 11.1, 13 2, 3.4, 4, 5, 11.1, 13
7. Meet product performance goals.	8.1 Estimate memory utilization. 8.2 Estimate processing capacity utilization. 8.3 Estimate I/O capacity utilization.	4, 11.1, 14.1 4, 11.1, 14.2 4, 11.1, 14.3
8. Minimize project risk.	9.1 Estimate risks.	12

Table 6-5. *General Management Goals, Measurement Activities, and Questions for Project Control*

Involved Group	Group Activities and Project Control Goals
Project/Program Management	Deliver product on schedule. Develop product within budget. Meet product specifications/requirements. Meet stated level of product quality. Minimize/eliminate project risk. Maximize profit. Maintain security. Maximize staff stability.

Table 6-6. *Decomposition of Project Control Goals*

information system item is supplied by a corresponding group supporting the goals of the main group. In other cases, another organization supporting the project control goals of the involved group supplies the individual information systems item.

Involved Group	Group Activities and Project Control Goals
Software Management	Deliver software on schedule. Deliver software within budget. Meet stated level of software quality. Stay within software size constraint. Keep development productivity above xxx SLOC/LM. Keep resources spent consistent with earned value attained.
Measurement	Track and monitor software development to anticipate problems. Provide metrics information to management to aid in corrective action. Collect software experience measurements for process and product improvement. Provide measurements to aid in incremental process improvement. Provide metrics to revise/improve software standards. Maintain a software development experience database.
Software Engineering	Design to requirements. Meet functional objectives. Meet software performance goals. Develop all software by structured methods. Develop software in a manner consistent with standards.
SEPG	Raise the process maturity level. Revise/improve the software development standards. Define new development processes and methods to lower cost and raise quality. Track the software action items (SAIs).
SQA	Train all software developers in design and code inspection methods. Maintain a quality experience database. Audit the development project for compliance to quality standards. Deliver software with an estimated latent defect density of at most 1.0.
CM	Organize a Software Change Control Board and meet regularly. Audit the project for compliance to configuration management standards. Review the configuration of every software build for correctness.
SE	Maintain a Engineering Change Proposal (ECP) database. Monitor the status of all ECPs. Maintain a Program Trouble Report (PTR) database. Monitor the status of all PTRs. Define and communicate all software requirements. Maintain and audit requirements traceability. Minimize interface problems.
Finance/Accounting	Establish and maintain a separate tier of cost accounts for each CSCI. Establish and maintain a separate cost account for every development activity. Audit and monitor project financial status.

Table 6-6. *Decomposition of Project Control Goals, continued*

6.5.2 Project Control and Process Improvement Questions

Table 6-8 shows the questions that you can ask in support of the goals of project control and process improvement. It also gives the association with the metrics presented in Sections 6.7 through 6.14. An asterisk indicates that the concerned group wants to determine the answer to the associated question, and a blank indicates that the concerned group is (probably) not interested in the associated question. A blank in the metrics column means that there is no metric to satisfy the associated question.

6.6 DERIVATION OF UNIT COSTS FOR NEW AND REUSED CODE

"Unit cost" is an important metric for activity-based modeling. This is so regardless of the activity or set of activities to which it applies. If you have no other information about the unit cost for an activity, you can estimate a value for this metric. The value selected can be an estimate based on industry experience, or it can be a unit cost goal selected by your management. However, if you have cost performance data based on past projects such as might be contained in your organization's experience database, then you can calculate unit costs by the method presented in this chapter.

Involved Group	Information System Support Items
Project/Program Management	Actual and planned schedule, budgets and effort expended, staffing levels, staff positions planned and filled, estimates of project risk, and required and estimated product quality
Software Management	Actual and planned software development schedule, software budgets and effort expended, required and estimated software quality, earned value, and productivity to date
Measurement	Metrics/measurements for size, cost, schedule, stability, status, quality, earned value, and computer resources
Software Engineering	Computer resources metrics, amount of function or code in compliance with standards, amount of function or code developed by the approved method
SEPG	Present and anticipated process maturity level, SAIs completed, and requirements designed
SQA	Number of developers trained, amount of design and code inspected, and estimated latent defect density
CM	Amount of function or code in compliance with CM standards
SE	Number of ECPs completed, number of PTRs completed, number of software requirements satisfied
Finance/Accounting	Budget and effort expended for project and for software

Table 6-7. Information System Support to Project Control Goals

Number	Question	Project Control	Process Improvement	Metrics
1	What is the overall schedule: estimated and actual?	*	*	3.1
2	What is the effort expended (cost) and budget by time, activity, and iteration?	*	*	2.1-2.4
3	What is the characterization of the activities that comprise the process?	*	*	
3.1	What is the number of input and output units?	*	*	1.7
3.2	What is the I/O count ratio?	*	*	1.7
3.3	What is the number of defects found in the verification portion of this activity?	*	*	4.1-4.4
3.4	How much effort will it take to transit each activity each time?	*	*	2.1
3.5	What is the staffing level for each activity?	*	*	2.4
3.6	How many times was each activity transited?	*	*	2.5
3.7	What is the time required to transit each activity?	*	*	3.1
4	What is the size of the new and reused code?	*	*	1.3
5	How many requirements will be added and deleted and when?	*	*	1.1
6	What is the product application environment?	*	*	5.1-5.10
7	What is the development environment?	*	*	6.1-6.10
8	Are there development constraints?	*	*	
8.1	Is there a severe cost constraint?	*	*	7.1
8.2	Is there a severe schedule constraint?	*	*	7.2
8.3	Is there a severe development personnel availability constraint?	*	*	7.3
9	What is the development personnel characterization?	*	*	8.1-8.4
10	What is the amount of support (effort) to the software development process of quality assurance, configuration managements, systems engineering, and finance?	*	*	2.1
11	What is the initial estimate and final actuals of the quantities in 11.1 through 11.4?	*	*	
11.1	What is the code size and documentation size for each software product?	*	*	1.3
11.2	What is the development effort by activity for each software product?	*	*	2.1
11.3	What is the development time by activity for each software product?	*	*	3.1

Table 6-8. *Questions Asked in Support of Project Control and Process Improvement Goals*

Number	Question	Project Control	Process Improvement	Metrics
11.4	What are the latent errors for each software product at delivery (original goal and estimated)?	*	*	4.1, 4.2
11.5	What is the design quality of each software product (original goal and estimated through development)? Does the code match the design?	*	*	4.4
12	What is the project risk?	*		
12.1	What is the cost risk?	*		1.3, 2.1
12.2	What is the schedule risk?	*		2.1, 3
12.3	What is the application performance risk?	*		5.1-5.10
12.4	What is the risk in requirements stability?	*		1.1
12.5	What is the risk in unstaffed positions?	*		2.4
13	What is the status?	*		
13.1	What is the status of each software product in each development activity?	*		1.1, 1.2, 1.3, 1.4, 1.5, 1.6, 2
13.2	What is the earned value of each software product?	*		1.7
13.3	What is the overall project status?	*		1.0, 2.0
14	What is the estimated utilization of the target processor?	*		
14.1	Memory?	*		5.8
14.2	Amount of processing capacity?	*		5.9
14.3	Amount of I/O capacity?	*		5.10

Table 6-8. *Questions Asked in Support of Project Control and Process Improvement Goals, continued*

6.6.1 Unit Costs

The cost of software development can be expressed as:

$$C = C_N + C_R$$

where C is the cost in LM (or LH) of the software product in question, C_N is the cost of developing new code for the product, and C_R is the cost of reusing code for the product. This cost includes the set of activities in your development process, typically all activities from design through integration and system test. It does not include any costs of amortizing the development of code that is reused. (A more general model does include the amortization costs, and more detail on this model can be found in Chapter 8.) Documentation costs (contract deliverables in the case of DoD development) are included; however, support costs are not included. You can express C_N and C_R as the product of a unit cost in LM/KSLOC (or LH/SLOC) and a size in KSLOC (or SLOC) for new and reused code, respectively, as:

$$C = C_{VN} \cdot S_N + C_{VR} \cdot S_R$$

where C_{VN} is the unit cost in LM/KSLOC of new code, C_{VR} is the unit cost of reusing code, S_N is the size of the new code in KSLOC, and S_R is the size of the reused code. Alternatively, you might express size in other units, such as "function points" or "feature points" or "number of objectives," rather than KSLOC.

Separate unit costs for new and reused code will usually not be directly observable (and measurable), although the overall cost of development and the sizes will be observable. The overall cost comes from accounting records, and the sizes result from counts of the SLOC. Since the individual unit costs are not observable, they are unknowns. However, you can estimate them as follows:

For simplicity in the mathematics, we denote the unknown unit cost parameters, C_{VN} and C_{VR}, by u and v and consider software product j. Then the general cost equation given above may be written as:

$$C_j = u \cdot S_N + v \cdot S_R$$

Assume that data on software size and cost for m similar development projects (similar applications developed using similar environments) is available. Since you are to calculate two parameters, u and v, you need data from at least two projects. However, if more than two project data sets are available, you should use all of the applicable data sets (i.e., those from similar development projects) since greater accuracy in the calculated unit costs will result. You can formulate this data in matrix form as follows:

$$
X = \begin{bmatrix} S_{N,1} & S_{R,1} \\ S_{N,2} & S_{R,2} \\ \cdot & \cdot \\ \cdot & \cdot \\ \cdot & \cdot \\ S_{N,m} & S_{R,m} \end{bmatrix}
\qquad
Y = \begin{bmatrix} C_1 \\ C_2 \\ \cdot \\ \cdot \\ \cdot \\ C_m \end{bmatrix}
\qquad
B = \begin{bmatrix} u \\ v \end{bmatrix}
$$

where $S_{N,j}$ and $S_{R,j}$ are the sizes in KSLOC (or SLOC or other appropriate unit) of new and reused code in project j, and C_j is the cost of software development in project j. To get the values of u and v, solve the matrix equations (Graybill 1961).

$$(X^TX)B = X^TY$$
$$B = (X^TX)^{-1}X^TY$$

Remember that the weights u and v are really the (estimated) unit costs of the activities of developing new code and of reusing code. You can use these unit costs for cost estimation as shown in Chapter 8. You can apply this mathematical technique, using all appropriate project cost and size data, to each development activity (e.g., design, implementation, and test), and you can compute separate unit costs for each of these activities. Furthermore, you can apply the technique, using all project data, to the constituent activities of the development process (if cost and size data are available) and compute separate unit costs for activities (or a group of several activities).

Of course, the values of u and v (i.e., C_{VN} and C_{VR}) you have computed apply to the distinct type of software product under consideration and the environment used in the development of the projects from whose cost and size data their values were estimated. You should not mix the cost and size data from different types of software when computing these unit costs. For example, display software and control software should have unique unit costs for development activities, so you should not mix their sizes and costs in this type of computation. Further, the values of C_{VN} and C_{VR} that you have computed can be connected and used only for some range of size values. The numerical relationship may change for a different range of size values.

As an example, suppose that data is available (perhaps from your experience database) for three previous projects as follows:

$$X = \begin{bmatrix} 25 & 75 \\ 110 & 35 \\ 90 & 55 \end{bmatrix} \qquad Y = \begin{bmatrix} 205.0 \\ 716.5 \\ 486.5 \end{bmatrix} \qquad B = \begin{bmatrix} 5.96 \\ 0.35 \end{bmatrix}$$

This data indicates that project 1 was composed of 25 KSLOC of new code and 75 KSLOC of reused code and that the total development effort was 205.0 LM. The other row vectors indicate similar information for projects 2 and 3.

The inverse of the X^TX matrix is:

$$(X^TX)^{-1} = \begin{bmatrix} 10.769 & -11.641 \\ -11.641 & 22.710 \end{bmatrix} \cdot 10^{-5}$$

Since the elements of the X matrix are KSLOC of new code and KSLOC of reused code and since the elements of the Y matrix are LM for development, the elements of the B matrix are LM/KSLOC for new code, u, and for reused code, v. The unit cost for new code, $u = C_{VN}$, is 5.96 LM/KSLOC, and the unit cost for reused code, $v = C_{VR}$, is 0.35 LM/KSLOC.

6.6.2 Equivalent Source Statements

The (cost) equivalent size of a system composed of new and reused code (Gaffney 1983; Cruickshank 1984 and 1988) is represented by the ESLOC metric which combines the two metrics of new and reused source statements into one size metric. You can define the metric either in terms of SLOC or KSLOC. It combines new code (N) and reused code (R) sizes into one size metric that is cost-equivalent to all new code. The definition is:

$$ESLOC = (SLOC)_N + w(SLOC)_R$$
$$KESLOC = (KSLOC)_N + w(KSLOC)_R$$

The ESLOC (or KESLOC) metric assigns a weight, w, of 1.00 to new SLOC and a weight of w<1.00 to reused SLOC. Experience shows that w typically has a value of 0.04 to 0.31, which means that reused code cost (on a per statement or per unit basis) is 0.04 to 0.31 as much as the new code to be included in the system being developed.Using a value of 0.30, a software product composed of 100 KSLOC of new code and 190 KSLOC of reused code has 100+(0.30)190=157 KESLOC. This example illustrates the representation of size by one number when there are two code types present.

In the example of C_{VN} and C_{VR} previously given, the weight for equivalent code is:

$$w = \frac{C_{VR}}{C_{VN}} = \frac{v}{u} = \frac{0.35}{5.96} = 0.06$$

These results are within the range of some specific experience with real-time embedded software development.

The ESLOC and KESLOC concepts allow you to compute overall size and unit cost or productivity metrics for software products that include both new and reused code. The ESLOC concept facilitates quality assurance size and productivity comparisons among computer programs and among development projects with varying code mixtures.

Your organization should determine a standard value for the weight (w) so that all definitions and calculations of ESLOC will be on the same basis and will be comparable. The precise value of w will be a characteristic of the development environment and process.

As used above, it is possible to define the ESLOC metric in terms of more than the two code types. For example, you could use the categories of new (N), modified (M), and reused (R). In this case ESLOC would be defined as:

$$ESLOC = (SLOC)_N + w_1 \bullet (SLOC)_M + w_2 \bullet (SLOC)_R$$

For this and similar definitions of ESLOC metrics, you have to derive numerical values for the weights, and such a derivation depends on a very detailed quantitative knowledge of your software development process and the unit costs that compose it. For convenience, it is usually assumed that modified code costs the same (and therefore has the same weight) as new code. In most cases, reusing code costs less than developing new code, as previously asserted. It is usually true that reused components cost less to use than modified components. (Cruickshank 1988).

It may be assumed that deleting or removing code has no cost, i.e., code deletion or removal has a unit cost of 0.00 LM/KSLOC or LH/SLOC. In this case, the cost impacts of deletion or removal are assigned to the costs of new code development. Generally speaking, by using this type of code in your cost calculations, you are assigning the costs to the categories of code even though there actually may be more than the two code categories of new and reused.

Since the weight for reused code is relative to new code, the weight for reused code in the ESLOC relation is w=(v/u), where the weights u and v are derived in the previous subchapter. You calculate ESLOC and KESLOC as:

$$ESLOC = (OR\ KESLOC) = S_N + (v/u)S_R$$

6.7 PRODUCT SIZE METRICS

Table 6-9 shows a set of software product size metrics.

You might define the number of requirements by counting the number of "shalls" in the specification. This guidebook assumes there is no formal mathematical notation for a requirements specification.

You should count SLOD when you use a PDL or equivalent design representation such as pseudocode or structured narrative. Count SLOD for both preliminary design and detailed design. Derive SLOC/SLOD ratios for use in estimating software size in SLOC when you only know SLOD in design.

Use Table 6-9 to select the size metrics for tracking the size of the software through the development life cycle and to compute costs. You can find additional data items in National Aeronautics and Space Administration (1990); IEEE (1992); Humphrey, Kitson, and Kasse

(1989); Grady (1992); and Grady and Caswell (1987) if you want to expand the list or if you want to make your own list of software size metrics.

Number	Type	Metrics
1.1	Requirements	Original and final number of requirements
		Number of requirements added and deleted during development
		Number of undefined requirements over the time of development
		Number of (function) boxes in system diagrams
		Number of (data) stores in system diagrams
		Number of (hardware) boxes in a computer network diagram
		Number of major subjects or headings in a system description diagram
1.2	Design	Number of design statements (source lines of design [SLOD]), program design language (PDL) statements, and structured narrative statements
		Number of pages in design documents
		Number of process "bubbles"
		Number of data "entities"
		Number of boxes or arrows in hierarchical input-output (HIPO) charts
1.3	Code	Number of source statements (source lines of code [SLOC]) by language, by type (new, added, modified, reused), and by line code count (physical and/or logical)
		Number of source statements delivered and not delivered by language
		Number of lines (physical and logical) of comments (casual, headers, prologs)
		Number of function points
		Number of feature points
		Number of object code instructions or bytes
		Number of words of memory
		Number of screens
		Number of operands and operators
		Number of tokens
1.4	Test	Number of tests
		Number of test procedure steps
		Number of test procedure steps completed at each activity
		Number of pages of test documentation (plan procedures, reports)

Table 6-9. *Software Product Size Metrics*

Number	Type	Metrics
1.5	Functions	Number of CSCIs, CSCs, and CSUs
		Number of hardware boxes (where there is primary computer software controlling secondary computer hardware functions)
		Number of inquiries
		Number of inputs and outputs
		Number of external interfaces
		Number of logical files
		Number of algorithms
		Number of function and feature points
		Number of iterations per activity combination in the evolutionary spiral process
1.6	Documentation	Number of pages of documentation by document name; pages can be classified as text, tables, or figures
		Number of documents by type
1.7	Status	Percent complete in each development activity of each software product; can be measured in software units such as CSCs, CSUs, requirements, SLOD, SLOC, or function points
		Earned value
		Percent of budget spent in each development activity of each software product
		Number of SAIs opened and closed
		Number of ECPs opened and closed
		Number of authorized positions staffed and unstaffed

Table 6-9. *Software Product Size Metrics, continued*

6.8 COST AND EFFORT METRICS

This chapter provides metrics for software development labor and for using a computer that supports development.

6.8.1 Labor Cost Metrics

This chapter focuses on the cost of development labor. In this guidebook, cost is expressed in terms of effort, i.e., LM or LH. Typically, no less then 80 percent of the cost to develop software modules is attributable to labor; therefore, cost metrics play a crucial role not only in estimating software development and maintenance costs but also in the management of software development. Use the size metrics presented in Section 6.7 with the cost metrics to produce estimates of software development costs shown in Chapter 8. Accurately estimating software costs is widely acknowledged to be a critical problem in the management of software development, so cost metrics are of great importance. Table 6-10 presents a set of software labor cost metrics.

Number	Type	Metrics
2.1	Effort (cost)	Initial estimate and final actuals of effort (cost) in LM, LH, and/or dollars for each activity in each software product
		Budgets in LM, LH, and/or dollars for each activity in each software product
		Amount spent in LM, LH, and/or dollars for each activity in each software product
2.2	Computer support	Budgets and actuals of computer dollars spent for each development activity for each software product
2.3	Risk management activities	Number of risk management activities (including risk aversion and iterations) associated with a development activity
2.4	Staffing	Number of full-time equivalent positions authorized and filled

Table 6-10. *Software Cost Metrics*

You can measure software costs labor by LM, LH, and dollars. In estimating costs, you estimate LM or LH first and then convert them to dollars. LM and LH are the primary measures of cost since using these cost measures facilitates comparisons among different projects at different times. State the costs of activities comprising the software development life cycle in terms of LM or LH. You can state these cost measures in terms of dollars once you determine the proper labor categories.

You can compare measurements of cost in LM or LH with other measurements in LM or LH that you made at different points in time, such as with previous projects. Measurements made in dollars are difficult to compare over time or among development projects done by different organizations because of variability in unit costs (in dollars) among organizations and in the value of the dollar and because of the changing cost of labor. You first make estimates in LM or LH and convert them to dollars for proposal and budgetary purposes. Normally, you use LM or LH as the primary estimation quantity. If you use LM, be sure to state the number of LH per LM.

Collect cost data in LM or LH for the total labor expended: normal time plus overtime. Keep separate cost accounts for each CSCI in the WBS, and keep a separate cost account for each of the activities in the WBS development process. The development activities' cost accounts should tier up to the CSCI total development cost account, and there should be a separate tiering structure for each CSCI. If parts of a CSCI use different development processes, each process should be a separate tiering structure. Such an accounting scheme makes budgeting more precise and makes collecting costs much easier.

This guidebook presents costs in terms of LM and LH, not dollars, since dollars per LM or LH differ substantially among organizations, locations, and labor category.

6.8.2 Labor Months and Labor Hours

It is important to note that where you use LM as the measure of effort, you should know and clearly state the number of hours per LM. Such a statement in cost reports facilitates the comparison and standardization of the LM measure among separate organizations. Collect all charges to each cost account and activity in a development project.

One measure of LM is 167 LH per direct LM. This figure is derived from observing that there are 52 weeks per year at 40 hours per work week or 2080 possible work hours per year. Subtracting 80 hours (10 days) of holidays yields 2000 work hours per year. Thus, there are 2000/12=167 hours per LM. However, the 167 hours/LM figure does not take into account vacations and sick time. If 120 hours is allocated for vacation and 40 hours for illness, the actual staffing LM is 1840/12=153 hours.

Because of possible confusion among the various definitions of an LM, it is desirable to use LH in preference to LM. If you use the LM measure, ensure that you define it in terms of LH, providing the rationale for the figure you chose.

6.8.3 Computer Usage Cost Metrics

The cost of computer support during software development is a measure that you collect if your project is charged for computer time. Some software development projects use both host and target computer systems. In many cases of DoD software development, the target computer is government-furnished equipment (GFE), but the host computer is a corporate computer. No charge is made for using the GFE system, but an internal procedure bills you for host computer time. Since the host system performs such tasks as simulation studies, data analysis, documentation production, and program conversion for execution on the GFE system, this cost can be a significant burden.

Most organizations base their billing procedures on the amount of computer time used, but this is a difficult quantity to estimate in advance since few developers know how fast their software will execute on the host or target system and how many runs they will need to make. If your organization keeps accounting records on the hours of computer time (internally or externally) billed and the LM or LH for software development, then you can derive an hours/LM or hours/LH metric. You use this type of metric for estimating future development computer costs by using the estimate of LM or LH for development and multiplying by the appropriate ratio.

More commonly, organizations keep accounting records for computer usage (where internal billing is involved) in dollars. In this case, you derive dollars/LM or dollars/LH metrics for computer usage. Furthermore, you develop separate metrics of dollars/LM or dollars/LH for the coding, documentation production, software integration testing, and system integration testing development activity. The values of these metrics will differ, but the use of unique computer cost ratio metrics for each activity in software development can lead to very accurate estimates of computer costs. There should be a date associated with each computer cost metric to indicate the time when the cost metrics were updated. This time label allows the adjustment of costs forward and backward in time.

6.9 SCHEDULE METRICS

Schedule is an important determinant of cost. If not enough time is available for the development of a software product, you will make errors and not discover them, and your costs will be high. If too much time is available, your productivity will be low and your costs will be high. It is important to have a reasonable schedule for development.

The most common schedule measurable is time in months, although you might use years. You may also use milestones and events as time or schedule measures. Table 6-11 presents a set of software schedule metrics.

6.10 SOME QUALITY METRICS

Quality of the software product and of the software development process is an important consideration. The basic quality measure is defects. To produce a high-quality product, you must attune your development process to a zero-defect goal method of operation. To produce a high-quality product at the lowest possible cost, you must remove defects at the earliest possible point in the development process. Concentrate on discovering and removing defects/errors at the earliest possible stage of development, i.e., in design and code inspections. Table 6-12 presents a set of quality metrics. See Chapter 10 for additional discussion and information about software defects and the selection of software quality metrics.

Possible categories for the types of defects include design, logic, syntax, standards, data, return message, prolog/comment, performance, and interface. You may count requirements defects, both the number of instances of incompleteness and the number of instances of inconsistencies, if requirements reviews are a formal part of your software development process.

The design quality metrics deserve some special discussion. You measure design defect density in design defects/KSLOC to get an indication of design correctness. Design defects can be discovered in any development activity from preliminary design to CSCI test.

Number	Type	Metrics
3.1	Schedule	Schedules and elapsed time in weeks, months and/or years
		Milestone or events (on an ordinal scale)

Table 6-11. *Software Schedule Metrics*

Number	Type	Metrics
4.1	Number of defects Number of each type of defect including program trouble reports (PTRs)	Number of valid and invalid defects including PTRs Number of defects discovered in each activity of development and/or by type of inspection or review (includes PTRs) Number of major and minor defects (on an ordinal scale) Number of valid field deficiency reports
4.2	Defects/product unit	Defects/KSLOC or defects/function point
4.3	Defect cost	LM, LH, or dollars of inspection/detection cost per defect Number of persons participating in inspections
4.4	Design quality	Design defects/KSLOC discovered during development (correctness) Average number of days to fix an error (maintainability) Average effort to expand the product divided by effort to develop the product (expandability) Average effort to verify the product divided by effort to develop the product (verifiability) Effort to port (apply to a new application) the product divided by effort to develop the product (portability) Effort to reuse the product divided by effort to develop the product (reusability) Number of two-way jumps + 1 (McCabe complexity) Halstead's difficulty metric (design goodness) Number of latent defects divided by number of life cycle defects (error discovery efficiency) Function of the number of unique inputs and outputs and the number of assignment statements (strength) Average number of input and output items shared by this product with others (coupling) Data bindings

Table 6-12. *Software Quality Metrics*

Measuring design defect density gives you a good indication of design quality, although your judgment of whether the measured design quality is acceptable or not will depend upon your experience in your environment. Any judgment of design quality acceptability will depend upon a comparison of the current measurement with a standard or an acceptable design performance in the past.

It is also worthwhile to note that defects/KSLOC is a metric for overall software product quality, whether measured throughout development or given as estimated latent defects/KSLOC at delivery. Experience with the measurement of overall product quality in defects/KSLOC for real-time embedded software shows that about 20 defects/KSLOC is a good level of performance over the development cycle (excluding requirements analysis).

Similarly, metrics for maintainability, expandability, verifiability, portability, and reusability be proposed as measures of design quality and of overall software product quality (see Chapter 10). The products could not be maintainable unless they are well designed. There is no quantitative guidance as to acceptable values of the metrics of these software attributes. You will have to develop your own standards based on past experience with like products.

Some of these design quality metrics relate to the software product, some relate to the development process, and some relate to both. The metrics suggested for maintainability, expandability, verifiability, portability, and reusability relate to the software product. The error discovery efficiency metric relates to the process. And the metrics for complexity and design goodness relate to both the product and the control process.

Control structure complexity is defined (McCabe 1976) as the cyclomatic number of the graph representation of a program and is computed by the formula:

$$V(G) = e - n + p$$

where V(G) is the cyclomatic complexity of a graph with (e) edges, (n) nodes, and (p) connected components. This quantity is equal to the number of two-way conditional jumps plus one. V(G) is a metric for the control complexity of a unit of software.

Halstead (1977) defined "difficulty"; and Christensen, Fitsos, and Smith (1981) proposed it as a measure of design goodness. The metric is:

$$\text{Difficulty} = \left(\frac{\text{unique\_operator\_count}}{\text{potential\_operator\_count}} \right) \left(\frac{\text{total\_operands}}{\text{unique\_operand\_count}} \right)$$

where operands are the variables or constants employed in the software algorithm or product and the operators are the symbols (e.g., instructions) that affect the values or ordering of the operands. The potential_operator_count is the minimum possible number of operators and is known to be equal to 2. Therefore, the difficulty metric becomes:

$$\text{Difficulty} = \left(\frac{\text{unique\_operator\_count}}{2}\right)\left(\frac{\text{total\_operands}}{\text{unique\_operand\_count}}\right)$$

The difficulty metric is a measure of the difficulty constants of writing (and reading) code and is the reciprocal of the level measure (Halstead 1977; Christensen, Fitsos, and Smith 1981). Christensen et al. discovered that the difficulty metric, especially its second factor, has a relatively high correlation with the number of defects discovered in the operation of a software system.

Defect (Error) discovery efficiency may be defined as:

$$\text{Defect\_discovery\_efficiency} = 1 - \frac{\text{latent defects}}{\text{total\_No.\_of\_defects\_injected}}$$

where the number of latent defects is the number of defects estimated to be remaining in the software after delivery, and the total number of defects injected is the number of defects injected during development and preliminary design through CSCI test.

Myers' (1975) two measures related to the structure of software and the goodness of a software design are strength (cohesion) and coupling. "Strength" is a measure of the degree of cohesiveness of the elements in a software product unit (a module). "Coupling" indicates the degree of interconnectedness of a number of such units.

Cruickshank and Gaffney (1980) proposed the strength metric:

$$\text{Strength} = (X^2 + Y^2)^{1/2}$$

where X is the reciprocal of the number of assignment statements in the module (product), and Y is the number of unique function (product) outputs divided by the number of unique function (product) inputs.

Cruickshank and Gaffney (1980) proposed the coupling metric:

$$\text{Coupling} = \frac{\sum_{i=1}^{n} Z_i}{n}$$

where:

$$Z_i = \frac{\sum_{j=1}^{m} M_j}{m}$$

M_j is the sum of the number of input and output items shared between component i and component j in the software product. Z_i is, therefore, the average number of input and output items shared over m components with component i. Therefore, the coupling metric is the average number of input and output items shared over all n components in the software product.

These metrics have not been widely used; however they do provide quantification of the coupling and strength concepts.

Selby and Basili (1991) developed another measure of a software system's structure, which essentially combines the strength and coupling measures. It is based on intrasystem interaction in terms of software data bindings. Selby and Basili (1991) define "data bindings" as "…measures that capture the data interaction across portions of a software system." These bindings are defined with respect to clusters of routines of the software system analyzed. This metric is defined as the ratio:

$$\frac{B}{b}$$

Where B = the number of data bindings between routines within the cluster and those outside of it, and b = the number of data bindings between routines within the cluster.

This number is interpreted as the ratio:

$$\frac{C}{c}$$

Where C = the coupling of the cluster with other clusters in the subsystem, and c = the internal strength of the cluster

6.11 PRODUCT APPLICATION ENVIRONMENT METRICS

The scaling measures of some subjective measurables (Tables 6-13 through 6-16) are based on orthogonal polynomials that assure statistical independence. These values not only scale the variable numerically but also ensure their mathematical independence in any statistical regression (or similar) studies. Table 6-13 presents the software product application environment metrics.

6.12 DEVELOPMENT ENVIRONMENT METRICS

Development environment metrics are quantitative measures of how software development is managed, including process, practice, and organizational aspects. Because the environmental scales are subjective and different for each of the metric types, the metrics have been

Number	Type	Metrics
5.1	Planning limitation	Bytes or words of memory used and bytes or words limitation
5.2	Processing capacity limitation	Mips used and mips limitation
5.3	I/O capacity limitation	I/O capacity used in terms of information per unit processing time
5.4	Reliability	Reliability level (very low=−2, low=−1, nominal=0, high=1, very high =2)
5.5	Embedded	Embedded (no=−1, yes=1)
5.6	Real-time	Real-time (no=−1, yes=1)
5.7	Complexity	Software product complexity (low=−1, medium=0, high=1)
5.8	Size limitation	Number of bytes or words of memory used and number of bytes or words limitation
5.9	Speed limitation	Mips used (needed) for product execution and mips permitted for product execution
5.10	Transactions limitation	Number of I/O transaction processed by unit time and minimum required number of I/O transactions processed by unit time

Table 6-13. *Software Product Application Environment Metrics*

quantized on an orthogonal scale. The orthogonal scales ensure the mathematical independence of these variables in linear regression studies. Table 6-14 presents the software development environment metrics.

6.13 DEVELOPMENT CONSTRAINT METRICS

Development constraint metrics are quantitative measures of the limitations placed on development costs, schedules, and staffing. Because the constraint scale is subjective, ranging from not severe to severe, the metrics have been quantized on a scale from −1 to 1. These values orthogonalize the scale and ensure their mathematical independence in linear regression studies. Table 6-15 presents the software development constraint metrics.

6.14 DEVELOPMENT PERSONNEL METRICS

Table 6-16 presents the software development personnel characterization metrics. Because the personnel characterization scale is subjective, ranging from low to high, the metrics have been quantized on a scale from −1 to 1. These values also orthogonalize the scale.

Number	Type	Metrics
6.1	Computer access	Development computer access (no workstation/remote mainframe=−1, shared workstation=0, individual workstation=1)
6.2	Practices	Use of modern programming practices and methods (very low=−2, low=−1, nominal=1, very high=2)
6.3	Tools	Use of programming tools (very low=−2, low=−1, nominal=0, high=1, very high=2)
6.4	Risk management	Use of development risk management techniques (low=−1, moderate=0, high=1)
6.5	Defined process	Use of defined process (low=−1, moderate=0, high=1)
6.6	Requirement stability	Product requirement stability (low=−1, moderate=0, high=1)
6.7	Process stability	Development process stability (low=−1, moderate=0, high=1)
6.8	Simultaneous development	Simultaneous hardware/software development (no=−1, yes=1)
6.9	Standards	Degree of enforcement of software engineering standards (low or no standards=−1, moderate=0, high=1)
6.10	Contract	Type of contract (cost plus fixed fee [CPFF]=−1, cost plus incentive fee [CPIF]=0, fixed price [FP]=1)

Table 6-14. Software Development Environment Metrics

Number	Type	Metrics
7.1	Cost	Cost constraint (not severe=−1, severe=1)
7.2	Schedule	Schedule constraint (not severe=−1, severe=1)
7.3	Staffing	Staffing constraint (not severe=−1, severe=1)

Table 6-15. Software Development Constraint Metrics

Number	Type	Metrics
8.1	Language familiarity	Development group familiarity with product implementation language (low = −1, moderate = 0, high = 1)
8.2	Experience	Development group software engineering experience (low = −1, moderate=0, high = 1)
8.3	Application familiarity	Development group familiarity with application (low = −1, moderate = 0, high = 1)
8.4	Management	Management personnel experience (low = −1, moderate = 0, high = 1)

Table 6-16. Software Development Personnel Characterization Metrics

6.15 PRODUCTIVITIES AND UNIT COSTS

Use the size metrics from Section 6.7 with the cost metrics from Section 6.8 to produce productivities and/or unit labor costs. Choose the metrics appropriate to your needs and compute the values of the metrics for the delivered product over the development process for each product. Also, separately compute the appropriate metrics for new and reused code for each activity, where applicable, using the method shown in Section 6.6. Some useful productivity and unit cost metrics are:

- SLOC per LM or per LH.

- LM per KSLOC or LH per SLOC.

- ESLOC per LM or per LH.

- LM per KESLOC.

- SLOD per LM or per LH.

- Words of object code per LM or per LH.

- Test procedure steps per LM or per LH.

- Pages of documentation per LM or per LH.

- Function points per LM or per LH.

You use SLOC/LM as the productivity metric or LM/KSLOC as the unit cost metric for the activities in development even though SLOC is not the output of some of the activities, such as design. SLOC may be actual or estimated. The design cost metric can be SLOD/LM. This metric requires estimates and counts of SLOD. When the development of the software product(s) has been completed, you revise the values of the productivity and unit cost metrics to reflect the actual value of the size of the product(s) or of the new and reused code they contain.

Unit costs are the scaled inverse of productivities. Alternatively, you use LM/KSLOC as a unit labor cost metric for either new or reused code. The advantage of using LH/SLOC or LM/KSLOC is that these unit costs are additive, so you can easily calculate the total unit cost for development from the individual activity unit costs. Productivities such as SLOC/LM are not additive, and thus they offer no such convenience of representation or calculation. Alternatively, you use LM/KESLOC or LH/ESLOC as overall unit cost metrics. Unit labor cost metrics such as LM/KSLOC and LH/SLOC are also called unit costs.

The conversion formulas between productivities and unit costs are:

$$SLOC/LM = 1,000/(LM/KSLOC)$$
$$SLOC/LH = 1/(LH/SLOC)$$

Your software development organization should derive a unit cost for every activity in its development process for each type of software product it develops. You view this set of unit costs as the "standard" or "baseline" set to guide or be used as a "menu" corresponding to the set of possible activities composing the software development process. This process consists of selecting the activities that form the standard or baseline set describing (modeling) the particular software process in question then modifying the standard unit costs, if necessary, for some of these selected activities.

Collect the number of iterations (or the number of prototypes) through the software development life cycle and the number of iterations through each of the activities that compose the spiral process. These quantities appear in the list of product size metrics given in Section 6.7. You should also determine the cost per iteration and the cost of the activities that compose each iteration if possible.

When you collect labor cost data, whether in LM or LH, it is important that you collect all of the applicable labor cost data. Since a software product is often produced with significant overtime and normal working time, you should capture all of this cost data. To consider only normal working hours tends to overstate productivity and understate costs.

6.16 SUMMARY OF RECOMMENDATIONS

The recommendations on the selection of metrics presented in Chapter 6 are:

- Define metrics relative to objectives and establish measurements in advance of project initiation. Use the GQM paradigm to identify the metrics you need.

- Relate metrics to problem (or potential problem) solutions.

- Count source statements and comments separately. Do not count noncomment blank lines.

- Compute cost estimates and initially state them in LM or LH. The LM or LH mode allows more precise comparisons between projects or activities. The value of the dollar constantly changes through time and by labor category, whereas LM or LH do not. Convert LM and LH to dollars when appropriate.

- Select metrics based on goals that a particular user group has established for information on project control and/or process improvement.

- Select the metrics you will use in a cost-effective manner.

Chapter

7

HOW TO ESTIMATE
SOFTWARE SYSTEM SIZE

7.1 SIZE ESTIMATION

The effort, cost, and length of time required to develop software all depend on the size of the software products to be developed. This chapter describes how to estimate software product size.

7.1.1 The Importance of Size Estimation

Size estimation is an important activity in the quantitative management of software projects because most cost estimation algorithms use size estimates as input, and the misestimation of size will lead to inaccurate cost estimates. The biggest difficulty in using the cost estimation algorithms available today is the problem of providing sound sizing estimates (Boehm 1983). Misestimation of software product size is probably a greater source of error in software cost estimates than misestimation of productivity or unit costs.

Software size estimation is also difficult because there is no fundamental size to accomplish a stated requirement. The size of the software component created to satisfy a requirement may depend upon the skill and experience of the software engineers assigned to the job (Boehm 1983). The nature of this dependence is not readily discernible.

7.1.2 Size Estimation Activities

This chapter is designed to help you answer the question, "How big will the system be?" It provides methods for estimating software size in terms of software statement or lines of code counts, emphasizing methods that you can apply early in the development cycle.

125

Estimating the size of a new software system is the key to estimating development cost, both in dollar terms and in the amount of labor and other resources required, since the size determines a large part of the cost of a software system. Errors in the estimate of a software system's size often exceed the estimation error for development productivity.

You should reestimate software product size throughout the development process. You should derive the initial estimate prior to the initiation of software development using your knowledge of the requirements. You can derive subsequent estimates during the development process based on increased knowledge about the software system as it evolves. You should derive this additional information from further elaboration and expansion of the requirements, the design, and other intermediate products of the process, e.g., documentation, as you create them during development. The methodology presented here uses knowledge about what is to be built, i.e., the requirements, as well as what has been designed and/or coded to date during the development process. However, the emphasis here is on the development of "front-end" estimates, those you make before you begin the actual development.

There are two principal types of measures of software product size:

- ***The Amount of Code.*** This is the number of source statements or number of SLOC, as discussed in Chapter 6. A SLOC count tends to vary with the language in which the software is written. That is, in general, a given system is expressible in fewer higher level language statements (e.g., Ada) than are required for lower level (e.g., assembly) language.

- ***The Number of Function (or Feature) Points.*** This is a measure of the amount of function provided by the software system, as defined in Section 7.5. It is independent of the language in which the system is written although the cost of development is not.

This chapter focuses on the estimation of code size in SLOC because it is the more general approach.

7.1.3 Size Estimation and the Development Cycle

This section is particularly concerned with estimating the size of a new software system very early in the development cycle, i.e., in the proposal or conceptual and requirements analysis activities. At this very early point in the development cycle, there is usually very little detailed information available about the intended software system. You may not yet have assigned new and reused code to the planned functions. Later in the development cycle, when you have assigned new and reused code to functions, you can estimate the size of the functions to be represented by new code using other methods presented in this chapter. When you identify the functions to be implemented by reused code, you can count the reused code.

7.1.4 Size Estimation and Process Maturity Levels

Software organizations at lower levels of process maturity typically concentrate on using methods that require a minimum of experience data. An organization at higher levels will typically use methods that emphasize the use of experience data to estimate size, incorporating lessons learned from results of the organization's process modifications and development experience.

Software size is the primary parametric input to most cost and schedule estimating algorithms, but the estimates of size used for these purposes are frequently based on guesses or anecdotal information. Inaccuracies in size estimates are the primary cause for inaccuracies in cost and schedule estimates. Even where you know your unit costs and where you have thoroughly analyzed your schedule constraints, the overall cost and schedule estimates for your software development projects may lack precision because your size estimates were not derived using systematic methods.

It is best if you estimate code size based on the past experience of your own organization. This experience should be accessible in terms of the data available in a formal database. This database should contain the sizes of CSCIs, the number of major inputs and outputs, the code counts, and other such information. You should take considerable care in making a direct comparison between projects, i.e., between the new project in question and a previous project as it appears in the experience database. You should make a careful analysis of both the similarities and differences of the functions in both projects before basing your size estimates on previous experience.

7.2 SIZE ESTIMATION DURING THE DEVELOPMENT CYCLE

This chapter shows you ways to estimate software product size throughout the development cycle.

7.2.1 Size Estimation by Development Activity

A software development organization that has a defined process (i.e., the process of an organization at SEI process maturity Level 3) should have accumulated enough data in its software experience database so that it can make reasonable estimates of size throughout the life cycle of the software. Your organization should use systematic methods for size estimation such as those presented in this chapter. The life cycle is composed of many activities, all of which you define and place under management control at SEI process maturity Level 3 or equivalent. You should make size estimates at several milestones during development.

Monitor a software development project, with all of its associated software products, throughout the development cycle using a continuous measurement process. Considerable variation characterizes software product size estimates done early in the development cycle because so little detail about the software is available. Size estimates you make later, during the design, code, and test activities are subject to much less variation since you have based them primarily on design and code counts made during development.

In general, when your software development project is in the system-level conceptual stage, you should use a technique such as function block counting (see Section 7.3) since you know very little else but the major functions included in the system. As the project moves from conception to proposal, techniques like I/O counting (see Section 7.6) come into play since you will have defined the main interfaces between the major functions. At proposal time, you can use function block and I/O techniques as cross-checks on each other to achieve a reasonable level of confidence that you made a suitable size estimate. At the design phase, you should count design statements (SLOD) and convert them to SLOC estimates by an SLOC-to-SLOD ratio derived from your organization's experience. As the project moves from design to coding and testing, use code counts to give very accurate estimates of final product cost.

7.2.2 Using Source Lines of Design to Estimate Software Size (SLOD)

During the conduct of the design activity, information in the form of SLOD counts is available if you use a design language. Preserve these SLOD counts in your software experience database. When the corresponding SLOC counts become available, compute a SLOC-to-SLOD ratio and preserve it. This ratio will aid you in converting SLOD-to-SLOC estimates during future project developments. You can use an estimate for this ratio based on past project development experience or other information that may be available to you. Alternatively, you can compute function point-to-SLOC ratios and use them for future estimates of the amount of design (in SLOD) that you will develop for a system of some given size in function points.

7.2.3 Size Estimation Steps

You should follow these steps in making size estimates:
- At the conceptual or requirements stages, compile the requirements for the system and its major parts, such as CSCI or a software product, whose size you wish to estimate.

- Get all of the data you can about the system you are to estimate (i.e., functions to be performed, counts of inputs and outputs, etc.).

- Get as much detail as you can. Get the data for as many of the (likely) component functions or parts of the system as you can. Consult with those who have the most expert knowledge of the components or functions in which you are interested. Take advantage of the fact that an underestimate of the size of one component often cancels the overestimate of the size of another component.

- Make several estimates at each stage of development based on different types of data, then compare them. If they differ beyond 10 to 20 percent, reconsider your assumptions and try again. Repeat the process.

7.3 FUNCTION BLOCK COUNT SIZE ESTIMATION

This chapter describes a method for estimating a software system's size based on the number of major software functions or subfunctions that you believe will compose the system. If you have very little information about the intended application system, you can make a rough estimate of the software system size using the counted or estimated number of CSCIs or CSCs or other units of code. This method has the advantage of requiring little information, so you can apply it very early in the development cycle. You can apply this method at the conceptualization or requirements stages when the size implication of a requirement is itself the input to a decision-making process, e.g., the decision to include the function or to bid on a contract. This method has the disadvantage of not directly including the effect of other information that may be available about the application system.

You can count major functions and equate them to the number of CSCIs or the number of CSCs. You can also count major functions as function blocks in a system description document or in a system-level block diagram or flow chart. At the conception of the system (when you are planning the system at the top level), you should identify the major software functions and count them as function blocks. A function block corresponds to a CSCI; and the next level of decomposition, major subfunctions, corresponds to a CSC. You can use a similar decomposition method if you don't employ CSCIs and CSCs.

You can apply the methods presented here at one or two levels of decomposition: at the CSCI or CSC level. Gaffney (1984b) and Britcher and Gaffney (1985) demonstrated that, under the assumption that most systems have the same number of decomposition levels, you can estimate the system's size as a function of the number of functional elements at any one level. Thus, you would not expect a larger system to have more (vertical) levels of decomposition than a smaller one. Instead, the larger system would have more units of code at each level: CSCI and CSC.

You can base your estimate of software system size on the number of CSCs or CSCIs that you expect to compose the system. Britcher and Gaffney (1985) present figures of 41.6 KSLOC and 4.16 KSLOC, respectively, for the expected values of size for a CSCI and a CSC. Experience suggests that the size of a CSCI can vary rather substantially among systems or even within a given system. It is quite reasonable to expect a substantial variation since the estimation process uses little information about the actual system such as what coding language is being employed in its composition. Some data on the experience of an aerospace contractor shows that the standard deviation of the sizes of a CSCI averages 27.5 percent of the expected value, s/E = 0.275 (see Section 7.4). The values presented here are undoubtedly application domain–dependent, and you should make great efforts to adapt these values to the domain or environment in question.

Your organization should collect data about the sizes of the CSCIs and CSCs and then develop average size figures to use in developing function block estimates as described here. However, if no such data is available, then you might use the figures of 41.6 KSLOC and 11.45 KSLOC (= 0.275 x 41.6), respectively, for the expected value and standard deviation of the size of each CSCI in the system whose size you wish to estimate. Then, based on the statistical concepts presented in Section 7.4, calculate the expected estimate of size in KSLOC and the estimated standard deviation of the size in KSLOC of the overall system using the equations:

$$E_{tot} = 41.6 \bullet N$$
$$\alpha_{tot} = 0.275 \bullet E_{tot}$$

where N is the number of CSCIs. Alternatively, you can multiply the number of CSCs by 4.16 KSLOC to produce an estimate of size. One of the estimates would be based on your estimate of the number of CSCIs, and the other estimate would be based on your estimate of the number of CSCs. You can use the two-product size estimates as a cross-check on each other.

In summary, the steps of the function block method are:

- Count or estimate the number of blocks at a given level of detail, i.e., at the CSCI or CSC level, or both.

- Multiply the number of blocks by the expected value of the size for that type of block. This is the expected size of the system overall.

- Compute the standard deviation of estimated system size.

- Compute the desired range of the system size for the probability levels desired per the method described in Section 7.4.

- Apply this method for both the count of CSCIs and for the count of CSCs, and pool the results. Do not apply this method when there are fewer than three function blocks.

7.4 STATISTICAL SIZE ESTIMATION

This chapter describes a systematic method for estimating the code size of a software system by estimating the ranges of size of the component elements such as CSCs and CSCIs that will compose it. This method enables you to make systematic estimates of the sizes of the software system's individual components that you are to develop. The method involves decomposing the system into a number of functions, considering each of them in turn, and then statistically operating on the data to obtain estimates of the overall size and the standard deviation of the estimate. This method enables you to reduce the effect of uncertainty in estimated sizes of the individual components and to obtain a better estimate of the overall system size. The source of the information for the size estimate typically is the sizes of components or units in similar jobs that your organization has done earlier, i.e., software product sizes from your software experience database.

The method presented here systematizes the estimation-by-analogy approach based on your organization's experience. Such estimates are done by an individual or by pooling the educated guesses of a group of people. The method is described in Putnam (1978). The steps in this process are:

- Determine the functions that will compose the new system.

- Compile size data about any similar functions previously developed.

- Identify the differences between the similar functions and the new ones.

- For each component (i)—function whose size you are to estimate—estimate three parameters:
  - The lowest possible number of source statements (or function points or other size measure), a_i
  - The highest possible number of source statements (or function points or other sizemeasure), b_i
  - The most likely number of source statements (or function points or other size measure), m_i

- Compute two numbers for the estimated size of each of the components, the expected value and the standard deviation. The formulas for calculating each of them are as follows:
  - The equation for estimating the expected value of the number of source statements (or function points or other size measure) in the ith unit of code, E_i, is:

$$E_i = \frac{a_i + 4m_i + b_i}{6}$$

where a_i is the lowest possible number, b_i is the highest possible number, and m_i is the most likely number.

- The equation for estimating the standard deviation of the number of source statements (or function points or other size measure) in the ith unit of code, α_i, is:

$$\alpha_i = \frac{(b_i - a_i)}{6}$$

- Tabulate the estimates for each of the components.

- Compute the expected value, E_{tot}, and the standard deviation, α_{tot}, for the overall system.

$$E_{tot} = \sum_{i=1}^{n} E_i$$

$$\alpha_{tot} = \left(\sum_{i=1}^{n} \alpha_i^2 \right)^{\frac{1}{2}}$$

Table 7-1 is an example of a table that you can use when applying the method just described. It illustrates a case in which there are four units of software to be built.

Function	Smallest	Most Likely	Largest	Expected	Standard Deviation
A	5,830	8,962	17,750	9,905	1,987
B	9,375	14,625	28,000	15,979	3,104
C	6,300	13,700	36,250	16,225	4,992
D	5,875	8,975	14,625	9,400	1,458
Overall				$E_{tot} = 51,509$	$\alpha_{tot} = 6,374$

Table 7-1. Size Estimation Table Example

You can approximate the uncertainty in the overall size of the system using the values just calculated for the overall expected value and standard deviation under the assumption that the size is normally distributed. You would expect this approximation to be more accurate for cases in which there are larger numbers of functions in the overall system. Some of the size uncertainty ranges are:

$$\text{68 percent range: } E_{tot} \pm 1 \; \alpha : 45{,}135 \text{ to } 57{,}883$$
$$\text{99 percent range: } E_{tot} \pm 3 \; \alpha : 32{,}387 \text{ to } 70{,}631$$

The percentage range figures hold under the assumption of normality. Normality is the most robust assumption that can be made. The 99 percent probability range is much wider than the 68 percent range. You can use the method described here to provide a range of size estimates for use in the calculation of cost risk as described in Section 7.5.

The method of calculating size uncertainty ranges presented here assumes that the estimate it produces is unbiased toward neither overestimation or underestimation. However, some experience indicates that the "most likely" estimates are biased more toward the lower limit than the upper one. The sizes of actual software products tend more toward the upper limit (Boehm 1981). This observation is in keeping with a common view that software estimators tend to underestimate the size of their products. Section 7.7 gives more detail on size growth.

7.5 FUNCTION POINTS

This chapter describes the nature of the function point size metric and how to compute and apply it. The function point metric is a measure of the size of the function rather than of the amount of code that implements it.

7.5.1 Definition of Function Points

The function point metric intends to measure the functionality of the software product in standard units, independent of the coding language. A "function point" is a measure of software functionality based on the counted or estimated number of "externals" (inputs, outputs, inquiries, and interfaces) of a program unit and the counted or estimated number of internal files of a program unit. This chapter briefly describes the nature of the function point measure and summarizes how you calculate it.

You calculate the function point metric based on the actual or estimated number of each of the four types of system externals, plus the count of internal logical files. As in the case of other software size metrics, the function point metric can be estimated before the software unit is actually constructed, or it can determined after the software unit has been fabricated. The statement of software system requirements often describes the externally visible behavior of the intended system. The function point measure relates directly to that view, as the counts of the four types of externals are measures from which it is calculated. Definitions of the five items that are counted (or estimated) in computing the function point measure are:

- *External inputs.* Unique data and/or control inputs that enter the external boundary of the system, which cause processing to take place. Specific examples include input files (data files, control files), input tables, input forms (documents, data entry sheets), input screens (data screens, functional screens), and input transactions (control discretes, interrupts, system messages, and error messages).

- *External outputs.* Unique data and/or control outputs that leave the external boundary of the system after processing has occurred. Specific examples include output files (data files, control files), output tables, output reports (printed and screen reports from a single interrupt, system messages, and error messages).

- *External inquiries.* Unique I/O queries that require an immediate response. Specific examples include prompts, interrupts, and calls.

- *External interfaces.* Unique files or programs that are passed across the external boundary of the system. Specific examples include common utilities (I/O routines, sorting algorithms), math libraries (library of matrix manipulation routines, library of coordinate conversion routines), program libraries (run-time libraries, package or generic libraries), shared databases, and shared files.

- *Internal files.* A logical grouping of data or control information stored internal to the system. Specific examples include databases, logical files, control files, and directories.

You estimate the complexity of each element of the five categories (e.g., external input) as low, medium, or high. Then, you multiply each count by the appropriate weight shown in Table 7-2 and sum it to determine the "function count."

Description	Complexity Weights		
	Low	Medium	High
External Inputs	3	4	6
External Outputs	4	5	7
External Inquiries	3	4	6
External Interfaces	5	7	10
Internal Files	7	10	15

Table 7-2. Function Count Weights for Complexity

The next step in the calculation of function points is to determine the "value adjustment factor," which is a function of the impact of 14 factors. These factors are:

1. Data communications
2. Distributed functions
3. Performance
4. Heavily used operational configuration
5. Transaction rate
6. Online data entry
7. Design for end-user efficiency
8. Online update (for logical internal files)
9. Complex processing
10. Reusability of system code
11. Installation ease
12. Operational ease
13. Multiple sites
14. Ease of change

These factors are evaluated on a scale that runs from 0 to 5 defined as 0 - factor not present or has no influence, 1 - insignificant influence, 2 - moderate influence, 3 - average influence, 4 - significant influence, 5 - strong influence.

After the 14 factors have been rated and summed, the total is converted to a "value adjustment factor," which is given by the following formula:

$$\text{Multiplier} = (\text{Sum of the factor values}) \cdot 0.01 + 0.65$$

Finally, you calculate the function point count by multiplying the "function count" by the "value adjustment factor." The result is the final "adjusted function point totals." More information about function points, including rules for calculating them, is given in Albrecht (1979), Albrecht and Gaffney (1983), Brown (1990), and Jones (1990 and 1991).

7.5.2 Example of Function Point Calculation

Jones (1991) gives an example of a low-complexity application with 1 external input, 2 external outputs, 1 logical file, and no interfaces or inquiries. The calculation uses the weights in Table 7-2 and gives 18 unadjusted function points. Of the 14 factors, online data entry and online update are rated at 2, end-user efficiency and operational ease rated at 3, and all the other factors are rated at 0. The total of the factors is 10. When this sum is entered into the above value adjustment formula, a value adjustment multiplier of 0.75 is obtained. Therefore, there is (0.75)(18) = 13.5 total adjusted function points.

7.5.3 Applications of Function Points

Function points correlate well with software cost, as do lines of code for management information systems (MIS) software. However, the cost per function point is not independent of the language used to implement the software. This is because the cost of development is a function of code size as well as the amount of functionality to be implemented (Gaffney 1986).

The function point size metric is consistent across languages and applications. When you know the SLOC-to-function point ratio for a particular language, you can use function points to estimate source code size in SLOC by multiplying that ratio by the number of function points. For example, Jones (1986) states that there are 106 COBOL statements per function point.

Experience with MIS and commercial software shows that, using function points, you can make an early estimate of size, generally quite successfully, for those classes of software. However, function point advocates typically use the counts of the five items cited above as the basis for calculating function points, as described above, and not as the basis for making an estimate of the count of source statements.

Jones (1991) presents a variant of function points called "feature points." Feature points are based on counts of the five externals discussed in connection with function points plus a count of the number of algorithms. Jones (1991) has asserted the utility of this metric for various real-time and system applications.

7.5.4 Calculation of Physical Program Size

Even if you can calculate the function point number relatively consistently and accurately, it does not provide all of the information that you need to answer all your questions about the size of a software product. It is likely that you can estimate the physical implementation size (in bytes) of a program or major functional unit such as a CSCI relatively easily from a KSLOC estimate. To do this, you should use data about the compiler's functioning, in particular the average expansion from SLOC to the number of object statements. Then, multiply this figure by the average size (in bytes) of an object statement, based on experience captured in the experience database. For example, some people have used a figure of 22 bytes per logical SLOC for Ada. However, it is well to note there is, in general, no fundamental (physical) program size to perform a given function. Indeed, Boehm (1983) reported on an experiment in which there was a severalfold variation in the size of the programs implemented to meet the same functional objectives but with different optimizing criteria.

7.6 HOW TO ESTIMATE SOFTWARE SIZE BY COUNTING EXTERNALS

This chapter shows how to estimate the size of a software system in KSLOC using external measures of the intended system's requirements. Here, aerospace software can be characterized as real-time command and control embedded software. This method is of particular interest since the measures used are counts of the four externals that are often available very early in the development cycle. The method is a generalization of the function point method described in Section 7.5. The four external measures used here are defined in Section 7.5.

The method described here is based on the use of data about aerospace systems (Gaffney and Werling 1991) and is based on the observation that the unweighted sum of the counts of the externals (the primitives from which you determine the function point value) correlates about as well with the source statement count as do function points. Since the calculation of function points involves a subjective estimation of some additional factors, including the appropriate weighting to apply to the counts of each of the primitives, use of the "raw" sum of the primitives could prove advantageous since it does not require making the additional subjective judgments implicit in the estimation of function points. Not doing the weighting and other processing of the raw counts is simpler and might result in a reduced degree of error in the source statement estimate and also the development labor estimate determined in part from it.

You can apply an empirical software size-estimating model, based on counts of the program externals defined here, to the estimation of both embedded and business software systems. The estimates of the parameters of such a model are best developed by the organization intending to use it, based on data from the experience of that organization. However, if such data is not available, you can use either of the two estimating equations presented here, one for the case of three externals and the other for four externals. They are based on data from Gaffney and Werling (1991).

The first estimating equation for estimating size from counts of externals is:

$$S = 13.94 + 0.034A$$

where S is the software system size in KSLOC and A is the sum of three program externals—inputs, outputs, and inquiries. The second estimating equation is:

$$S = 12.28 + 0.030E$$

where S is the software system size in KSLOC and E is the sum of all four program externals.
The estimation procedure is:
- Collect counts of program externals and of product size (KSLOC) for software products developed by your software experience database.

- Develop an organization- and domain-specific estimating formula for estimating size from counts of externals. To derive such a formula, use the project data in the organization software experience database to plot size (on the y-axis) against counts of externals (on the x-axis), and fit a line that seems to best represent the data. Although a visual fit can be made, it is preferable to use a linear regression fit, as described in Graybill (1961) and other standard texts on linear statistical models.

- To estimate size for a new proposal, identify the number of program externals for each major program unit (such as CSCI).

- Estimate size in KSLOC by using the formulas above or those derived from your experience data, and the appropriate counts of externals.

You can obtain the data for the estimating model and use it to develop an estimate of software size for your project at requirements time. This allows you to make a more accurate estimate of development costs earlier in the project. You can pool this estimate with size estimates developed using other techniques.

7.7 SOFTWARE PRODUCT SIZE GROWTH

The size of software products of all types tends to grow from the time you initiate development to the time you deliver the product. Such growth could tend to add to the originally estimated development cost.

Code growth should be reduced as your organization becomes more mature. A major aspect of more mature organizations is that their performance is more predictable than organizations at lower levels.

Code growth can occur because you underestimate size at the conceptual, proposal, and requirements phases of the software project. You tend to be optimistic and may not know or fully understand the requirements, and both of these factors cause underestimation. Code growth can also occur due to the addition of requirements (functional growth) during the development process. Since this code growth can add to cost, staffing, and schedule problems, you should be aware of its likely occurrence.

The proportion of code growth over the development cycle can be defined as:

$$\text{Growth} = \frac{(\text{Delivered\_Size}) - (\text{Initial\_Estimate})}{(\text{Initial\_Estimate})}$$

where size is given in SLOC, function points, etc.

Cruickshank (1985) gives some experience with code growth in aerospace software development. Table 7-3 summarizes this experience, based on 16 projects in the 200 to 400 KSLOC range.

For example, based on this data you would expect a software development effort scheduled to take 24 months from preliminary design through functional (CSCI) test to grow 19 percent from the original estimate. If the predesign estimate is 320 SLOC, then the estimate of the delivered size will be (320)(1.19) = 380.8 KSLOC. You should collect data about code growth and include it in your experience database. You should factor likely code growth into your size estimates.

Development Time in Months (Design through CSCI Test)	Percent Growth, Initiation to Delivery
12	11
24	19
36	32
48	55

Table 7-3. Code Growth Factors

7.8 COMBINING ESTIMATES

You should develop several independent estimates of size, if possible. This can be done in terms of the method used and/or in terms of the people who develop the estimate using some particular method. Different methods of size estimation might use different information about the application. Hence, if the application of two different methods yields relatively close estimates, then you would tend to feel comfortable about them. However, if they differ considerably, this should be cause for you to examine why this is so. One reason could be that the assumptions underlying the two estimates are incompatible. You also might use several people to develop an estimate using a single method. For example, using the statistical size estimation procedure described in Section 7.4, different individuals might be responsible for developing the estimates of each of the functions (i.e., A, B, ...0). Alternatively, several people might develop estimates of the size of each function. Then, the parameter values smallest, largest, and most likely (see Section 7.4) would be computed. This is an application of the well-known Delphi technique, which is used to combine information from several experts in a field of knowledge. In summary, it is always better to have a number of independent estimates in terms of both people and method.

Another approach is to combine several estimates of size for an entire software product or for each of the functions that compose it. This approach combines several estimates by developing a weighted average of them according to your estimates of the probabilities of correctness of each of them. Of course, you should be sure that the sum of their probabilities is 1.0. Such a set of estimates might span the range from optimistic (it will be small!) to pessimistic (we do not understand the application!).

KSLOC Estimate	Probability
100	0.20
150	0.30
200	0.50

Table 7-4. Sample Software Product Size Estimates

Now, we consider an example of this approach. Consider the hypothetical data in Table 7-4. Suppose you have three different size estimates and you associate each with a weight that is an estimate of the probability of correctness as follows:

The combined (weighted average) estimate is 165 KSLOC. Alternatively, you might use each of the size estimates, together with its probability weighting, to develop a cost risk (see Chapter 8).

7.9 SUMMARY OF RECOMMENDATIONS

General recommendations on size estimation are:

- Estimate the size of every major component of your prospective product (at least each CSCI) separately.

- Test the estimated size for compatibility with the schedule and estimated development effort.

- Do size/development effort trade-offs.

- Make sure that methods for size estimation, compatibility testing among size, effort, schedule, and trade-offs are part of your software standards.

- Track code growth during development.

- Develop and use an experience database for **your** organization to aid in size estimation.

- Form your estimate independently of market pressures.

- Help management establish the level of risk.

- Provide information to help management make informed decisions.

- Key your cost and schedule estimates to the size estimate.

- Estimate size in several ways.

- Update your size estimates several times during development to take advantage of new/better information about the software system that you are developing.

- Base your estimates of size on **your organization's experience**, retained in its database.

- Relate code size to the size of other products of the software development process such as the amount of design. This technique facilitates making updates during the development process.

- Develop a good estimate of size as key to a good estimate of cost.

- Choose from among various ways to estimate size.

- Form your estimate based on **counting** available functions, input/output, etc., of your project.

- Update your estimate throughout the development process.

Chapter

8

HOW TO ESTIMATE SOFTWARE COST

8.1 OVERVIEW

This chapter presents methods to estimate software development costs. These methods can also be applied to estimating maintenance costs. Maintenance projects can be considered development projects in which a software product is modified to: rectify errors, add functionality, or remove functionality. For the most part, "cost" is equated with "labor hours" (LH) or "labor months" (LM) in this chapter. You can readily convert from either LH or LM to dollars based on the cost structure of your organization. This chapter presents three types of cost models: holistic cost estimation models, activity-based cost estimation models, and system cost models. Holistic models are overview models that yield estimates of the total software development labor cost and/or schedule. Activity-based models use a bottom-up approach to software development cost estimation based on an analysis of the costs of the individual activities that compose the software development process. Activity-based models are especially effective in an environment in which you have established a software experience database and where you use that database to feed back information about the process to improve the process. The use of activity-based cost models enables you to examine the effect of process and/or personnel changes on specific activities of software development when you estimate the cost of a new project using data from prior projects. System cost estimation models are based on top-level system knowledge of the hardware and software to be developed. The software development costs are estimated from an analysis of the system cost structure. This chapter also discusses software cost risk and cost risk management.

The cost estimation methods presented in this chapter use estimates of the software product size as the primary independent variable. For any given application domain, cost is more a function of size than of any other factor. You can estimate size by the methods presented in Chapter 7. In turn, the development schedule estimating methods shown in Chapter 9 use the cost estimates produced by the methods presented in this chapter. The size, cost, and schedule parameters are closely related.

8.2 COST ESTIMATION OVERVIEW

This section defines units for quantifying software development labor and relates cost estimating methods to software process maturity levels.

8.2.1 Units of Cost

Software development labor costs are presented in this section and in this guidebook in terms of units of effort such as LM and LH. In short, cost is synonymous with effort in this guidebook. Do your estimates of cost in LM or LH and convert them to cost or sell price dollars as required. No attempt is made to convert effort to dollars since labor costs have very different dollar equivalents from one environment to another and from one year to another. When you have estimated your software development labor effort, you can easily convert effort in LM or LH to dollars. Using LM or LH as your primary cost unit enables you to compare costs and productivities for projects conducted at different times and at different places.

8.2.2 Cost Estimation and Process Maturity Levels

The methods presented here roughly correspond to a progression through the SEI process maturity levels. If your software development organization is at process maturity Level 1, the initial level, you probably have no experience data in a database. In this case, you should estimate costs with the holistic models shown in Section 8.3. By the time your software development organization is at SEI process maturity Level 2, the repeatable process level, you will have established a software experience database and accumulated sufficient data so that you can calculate unit costs for the main activities of software development (e.g., requirements definition, design, code and test, integration and test) and apply them on a project basis (shown in Section 8.4). Even if you do not use the SEI maturity scale, you can equate your organization's "process maturity level" to some point on this scale.

When your organization reaches SEI process maturity Level 3 (or equivalent), the defined level, you will have had sufficient experience and data to do more precise cost estimation (shown in Section 8.4) and to estimate the costs of documentation, testing, and support to software (shown in Sections 8.7 and 8.9). When your organization reaches process maturity Level 4 (or equivalent), the managed level, you will have had sufficient expertise to use top-down methods (shown in Section 8.8). Finally, at Level 5, the optimized level, your organization will be sophisticated enough to routinely handle cost risk (Section 8.10) and the cost of software maintenance (Section 8.11).

As your process maturity level increases, you will have a software experience database that will provide you the information you need to use your own parameter values in the estimation equations given in this chapter. You should apply the estimating methods presented in an iterative way, continuously throughout the development cycle. You should apply each of these methods within the scope of your organization's cost management policies, plans, and procedures.

8.3 HOLISTIC MODELS

A holistic model uses the size of the prospective software product to estimate the development effort and/or schedule as a whole without considering in detail the costs of the individual activities that compose the development process. A holistic model associates size, effort, and development schedule using one or more equations and uses the relationship(s) for the exploration of trade-off possibilities. A holistic model may apply a percent corresponding to each activity to the overall cost or schedule to get the relative costs for the individual activities. These percents differ for each activity and often vary from one application domain to another.

8.3.1 COCOMO (Constructive Cost) Model

The COCOMO (Constructive Cost Model, Boehm 1981) is probably the most widely employed holistic model. If you do not have any productivity data of your own, then you can use the data that is incorporated into the parameter values of COCOMO. However, if you have experience data, you should use parameter values derived from your organization's experience.

There are three basic modes or application types in the COCOMO model: organic, semidetached, and embedded. There are also three principal levels of the COCOMO model: basic, intermediate, and detailed. In addition, there is an Ada-COCOMO model. This section describes the three modes and the three levels as well as the Ada process model. Models similar to the basic COCOMO for the estimation of effort and schedule are given by Walston and Felix (1977). Table 8-1 summarizes the basic model.

Mode	Effort (Cost)= $a(KDSI)^b$	Schedule Time= $c(LM)^d$ (months)
Organic	$LM=2.4(KDSI)^{1.05}$	$TDEV=2.5(LM)^{0.38}$
Semidetached	$LM=3.0(KDSI)^{1.12}$	$TDEV=2.5(LM)^{0.35}$
Embedded	$LM=3.6(KDSI)^{1.20}$	$TDEV=2.5(LM)^{0.32}$

Table 8-1. Basic COCOMO Model Effort and Schedule Equations

8.3.1.1 Basic COCOMO Model

In Table 8-1, LM is labor months, KDSI is thousands of delivered source instructions, and TDEV is development time in months. Delivered source instructions include a count of physical source statements for new and reused code but exclude undelivered support software such as test drivers. KDSI includes format and data declarations and excludes comments and unmodified utility software. Total KDSI is equal to total KSLOC for the same code categories as described. The LM estimated by the basic COCOMO effort-estimating equation includes the direct effort for product (top-level) software design through integration and acceptance testing. It includes project management, program librarians, documentation effort, quality assurance, and configuration management. However, it does not include personnel, the computer center, clerical help, facilities, and higher management effort.

The organic mode applies to a small to medium-sized product development in a familiar in-house development environment. The embedded mode represents a tightly constrained software product development situation where the product must operate in a complex hardware/software, interactive, and procedure-driven system. Military mission-critical and real-time command and control software and air traffic control systems are examples of such products. The semidetached mode is intermediate between organic and embedded.

Boehm (1981) gives the distribution of effort and schedule for the main activities of development for each mode and for a variety of development system sizes. As an example, Table 8-2 shows these distributions for a very large system of 512 KDSI for the embedded mode. For data on systems of other sizes, see page 99 of Boehm (1981). Gaffney (1982) presents a different set of activity distributions and notes that the distribution of effort among the development activities is a function of the development productivity. Gaffney also found higher productivity to be associated with higher proportions of the development effort in front-end activities.

Activity	Percent Effort	Percent Schedule Time
Product design	18	38
Detailed design	24	16
Code and unit test	24	16
Integration test	34	30
Total	100	100

Table 8-2. *Embedded Mode Activity and Schedule Distributions*

8.3.1.2 Intermediate COCOMO Model

The COCOMO intermediate model expands the basic model to include cost multiplier factors, which modify the cost estimates (LM) developed from the basic models shown in Table 8-1. Table 8-3 presents these cost multipliers. You can use your subjective judgment to select a ratings level. More detailed definitions of the ratings levels are in Boehm (1981).

Cost Drivers	Ratings (Mi)					
	Very Low	Low	Nominal	High	Very High	Extra High
Product Attributes						
RELY Required software reliability	0.75	0.88	1.00	1.15	1.40	
DATA Database size		0.94	1.00	1.08	1.16	
CPLX Product complexity	0.70	0.85	1.00	1.15	1.30	1.65
Computer Attributes						
TIME Execution time constraint			1.00	1.11	1.30	1.66
STOR Main storage constraint			1.00	1.06	1.21	1.56
VIRT Virtual storage volatility		0.87	1.00	1.15	1.30	
TURN Computer turnaround time		0.87	1.00	1.07	1.15	
Personnel Attributes						
ACAP Analyst capability	1.46	1.19	1.00	0.86	0.71	
AEXP Applications experience	1.29	1.13	1.00	0.91	0.82	
PCAP Programmer capability	1.42	1.17	1.00	0.86	0.70	
VEXP Virtual machine experience	1.21	1.10	1.00	0.90		
LEXP Programming language experience	1.14	1.07	1.00	0.95		
Project Attributes						
MODP Use of modern programming practices	1.24	1.10	1.00	0.91	0.82	
TOOL Use of software tools	1.24	1.10	1.00	0.91	0.83	
SCED Required development schedule	1.23	1.08	1.00	1.04	1.10	

Table 8-3. *Intermediate Model Effort Multipliers*

The general formula for effort (cost) estimation of the COCOMO model is:

$$LM = a(KDSI)^b \cdot \prod_{i=1}^{n} M_i$$

where Table 8-1 gives values for the parameters a and b. The values of the parameter Mi, the selected cost multiplier, are found in Table 8-3.

Using Tables 8-1 and 8-3, the cost of developing a 512 KDSI (very large), semidetached software product with a high product complexity, low programmer capability, very low virtual machine experience, and very low use of modern software practices (all other factors nominal) is:

$$3.0(512)^{1.12}(1.15)(1.17)(1.21)(1.24) = 6,555 \text{ LM}$$

These multipliers are not totally independent of each other, although under the COCOMO model they are applied as though they were. There is a cost-effect overlap between any two and among any group of COCOMO cost multipliers. Where only a very small group of cost multipliers (say, two or three) is applied, the effect of this cost overlap is minimal. But if you use a large number of multipliers, the cumulative effect of the overlap may be serious. The estimated costs may be too high or too low. You should be aware of this situation when developing cost estimates using COCOMO and act accordingly.

8.3.1.3 Detailed COCOMO Model

The detailed COCOMO model provides two capabilities not in intermediate COCOMO:

- *Phase-Sensitive Effort Multipliers.* The effects of the cost multipliers differ by development phase.

- *Three-Level Product Hierarchy.* Cost drivers are applied at three levels of the software product hierarchy, as appropriate. The three levels are: module level, subsystem level, and system level.

8.3.1.4 Reuse with the COCOMO Model

You can also use the COCOMO model to estimate development costs in situations involving the reuse or the modification of code for a new application as well as to estimate maintenance costs. You calculate equivalent delivered source instructions (EDSI) as shown in the example presented in this section. EDSI is actually the weighted sum of the constituent percent changes in each of the major development activities, where the weights are the relative costs for each of these activities. EDSI is somewhat different from ESLOC (defined in Section 6.2). ESLOC is the weighted size of new and reused code.

The EDSI is defined as:

$$EDSI = ADSI(AAF/100)$$

where ADSI is the number of delivered source instructions (statements) adapted from existing software.

The application adjustment factor (AAF) is defined as:

$$AAF = 0.40(DMa)+0.30(CMA)+0.30(IMa)$$

where DMa is the percentage of the adapted software's design that is modified; CMa is the percentage of the adapted software's code that is modified; and IMa is the percentage of effort required to integrate the adapted software into an overall product and to test the resulting product as compared to the normal amount of integration and test effort for software of comparable size. Table 8-4 gives the quantities to apply in calculating the EDSI for various reuse and adaptive situations.

Adjustment Factor Components	Adaptive Percent Changes			
	Simple Conversion	Complex Conversion	Extensive Conversion	Component Conversion
Design modification (DMa)	0	15	35	5
Code modification (CMa)	15	30	60	15
Integration modification (IMa)	5	20	140	25

Table 8-4. *Adaptive Quantities by Activities for Equivalent Delivered Source Instructions*

Thus, for a simple conversion (i.e., a simple reuse application) involving 500 statements, in which there is 0 percent change in design, 15 percent change in coding, and 5 percent change in testing:

$$AAF=0.4(0)+0.3(15)+0.3(5)=6.0 \text{ AND } EDSI=500(0.06)=30.0$$

The KDSI and EDSI models assume known and stable requirements. The EDSI model accounts for using only existing code and does not cover the use of existing domain and design information, including the effort to locate and evaluate reusable code.

Balda and Gustafson (1990) present a COCOMO-related reuse model that overcomes these difficulties. The model is:

$$LM = aN_1^b + 20\gamma aN_2^b + \gamma aN_3^b$$

where a and b are the multipliers and the exponents, respectively, from Table 8-1; and γ (gamma) is the cost ratio of developing a reusable component to the cost of developing a unique component. The range of γ is from 0.06 to 0.24; so for real-time command and control software, γ will have a value of about 0.2. For MIS software, γ will have a value of about 0.1. N_1 is the number of unique KDSI developed, N_2 is the number of KDSI developed to be reusable, and N_3 is the number of unchanged reused KDSI.

Balda and Gustafson (1990) also present a COCOMO-based prototype cost model for the evolutionary spiral process (see Section 8.4) of the form:

$$LM = aP^b + aI^b + aT^b$$

where a and b are the multipliers and exponents, respectively, from the effort column of Table 8-1. As with the basic COCOMO model, you must select the proper software development mode. P is the SLOC developed for the initial prototype. I is the number of SLOC developed during iterations of the process and is the total of SLOC added, removed, and modified. T is the number of SLOC developed specifically to convert the software to a deliverable product. (This prototype cost model is considered to be an initial model.)

8.3.1.5 Ada Process Model

The Ada Process Model (Boehm 1987) is a variation of the COCOMO model. It incorporates the effects of the use of Ada, rapid prototyping, risk management, the spiral model, and certain modern software development practices (as shown in Table 8-3 and in Boehm [1987]) into one model. The Ada version of COCOMO, which incorporates the effects of the use of Ada and the Ada Process Model, is:

$$LM = 2.8(KDSI)^{1.04 + \sum_{i=1}^{4} W_i}$$

where the weights W_i are given in Table 8-5.

Weights W_i	Experience With Ada Process Model	Design Thoroughness at PDR: Specifications Compiled	Risks Eliminated by PDR	Requirements Volatility during Development
0.00	Successful on >1 mission-critical project	Fully (100%)	Fully (100%)	No changes
0.01	Successful on 1 mission-critical project	Mostly (90%)	Mostly (90%)	Small noncritical changes
0.02	General familiarity with practices	Generally (75%)	Generally (75%)	Frequent noncritical changes
0.03	Some familiarity with practices	Often (60%)	Often (60%)	Occasional moderate changes
0.04	Little familiarity with practices	Some (40%)	Some (40%)	Frequent moderate changes
0.05	No familiarity with practices	Little (20%)	Little (20%)	Many large changes

Table 8-5. *Weights for the Ada-COCOMO Model*

Using the guidance in Table 8-5, a software development environment with no familiarity with the Ada Process Model or with the modern software practices of design thoroughness and risk management in an environment of changing requirements would rate a value of 0.05 in all four categories of software practice. Then the Ada-COCOMO estimating equation for 512 KDSI would be:

$$LM = 2.8(512)^{1.24} + 6,407$$

Table 8-6 gives some values of LM from the Ada-COCOMO model with the associated productivities.

Sum W_i	100 KDSI		500 KDSI	
	LM	SLOC/LM	LM	SLOC/LM
0.00	336	298	1,795	279
0.04	405	247	2,302	217
0.08	487	205	2,951	169
0.12	585	171	3,784	132
0.16	703	142	4,852	103
0.20	846	118	6,221	80

Table 8-6. *Sample Effort and Productivities for the Ada-COCOMO Model*

8.3.2 The Software Development Model

The software development model (Putnam 1978) is a widely used holistic model. This section describes this model and presents some of its applications.

8.3.2.1 The Software Development Model Equation

The software development model equation is:

$$S = C \cdot K^p \cdot t_d{}^q$$

where S is the software system size in SLOC (excluding comments); C is the technology constant that represents both the sophistication of the development environment and the nature of the software to be developed; K is the development effort in labor years; and t_d is the development time in years. ESLOC may be used in place of SLOC when reused code is involved (see Chapter 6). The parameter K covers all development activities from design through installation of the software system.

C reflects both the nature of the process to be used in developing the software product and the complexity of the product. Some sample values of C are shown by process maturity level in Table 8-7 (later in this chapter).

Putnam (1978) gave the parameters p and q the values 1/3 and 4/3, respectively. Gaffney (1983) calculates the values of p and q to be 0.6288 and 0.5555, respectively, based on development data from an environment that produces real-time command and control software. Other researchers have different values of parameters (see below). Chapter 9 discusses the effect of these parameters, p and q, on schedule and productivity.

As described in Section 9.5, the software development equation is useful as a basis for testing the mutual compatibility of the values of K, t_d, and S. For example, with size (S) established, you can use a value of effort (K) in the model to see if the resulting value of the schedule (t_d) is reasonable.

8.3.2.2 Production Team Efficiency Indicator and the Model

The values of the parameters p and q for your organization can tell you something about its software development efficiency. Tausworthe (1982) demonstrated that the ratio r, where r = q/p (see definition of q and p above), defines the degree of inefficiency of the production (development) team and the process it uses. As Tausworthe indicates, "The larger r is, the larger the increase in effort required to shorten the schedule, and the larger the production team inefficiency."

Tausworthe further states:

Low values of r in an organization are a mark to be proud of, showing efficiency in terms of structuring subtasks for clean interfaces. High (or negative) values of r may be indicative of overall task complexity, volatility of requirements, organizational inefficiency, or any number of other traits that tend to hinder progress.

Three empirical values of r are:

- Putnam, r = 4

- Gaffney, r = 0.88

- Freiburger and Basili (1979), r = 1.0

Notice the close degree of agreement between the last two values for r. Use your experience data as the basis for estimating the values of the parameters c, p, and q.

8.3.2.3 Incremental Changes with the Model

You can use the derivative form of the software development model equation to determine the amount of change in one or two process variables given a small change in the third variable.The incremental change equation (Gaffney 1982) is derived from the full differential of the software life cycle model. Its form is:

$$\frac{\Delta S}{S} = \frac{\Delta C}{C} + p \cdot \frac{\Delta K}{K} + q \cdot \frac{\Delta t_d}{t_d}$$

where $\Delta K/K$, $\Delta C/C$, $\Delta S/S$ and $\Delta t_d/t_d$ are small percentage changes. If size and technology are held constant:

$$\frac{\Delta K}{K} = -\left(\frac{q}{p}\right) \cdot \left(\frac{\Delta t_d}{t_d}\right)$$

Thus a 5 percent shrinkage in schedule might be expected to induce a 4.4 percent increase in effort.

$$-0.8834 \cdot = \frac{\Delta K}{K} = 4.4$$

The incremental change equation can be used to relate estimates of the effects of small changes in size or technology on effort and/or schedule. Alternatively, you might want to estimate the effect of small relative reductions in effort (K) and schedule (t_d) on the technology constant (C) such as might be expected from the introduction of a new tool or technology into the development process.

8.3.2.4 Calculation of the Technology Constant

You can estimate the value of the technology constant C for a new development project by use of the following equation:

$$C = \left(\frac{S}{t_d^q \cdot K^p} \right)$$

where the values of q and p are based on your organization's experience. In the absence of such experience, you can use published values. The values of the three variables t_d, K, and S should be from (in your experience database) similar applications as the one that you are estimating, C. If you have several similar previous applications, calculate C for each and average them to get your new application. You should keep in mind that values of C will vary by type of application and by development environment.

The technology constant C may be understood as representing two principal categories of factors affecting software development: the complexity of the software to be developed and the nature of the tools (Gaffney 1982). It really includes more factors than just those that can be grouped under the term "technology." Walston and Felix (1977) identify 29 of these factors.

If you do not have sufficient software development experience data to calculate the value of the technology constant C, you might consider estimating it with the help of Table 8-7. Table 8-7 presents sample values of C (Putnam 1990) that assume the use of a basic software development environment and the three modes of the COCOMO model. (If a more sophisticated environment is expected, higher values of C would be appropriate since higher values represent higher productivity and shorter schedule.) You can use these values as guidance in estimating the value of C for your environment and your application.

SEI Process	Value of Technology Constant (C) for Software Mode		
Maturity Level	Organic	Semidetached	Embedded
1	12,000	10,000	6,000
2	30,000	25,000	15,000
3	42,000	35,000	21,000
4	54,000	45,000	27,000
5	78,000	65,000	39,000

Table 8-7. *Sample Technology Constant Values*

8.3.3 The Cooperative Programming Model

The Cooperative Programming Model (COPMO) is another type of holistic model (Conte, Dunsmore, and Shen 1986). COPMO is designed to explicitly reflect the effect of development team size on effort. The effect of team size on development effort is especially strong in large projects where the complex nature of the software causes communication among the technical staff and among management to be difficult thus causing costs to rise dramatically. For large, complex projects, cooperation and communication must be effective to hold costs down.

The COPMO model is:

$$E = E_p + E_c$$

where E_p is the effort in LM for programming and technical development of the software product and E_c is the effort in LM for communication among the development staff. The programming effort is given by:

$$E_p = e + f \cdot S$$

where S is the software size in KSLOC and e and f are constants. The communications effort is given by:

$$E_c = g \cdot L^h$$

where L is the average staffing level in LM per month over the duration of software development.

Some parameter values empirically derived from actual development data are e=48.0, f=0.33, g=2.02, and h=1.67. Conte, Dunsmore, and Shen (1986) give similar values.

8.3.4 How to Apply Holistic Models for Cost Estimation

If your organization has little or no accumulated software development experience, you can apply holistic models such as COCOMO, the software development model, and COPMO using the parametric values presented here. As you gain and record software experience, you should modify or customize the holistic model parameter values to more closely represent your own software process.

Regardless of the degree of development of your estimating process, you can use the holistic models as a cross-check on each other. Make estimates for any situation by using two or more models, and you should compare their results. If the results differ by more than 10 to 20 percent (either cost or schedule time), then you should closely examine your assumptions and data about the software project in question.

As an example of cross-checking, suppose that you use the basic COCOMO semidetached model to estimate the cost of developing 660 KDSI. The estimate is $3.0(660)^{1.12}$ = 4,315.3 LM. If you also use the software development cycle equation to calculate the effort involved in developing 660 SLOC in 3.5 years with a technology constant of 10,000, the result involves solving the following relation for K (using the values for Use parameters p and q given by Gaffney, 1983):

$$660,000 = 10,000 \cdot K^{0.6288} \cdot 3.5^{0.5555}$$

The result is 258.8 labor years, or 3,105.6 LM, a value that does differ by about 28 percent from the COCOMO-generated value. However, if you remember that the COCOMO value includes quality assurance, configuration management, and software builds that are an additional (estimated) 19 percent cost increment (see Section 8.9), then the COCOMO value becomes 4,315.3/1.19 = 3,626.3 LM. This value is only 14 percent different from the software development equation value, so you can consider the two values to be essentially the same.

In general, when two estimates do not compare in a cross-check, look for differences in the definition of work to be done. Since KSLOC and KDSI are essentially the same, the difference is in the range of activities implied by each model. Check for size/effort/schedule compatibility as shown in Chapter 9.

If your organization is at process maturity Level 1 or 2 (or equivalent), use holistic models for cost and schedule estimation and for cross-checking purposes. You should initiate a software experience database to preserve cost experience, and use the data to customize the holistic model parameter values to your development environment.

8.4 ACTIVITY-BASED MODELS

This section describes activity-based cost models and how you can apply them to do cost estimates for your projects. For cost estimation, holistic models represent a great improvement over the ad hoc cost estimation methods of the past; however, they are not as precise as the activity-based models when applied with your own experience data. Using activity-based models may enable you to develop more accurate estimates than possible when using holistic models, because you can consider the effects of process, personnel and other factors on each of the development activities rather than on the development process overall. You should also use a holistic model as an approximation to provide a cross-check on your estimate derived using an activity-based estimate.

8.4.1 The Activity-Based Cost Model

An activity-based cost model enables you to consider the costs of each of the activities in the development cycle, such as requirements analysis, preliminary and detailed design, code and unit test, CSC integration test, and CSCI system test. You build an activity-based cost model by considering the activities that compose the development process to be used to produce the intended software product. The activities that form your development process may be from a previously used process, or they may come from a modified version of a previous process with some activities removed and other activities added, or there may be a selected subset of activities from a "menu" of activities. Your project may not use all of the "repertoire" of possible activities available to it. For example, if you are developing a new version of an existing system, you may not have any preliminary design in your development process. You usually measure unit costs in LM/KSLOC or LH/SLOC, although other metrics may be appropriate under certain circumstances. You should define your software development cycle in terms of known and measurable activities based on your organization's experience as contained in your experience database.

The activity-based model assigns a unit cost to each activity and estimates costs in LM or LH by multiplying the size of the software product (KSLOC or SLOC) by the assigned unit cost (LM/KSLOC or LH/SLOC). The general form of the activity-based model is based on the operations of adding, modifying, reusing, and removing code as discussed in Chapter 6. The general form of the model using (LM/KSLOC) is:

$$TLM = \sum_{i=1}^{n} (LM/KSLOC)_{i,added} \cdot KSLOC_{added} + \sum_{i=1}^{n} (LM/KSLOC)_{i,modified} \cdot KSLOC_{modified}$$

$$+ \sum_{i=1}^{n} (LM/KSLOC)_{i,reused} \cdot KSLOC_{reused} + \sum_{i=1}^{n} (LM/KSLOC)_{i,removed} \cdot KSLOC_{removed}$$

where TLM indicates the total effort in LM for all n activities and $(LM/KSLOC)_{i,j}$ indicates a unit cost in LM/KSLOC for activity i and code category j.

You can simplify this general form by weighting the modified code the same as added code (since both can be assigned the same unit cost) and then combining the added and modified code into the new code category. You can also assign the removed code a unit cost of 0.0. This procedure reduces the above equation to:

$$TLM = \sum_{i=1}^{n} (LM/KSLOC)_{i,new} \cdot KSLOC_{new} + \sum_{i=1}^{n} (LM/KSLOC)_{i,reused} \cdot KSLOC_{reused}$$

where TLM indicates the total effort in LM for all n activities and $(LM/KSLOC)_{i,j}$ indicates a unit cost in LM/KSLOC for activity i and code category j. You can use either actual or estimated size data.

This form of the cost (effort) estimating equation employs the categories "new" and "reused" code only. A modified form of this equation uses the LH and SLOC, rather than the LM and KSLOC metrics. It is the recommended format to employ (IEEE 1992; Gaffney and Cruickshank 1991a and 1991b). It is:

$$TLH = \sum_{i=1}^{n} (LH/SLOC)_{i,new} \cdot SLOC_{new} + \sum_{i=1}^{n} (LH/SLOC)_{i,reused} \cdot SLOC_{reused}$$

where TLH indicates the total effort in LH for all n activities and $(LH/SLOC)_{i,j}$ indicates a unit cost in LH/SLOC for activity i and code category j. You can use either actual or estimated size data. Other categories of code can be used with this type of activity-based model. Section 6.6.1 explains how you can estimate the unit costs for use in the activity-based cost model.

Activity-based costs models are linear models. Actually, software cost estimation models may not be linear in size. The COCOMO and development life cycle models previously discussed are examples of such nonlinear models. The unit costs of activities may be nonlinear over the wider range of software product sizes, but they can be treated as linear over shorter ranges.

You should observe that the linear model focused upon in Chapter 8 is of the form:

$$C_{Ai} = C_{Ui} \times S \;;\; C = C_{A1} + C_{A2} + \dots C_{An}$$

where: C_{Ui} is the unit cost of the ith activity; C_{Ai} is the cost of the ith activity; S is the size of the software product; and n is the number of activities composing the software development process.

There are various alternative linear forms that could be used, such as

$$C = A + (C_{A1} + C_{A2} + \ldots C_{An})$$

where C_{A1}, etc. is as defined above. However, such forms are not as easy to work with as that elaborated upon in Chapter 8.

8.4.2 A Basic Activity-Based Cost Model

Table 8-8 contains activities from DOD-STD-2167A (Department of Defense 1988) and DOD-STD-1521B (Department of Defense 1985) and unit costs that were derived from actual experience in developing embedded software in the aerospace industry during the development of 25 large (over 500 KSLOC) real-time command and control software systems. Cruickshank and Lesser (1982) present similar activity unit costs for a related sample of activity-based models. You may use the activities in Table 8-8 as a "menu" from which to select activities, if appropriate, to form your development process. The ordering of the activities in Table 8-8 is a natural order for presentation, but they are not necessarily the expected order of development. The unit costs shown in this table are for guidance, and your goal is to create your own set of unit costs based on your organization's experience. The menu of activities shown on Table 8-8 are applicable to both government and commercial software development efforts. Although most commercial development organizations might not use government terms such as "CSU," "CSC," etc., they probably have analogous terms for components of their products. Similarly, process-oriented terms such as "Preliminary Design" would be expected to have commercial equivalents.

The LM in Table 8-8 are based on 167 LH per LM, and the unit costs for new and reused code for each activity include the costs of multiple iterations through that activity. Your organization might have some other value, such as 140 or 152. The model of the software development process presented in Table 8-8 is a stagewise model in that it is composed of a succession of activities. The model incorporates the possibility of iteration between successive major steps. The costs of a normal amount of iteration are incorporated in the unit costs given. While it would be desirable to have it, the cost for each iteration is not normally available.

The unit costs in Table 8-8 include the costs (about 13 percent) for first-line management and applicable second-line management (Cruickshank 1988). Section 8.9 discusses additional costs for quality assurance, configuration management, and program management.

Activity	Subactivity/Product (DOD-STD-1521B and DOD-STD-2167A)	Unit Cost (LM/KSLOC)	
		New	Reused
Requirements analysis	System/segment design document	0.31	0.020
	Software development plan	0.13	0.010
	Preliminary software requirements specification	0.25	0.020
	Preliminary interface requirements specification	0.04	0.002
	Software requirements specification	0.39	0.030
	Interface requirements specification	0.04	0.002
Preliminary design	Software design document—preliminary design including design reviews	0.52	0.030
	Preliminary interface design document	0.07	0.005
	Software test plan	0.13	0.005
	CSC test requirements	0.01	0.000
Detailed design	Software design document—detailed design including design reviews	0.82	0.050
	Interface design document	0.07	0.005
	CSU test requirements and test cases	0.01	0.000
	CSC test cases	0.02	0.000
	Contents of CSU and CSC software development files	0.00	0.000
	Software test description—test cases	0.04	0.006
Coding and CSU testing	Implement source code including code inspections	1.48	0.070
	CSU test procedures	0.03	0.000
	CSU testing	0.73	0.050
	CSC test procedures	0.25	0.030
	Contents of CSU and CSC software development files	0.00	0.000
CSC integration and testing	CSC integration testing	0.74	0.200
	Software test description—formal test procedures	0.10	0.020
	Updated source code—error correction	0.10	0.010
	Contents of updated software development files	0.00	0.000
CSCI testing	CSCI testing including acceptance testing	0.73	0.150
	Software test report	0.01	0.000
	Updated source code—error correction	0.05	0.010

Table 8-8. An Example Set of Activity-Based Unit Costs

8.4.3 Estimating Costs Using Activity-Based Models

This section tells you how to estimate unit costs for the various software development process activities. Also, Section 6.6 deals with this subject.

8.4.3.1 Assignment of Costs

The basic procedure in estimating costs with activity-based models is to estimate a unit cost for each of the activities in the process being estimated and then to compute the total unit cost estimate. This procedure consists of the following steps:

1. Decompose your project software development process into its constituent activities List the activities of the software development process.

2. Assign a unit cost (LM/KSLOC, LH/SLOC, LH/Function Point, etc.) to each of the activities. You can sample the unit costs for the activities in Table 8-8 for guidance if this table contains activities that are similar to those in your development process, or you can use the existing unit costs of the development process being modeled. If you do not have any unit cost figures, then you may be able to derive them from the information in your experience database using the methodology presented in Section 6.6.1.

3. Modify the unit costs selected to be consistent with the development environment as discussed in the following sections.

4. Estimate the size of the new and reused code in the software product for which the development cost is being estimated.

5. Estimate the cost of each activity and total the costs of the activities in the process.

8.4.3.2 Example of Activity-Based Cost Estimation

The general cost model for a software product containing new and reused code is:

$$C_S = C_{VN} \cdot S_N + C_{VR} \cdot S_R$$

where:

C_S = The total cost of the software product.

C_{VN} = Unit cost of new code developed for this product.

C_{VR} = Unit cost of reusing code in this product. It represents the unit cost of reused code in the case where the components can be inserted directly into the product with no modification.

S_N = Amount of new code in source statements developed for this product.

S_R = Amount of reused code incorporated into this product in source statements.

As an example, suppose that you are to develop software consisting of 450 new KSLOC and 710 reused KSLOC and that you are to perform the activities of preliminary design, detailed design, coding and CSU testing, CSC integration testing, CSCI testing, and error correction. Further suppose that line management determines that the new requirements are not well defined; therefore, design for new code is estimated to cost 20 percent additional, i.e., 20 percent above the base unit costs for design. You derive such modifier factors as the 20 percent on the basis of a systematic evaluation based on past experience from a development environment similar to that to be employed in the development of your software system. Also, suppose that the programmers involved lack sufficient experience in the language selected so that coding and unit testing will cost an additional 10 percent, again based on a systematic, subjective evaluation. Using the unit costs in Table 8-8 as base unit costs, you then estimate the costs for your project using a worksheet such as shown in Table 8-9.

Using the total costs from Table 8-9, you can estimate the new code productivity to be 160.0 SLOC/LM (= 450,000/2,866.5) over all of the activities in the development process that you intend to use in creating the new software product. Assuming that reusing code costs 30 percent of developing new code, then KESLOC is 450+(0.30)(710)=663. The overall equivalent to new code productivity is (663,000/3,249.8)=204.0 ESLOC/LM. Also, the overall (delivered) product productivity is 357 SLOC/LM (=1,160,000/3,250.0). Comparing this productivity figure to that for new code, one observes the dramatic effect of code reuse on the productivity realized in the creation of the software product.

Project Name	EXAMPLE		Date	11/3/92
CSCI/Product Name	CSCI 19		Language	JOVIAL
Unit Cost Measurement	(LM/KSLOC, LH/SLOC, etc.)		LM/KSLOC	
New Code Size	450		Reused Code Size 710	

		New Code		
Activity	Base Unit Cost	Modifier	Estimator Unit Cost	Cost (LM)
Preliminary design (incl. documentation)	0.59	1.20	0.71	319.5
Detailed design (incl. documentation)	0.89	1.20	1.07	481.5
Code and CSU test	2.21	1.10	2.43	1,093.5
CSC integration test	0.74	1.00	0.74	333.0
Error correction (for CSC test)	0.41	1.00	0.41	184.5
CSCI test	0.73	1.00	0.73	328.5
Error correction (for CSCI test)	0.28	1.00	0.28	126.0
Total	**5.85**		**6.37**	**2,866.5**

		Reused Code		
Activity	Base Unit Cost	Modifier	Estimator Unit Cost	Cost (LM)
Preliminary design (incl. documentation)	0.035	1.00	0.035	24.9
Detailed design (incl. documentation)	0.055	1.00	0.055	39.1
Code and CSU test	0.120	0.00	0.000	0.0
CSC integration test	0.200	1.00	0.200	142.0
Error correction (for CSC test)	0.060	1.00	0.060	42.6
CSCI test	0.150	1.00	0.150	106.5
Error correction (for CSCI test)	0.040	1.00	0.040	28.4
Total	**0.660**	**1.00**	**0.540**	**383.5**
Overall Total LM				**3,250.0**

Table 8-9. Worksheet Cost Calculations for an Activity-Based Model

8.4.3.3 Adjustment of Unit Costs

View the unit costs in Table 8-8 as an example or as guidance based on some specific experience in the aerospace industry with developing real-time command and control software. The methodology used in the example can be employed for estimating the costs of developing software for different applications. Your organization's experience coupled with your judgment as a cost estimator may lead to a modification of some or all of these unit costs—up or down. For example, in a situation where your organization wants to integrate many CSCs, you may want to increase the unit cost for CSC integration test to account for additional complexity. The same is true of the functional testing of the software system where you integrate many CSCIs in the CSCI test. More generally, you can use this approach for a different set of developments that your organization might have. For example, your development process might not include an activity labeled "CSC Integration Test."

Do not view either these unit cost values as fixed quantities or the activities to which they apply as items that must be applied with no modification. They represent guidance to the cost estimator and should be modified to represent the software development environment in question. For example, suppose that the unit cost for implementing source code as shown in Table 8-8 had to be modified, in the judgment of the estimator, to reflect the fact that the programming staff is inexperienced in using the target coding language. Then, the estimator might assume that developing the code would cost 20 percent more than the unit cost in the table, and of a strong management team, which would cost 10 percent less than the given unit cost, then the modified unit cost for the coding activity would be 1.48 (1 + .20 − .10) = 1.63 LM/KSLOC.

The optimum estimation situation, both for estimating cost and software size, is one in which your organization maintains a database of actual software and documentation sizes and costs recorded by software development activity. Such a database allows you to create unit costs and overall cost estimates tailored to your software development environment.

If a set of standard or guideline unit costs based on such a database, as suggested above, is not available, you can use the COCOMO detailed model, specifically the modern programming practices (MODP) effort multipliers shown in Boehm (1981, Table 27-1). Using this scheme, you can modify the baseline unit cost for each activity from requirements through integration and test by a multiplier factor to adjust for the degree of adherence to modern programming practices. Boehm (1981) gives a set of factors to be used in this case.

Unit costs for each language used and for each application domain must be periodically recalculated since they change as more experience is recorded and as the development process is improved. Unit cost values are likely to decrease in the long term as the cumulative effects of technological change take effect.

8.4.4 Other Activity-Based Models

Table 8-10 presents the unit costs for the Ada language for embedded software development (Cruickshank and Gaffney 1992).

Activity	Ada Model	
	LM/KSLOC	Percent
Requirements Analysis	0.74	7.4
Preliminary Design	1.67	16.7
Detailed Design	2.22	22.2
Code and Unit Test	2.22	22.2
CSC Integration Test	1.60	16.0
CSCI Test	1.55	15.5
Total	10.00	100.0

Table 8-10. Ada Development Model

8.4.5 General Software Development Process Models and Risk Management

Spiral models (Boehm 1988) of software development subsume all other software development models such as the basic activity-based model previously discussed. Spiral models are general models in the sense that they incorporate a formal risk management process that includes analysis and the determination and evaluation of risk, i.e., the objectives, alternatives, and constraints of proceeding to the next activity. Risk management includes measurement, analysis, and taking action. The action might be to do nothing but await the completion of another process activity. If the level of the risk(s) is evaluated to be unacceptable, then the developer should not proceed to the next activity but should perform risk aversion (or mitigation) until the risks are under control. Risk aversion can take the form of remaining in the present activity, going to another activity further "downstream" from the present activity, or working on some other software component.

Risk aversion can also take the form of working to make the risk in the next activity be at an acceptable level, i.e., risk mitigation. Basically, the risk analysis helps the developer decide when to go to the next activity and when not to go to the next activity. This risk analysis procedure can be applied separately to each component of the software under development so that the developer will proceed with some components and not proceed with other components.

For example, you might determine during the risk analysis activity performed at the end of design that the cost risks of proceeding to code and unit test are too high because of unacceptable risks, e.g., the unavailability of programmers with experience in the implementation language. Therefore, you decide that it is less risky to postpone code and unit test activities until the code and unit test risks have stabilized at an acceptable level. Presumably, this stabilization occurs when experienced programmers are assigned to the project.

The unit costs given earlier in this section contain the total costs of all risk aversion subactivities. However, those risk aversion subactivities were not visible and their costs were not known explicitly. It is likely that more advanced software process designs would devote more effort to risk management activities than that included in the unit costs presented earlier. In instances of the application of spiral models, record the number and costs of risk management activities, if possible, in your experience database as valuable pieces of information. For example, one form of risk aversion might be to iterate back through the present development activity until the risks associated with the following activity have stabilized at an acceptable level. Then record the number of iterations through this activity in your experience database.

8.5 ADJUSTING COST ESTIMATES

This section describes how you can pool several cost estimates. It also tells you how to adjust your estimates to represent the impacts of various factors, such as the level of the coding language to be used.

8.5.1 Pooling Estimates

It is vital that you be familiar with the software development process for which you are making a cost estimate. Knowledge of the process means detailed knowledge of the activities that compose the process. You should determine the nature of the activities that compose the process you are estimating. Typically, the activities would be expected to be included in the list in Table 8-8. If you have no other information, you might modify the given unit costs to suit your situation. If no activity in these tables corresponds to an activity in your intended development process, you must find some other way to estimate the corresponding unit cost. Often, it helps to find an analogous activity in a past development project and use the associated unit cost data. This selection and modification process is an aspect of modeling the software development process.

It is often helpful to make a cost estimate first, using an activity-based model and then cross-check the estimate by using one or more of the holistic models. If the estimates do not differ by more than 10 percent to 20 percent, you can conclude that the results from all the estimating techniques and models are giving a consistent result. In the event that this desirable state of affairs does not exist (i.e., that some of the models give significantly different cost estimates), you must analyze the data and the models themselves to find an explanation. It may be that some of the models are not suitable for application to the situation at hand. Experience will show which cost-estimating models and techniques are best for your software development environment.

8.5.2 Point and Interval Estimates of Cost

If the unit costs of the activities in your development process are known from experience for a specific type of software product and a specific environment, there is little need to be concerned with the amount of statistical variation in the values. The values of unit costs derived from experience will be estimates of the "true" values, with little inherent variation. However, estimates of software size tend to have much more inherent variation. When used with a single estimate of size, unit costs such as those in Table 8-8 will produce a point estimate of cost, i.e., a single estimate of cost with no information about variation or about an implied statistical distribution. In addition to the point estimate, you should try to produce an interval estimate, i.e., a range of possible cost values with the statistical distribution of values. One possible way to do this is to estimate costs based on a sample of estimated software sizes with each of the size estimates produced by a different method. Chapter 7 presents several sizing methods that are useful in this context. You can process such information on the basis of unit cost and size estimate such as described later in this section.

When your unit costs are estimates based on little or no experience or other information, you must estimate costs based on a sample of sizes each with an assigned probability, spanning a possible range of sizes, and based on a sample of possible unit costs with an assigned probability spanning a range of possible unit costs. Of course, the ranges of size and unit costs should be such that each set of probabilities totals 1.0. This method will generate an interval estimate of cost. Section 8.10 gives an example of this method in the context of computing an estimate of cost risk.

8.5.3 The Cost Effect of Using a Higher Order Language

Using a higher order language (HOL) has an effect on software development costs. Gaffney (1986) establishes that the cost ratio of development in an HOL to development in assembly-level language is:

$$M = \frac{1 + \frac{c}{X}}{1 + c}$$

where c is the ratio of the (estimated) costs of software design and system testing costs to the software coding and unit test costs, and X is the ratio of the size of the software function or product in assembly-level code to the size in HOL, i.e., the inverse of the language level. Gaffney (1986) gives a value of 0.59 for C and 3.0 for X for one development situation. You can use M as a multiplier on software development costs in situations where you wish to account for the effect of using an HOL on software development costs.

You can also apply this formula (make ratios) to estimate the relative costs of developing software in two different HOLs.

8.5.4 The Cost Effect of Software Product Size

Check for the effect that the software product size has on unit costs. As software product size increases beyond some given size, the unit costs generally rise. Gaffney and Werling (1990) show unit cost as a function of size for a set real-time embedded (aerospace) software system:

$$U_{RTE} = 5.091 \cdot S^{0.0559}$$

where U_{RTE} is the unit cost for aerospace software in LM/KSLOC and S is the software product size in KSLOC. The relationship also holds if you measure unit cost in LH/SLOC and size in SLOC, but you would have to calculate revised parameter values accordingly.

For MIS (management information systems) software, a quadratic model does a somewhat better job of predicting unit costs than an exponential model. Such a model for MIS software is:

$$U_{MIS} = 106.076 - 0.6542 \cdot S + 0.00439 \cdot S^2$$

where U_{MIS} is the unit cost for MIS software in LM/KSLOC and S is KSLOC.

These relationships between unit cost and size were derived using new code development data. You should explore the sensitivity of your project unit costs by inserting several size values in KSLOC above the current estimate of size and observing the effects on U. If U increases by more than 10 percent, there is probably a risk exposure. Each set of unit costs relates to a specific range of sizes, and when you estimate costs outside of your normal range of sizes, you may have to use a different set of unit costs. Alternatively, you might use a set of linear approximations to the relationships between size and unit cost. This approach underlies the approach to applying the activity-based, unit cost models in this guidebook.

8.5.5 Cost Effects of CASE Tools

When considering the use of a CASE tool, you must estimate its effect on specific activities in the software development process. For each activity, you should determine the impact of the CASE tool application on:

- The reduction in the unit cost of doing the activity.

- The additional cost, if any, on this and any other activity of applying the CASE tool.

- The inputs to and the outputs from the activity.

- The determination of how and when the activity is completed.

- The quality of the activity.

- The sequence of activities to be performed in the execution of the process.

You cannot effectively assess the (potential) impacts of a CASE tool without the detailed knowledge of the process that an activity-based model, backed up by an extensive experience database, provides. As an example, suppose that your development unit costs and activities are like those in the Ada model shown in Table 8-10. Also suppose that you estimate that the application of the CASE tool will result in a 30 percent reduction in the detailed design costs. The unit cost of detailed design will become $(2.22)(0.70)=1.55$ LM/KSLOC, all other activities being unaffected. This will reduce the overall unit costs from 10.00 to 9.33 LM/KSLOC.

8.6 THE COSTS OF SOFTWARE REUSE

Section 8.4.3 shows how to estimate software development costs using the activity-based cost model for a software product involving new and reused code. This section expands on that cost model by showing the effects of investment in a domain on the total cost of a software product. The material in this section applies to the use of COSS software as well, because the use of COSS is just another form of (software) reuse.

8.6.1 Systematic Reuse

The reuse economics model presented here focuses on the systematic reuse (Campbell, Faulk, and Weiss 1990) of large-scale functional objects. You should view systematic reuse in the reuse economics model as consisting of two principal activities: domain engineering and application engineering. Domain engineering is the capital investment involved in creating reusable software objects that can be employed in a number of specific software systems or application systems. Capital investment here means the initial investment in terms of effort to create the means to produce application systems before those application systems are actually produced. This investment may be made all at once for the entire domain investment, or it may be made incrementally over the life of the domain, i.e., as long as the domain is used to produce application systems. The term capital investment here does not imply any specific contractual arrangement.

Application engineering is the set of activities involved in creating a specific application system from new and reused code (covered by the equation at the beginning of Section 8.4.3.2).

8.6.2 The Basic Economics Model of Software Reuse

This section describes the basic reuse economics cost model with all of the domain engineering or capital investment done up front.

8.6.2.1 Reuse Economics Model With Up-Front Domain Engineering

The basic reuse economics model (Gaffney and Cruickshank 1992; Cruickshank and Gaffney 1991a and 1991b) is designed to reflect the total costs of applying a reuse scheme. The model treats the cost of an application system as the cost of the capital investment in domain engineering apportioned over the expected N application systems plus the cost of application engineering (the cost of creating that particular system). Thus, the cost of an application system, CS, equals the prorated cost of domain engineering plus the cost of application engineering. Further, the cost of application engineering is the cost of the new code plus the cost of the reused code in the new application system, and R is the proportion of code that is reused code. Then:

$$C_S = C_{DP} + C_A$$
$$C_S = C_D/N + C_N + C_R$$
$$C_{DP} = C_D/N \text{ and } C_A = C_N + C_R$$

where:

C_S = The total cost of an application system.

C_D = The total cost of domain engineering.

C_{DP} = The pro rata share of domain engineering distributed between each of the N application systems.

C_A = The cost of an application system.

C_N = The cost of the new code in the application system.

C_R = The cost of the reused code in the application system.

Each of the costs, C_D, C_N, and C_R, is the product of a unit cost (LM/KSLOC) and an amount of code (KSLOC).

Then:

$$C_D = C_{DE} \cdot S_T$$
$$C_N = C_{VN} \cdot S_N$$
$$C_R = C_{VR} \cdot S_R$$

Therefore, the basic reuse cost equation, the average cost for each of the N systems over which the capital investment of domain engineering is to be apportioned, is:

$$C_S = C_{US}S_S = C_{DE}\, S_T/N + C_{VN}S_N + C_{VR}\, S_R$$

where:

C_{US} = Unit cost of the application system.

C_{DE} = Unit cost of domain engineering.

C_{VN} = Unit cost of new code developed for this application system.

C_{VR} = Unit cost of reusing code from the reuse library in this application system. It represents the unit cost of reused code where the library components can be instantiated directly into the application system with no modification.

S_T = Expected value of the unduplicated size of the reuse library, i.e., the available, reusable functionality (software objects measured in source statements) in the library.

S_N = Amount of new code in source statements developed for this application system.

S_R = Amount of reused code (from the reuse library) incorporated into this application system in source statements.

S_S = Total size of the application system in source statements.

Code sizes S_N, S_R, S_S, and S_T are denominated in source statements, either physical or logical (Gaffney and Cruickshank 1991a and 1991b). These code sizes could be denominated in function points (Albrecht and Gaffney 1983) or their variations (such as feature points). The important thing is that consistent units of code size be used.

Let $S_N/S_S = 1 - R$ and $S_R/S_S = R$, where R is the proportion of reuse, dividing through by S_S and rewriting:

$$C_{US} = \frac{C_{DE}S_T}{NS_S} + C_{VN}(1-R) + C_{VR}R$$

Now let $S_T/S_S = K$, the library relative capacity. Thus:

$$C_{US} = \frac{C_{DE}}{N} \cdot K + C_{VN} - (C_{VN} - C_{VR}) \cdot R$$

This is the basic reuse unit cost equation. On the average, it presumes a single reuse of S_R units (SLOC, KSLOC, function points) in each of the N application systems. Thus, this equation is most applicable to systematic reuse of code units having a relatively large amount of functionality.

8.6.2.2 Library Efficiency

You can construct a reuse library to cover the expected variation of a unit of function with any number of alternative or duplicate units of code (or reusable software objects). Let S_T be the "unduplicated" size of the library or its capacity. There may well be alternate or duplicate implementation functionality in the reuse library (source codes, as just stated), but that alternate or duplicate functionality does not add to the size of S_T. The case of alternative implementation of source code or all of the functionality of size S_T is covered in the cost model by an appropriate selection of the value of the unit cost parameter, C_{DE}.

The factor K (= S_T/S_S), the library relative capacity, represents the average proportion (over the N application systems) of functionality of an application system covered by the reuse library. If S_S represents the average application system size in the domain of interest, K is the upper bound for R, or $R < K < 1$.

The efficiency of the library infrastructure, E, is the ratio of the amount of reused code in the application system to the available reusable code.

$$E = \frac{R}{K} = \frac{S_R/S_S}{S_T/S_S} = \frac{S_R}{S_T}$$

where $0 \le E \le 1$.

The factor E indicates the extent to which the developer of a new application system has been able to make use of the library of reusable components in the new system. E can be viewed as the proportion of reuse that is attained relative to what could be attained. Consideration of the meaning of E suggests that you organize your reuse libraries to focus on a particular subject or domain to achieve higher efficiencies and larger returns on invest-ment (Cruickshank and Gaffney 1991a and 1991b; Gaffney and Cruickshank 1992).

E is a measure of the systematic reuse application process efficiency. It is desirable that E be equal to 1.0 or slightly less than 1.0; application engineers, on average, are expected to reuse as much code as possible when composing an application system.

8.7 HOW TO ESTIMATE DOCUMENTATION COSTS

Sections 8.7 through 8.9 present methods of estimating documentation costs and software development activities costs, in which documentation is the main product. Although the method is applied to the case of software developed for DoD applications, the principles underlying can be applied to other software development situations as well. You can use these estimating formulas if you do not have any data about documentation sizes and costs in your experience database. If you do have data, you should develop similar estimating formulas based on your own experience. You can use your experience data as the basis for determining parameter values that you can insert into the estimation algorithms shown here.

Hancock (1982) and Cruickshank (1984) give formulas for estimating the number of doc-umentation pages from program size (SLOC) information and for estimating the documentation effort (LM) from the estimated pages. Table 8-11 provides their formulas that you can use for estimating the number of documentation pages from (estimates of) software size if you do not have data about your organization's software development experience. If you do have such data, you can use it to develop formulas similar to those provided here. In Table 8-11, P stands for pages and S stands for KSLOC. The methods, equations, and parameter values shown are based on the analysis of the software experience database (actu-al costs) of an aerospace developer of real-time command and control software. The database contains over 6 million source statements (new and reused) developed with more than 1,000 labor years of effort over 40 major software products developed during the years 1976 to 1988 (Cruickshank 1984, revised).

The estimating formulas in Tables 8-11 and 8-12 must be separately applied to each required document. As an example, suppose that you are to develop a computer program of 150 KSLOC, and you want to estimate the effort to develop the first draft of a prelimi-nary design document and a detailed design document. Using Table 8-11 to estimate the pages involved, the preliminary design document is estimated to be (4.99)(150) = 749 pages, and the detailed design document will be (8.01)(150)=1202 pages. Using Table 8-12 to estimate effort, the estimated effort for the Preliminary Design Document will be (105.6)(749/1000) = 79.1 LM, and the estimated effort for the Detailed Design Document will be (79.8)(1202/1000) = 95.9 LM. These pages could be a mixture of text, figures,

Document	DoD-STD-2167A Document	Estimating Formula	KSLOC Range
System requirements Software requirements Interface requirements Software development plan	SSS, SRS, IRS, SDP	$P = 10.0\,S - 0.073\,S^2$	Below 68
		$P = 5.04\,S$	Above 68
Preliminary software design document Preliminary interface design document	Preliminary SDD Preliminary IDD	$P = 10.0\,S - 0.044\,S^2$	Below 114
		$P = 4.99\,S$	Above 114
Detailed software design document Detailed interface design document	Detailed SDD Detailed IDD	$P = 16.0\,S - 0.085\,S^2$	Below 94
		$P = 8.01\,S$	Above 94
Software test plan Software test description Software test specification	STP, STD	$P = 7.0\,S - 0.034\,S^2$	Below 103
		$P = 3.50\,S$	Above 103
Software test procedures Software test cases	CSU and CSC Test Procedures	$P = 24.0\,S - 0.140\,S^2$	Below 86
		$P = 11.96\,S$	Above 86
User's manual Operator's manual Version description document	SUM, VDD	$P = 5.0\,S - 0.020\,S^2$	Below 125
		$P = 2.50\,S$	Above 125

Table 8-11. *Estimating Pages from Software System Size*

Document	Estimating Formula (LH)	Estimating Formula (LM)
System and software requirements, preliminary design documents	$LH = 17.6\,P$	$LM = 105.6\,PK$
Detailed design documents, test plans and requirements	$LH = 13.3\,P$	$LM = 79.8\,PK$
Test procedures and cases	$LH = 7.1\,P$	$LM = 42.6\,PK$
User and operator manuals	$LH = 3.7\,P$	$LM = 22.2\,PK$

Table 8-12. *Estimating Documentation Effort from Document Size*

tables, and listings of a design language. When the impact factor for this situation is taken into consideration, the total effort is (79.1 + 95.9)1.38 = 241.5 LM.

You must apply the method separately to each required document. Also, to estimate effort from the estimated pages, you must use the formula based on a per thousand pages (pages/1000) basis. For certain development activities, such as design where the output is a document (electronic or hard copy), the estimate of documentation costs can serve as a cross-check on the estimate of design activity costs using LM/KSLOC. (The next subsection gives an example of cross-checking documentation costs.) You must remember that the unit costs for many development activities include the costs of documentation as a separate minor activity or subactivity. You use these estimating formulas for documentation size and costs when you want to estimate the cost of documentation as a separate activity or when you want to cross-check an estimate of documentation costs made with the use of unit costs.

The relationships shown in Table 8-11 came from data generated before the publication of DOD-STD-2167A (Department of Defense 1988), but these relationships have been extensively tested and used in estimating situations since the publication of DOD-STD-2167A.

Table 8-12 provides the formulas for estimating the documentation effort for a first draft in LH and LM from the estimated number of pages. The effort shown here includes the analysis time and writing a first draft. In Table 8-12, P stands for the number of pages and PK stands for 1,000 pages. Therefore, the effort in LH is on a per-page basis, and the effort in LM is on a per-thousand-page basis.

Estimates produced by using the formulas in Tables 8-11 and 8-12 are for a first draft of a document. There is an additional cost for producing a final document from the first draft. You may wish to include this additional cost in some cases. For example, the overall cost of documentation is the cost of getting the document completed, which includes not only writing but also reviews and revisions, customer interfacing, and management. Reviews and revisions to the draft and preliminary versions of the document will cost an additional (to the first draft costs) 17 percent, customer interfacing will cost an additional 8 percent, and management will cost an additional 13 percent. So the total impact factor is 1.38, and you must multiply the cost or effort of writing the document by the appropriate value of the impact factor to get the true cost of the document.

Suppose that you are to develop a computer program of 450 KSLOC, and you want to know how much the preliminary and detailed software design documents (SDD) will cost. Using Table 8-11 to estimate the pages involved, the preliminary design documentation will be (3.5)(450) = 1,575 pages, and the detailed design documentation will be (2.0)(450) = 900 pages. Using Table 8-12 to get costs, the preliminary design documentation will cost (105.6)(1.575) = 166.3 LM, and the detailed design documentation will cost (79.8)(0.900) = 71.8 LM. These pages could be a mixture of text, figures, tables, and listings of a design language. When you take the impact factor into consideration, the total cost is (166.3 + 71.8)1.38 = 328.6 LM.

8.8 TOP-DOWN ESTIMATION OF TOTAL SYSTEM DEVELOPMENT COSTS

As an estimator, you will sometimes be asked to answer questions such as, "Given a development program with a total estimated cost of (say) $50 million, beginning in two years, what will be the breakdown on the costs of major products and activities (i.e., cost drivers)?" You might also be asked, "How much software can we produce for this program?" The methods presented in this section can help you to answer such questions.

Often, projects entail the simultaneous development of computer hardware and software for a new system. Here system means an interacting group of target computer hardware and software items developed simultaneously. This section presents a top-down method for estimating the allocation of cost resources to all of the major aspects of system development. The methodology is called "top-down" since the only inputs to the methods are the total amount of resources (in dollars or LM) and the applicable aspects of the developmental system.

The top-down estimating method represents the view that the total system costs (of which software is a part) are proportional to the costs of the major cost drivers such as the example proportions shown in Table 8-13 (Cruickshank 1988). You can use estimating algorithms to calculate the costs corresponding to each of these cost drivers. In addition, the method represents the costs of all the major cost drivers as proportional to the software development costs. Table 8-13 shows an example of estimating algorithms for a developmental system. This includes all the major cost drivers of a full-scale program involving the

Program Cost-Driver	Proportion	Algorithm
Software development (SW) (including builds and libraries)	0.22	
Computer hardware development (HW design and model)	0.14	0.65 SW
Systems engineering (SE)	0.10	0.30 (HW+SW) or 0.50 SW
Test and evaluation (TE) (software and system testing/validation)	0.11	0.25 (SW+HW+SE) or 0.50 SW
Manufacturing (MFG) (full-scale development)	0.12	2 to 5 systems
Product support (logistics)	0.06	0.09 (SW+HW+SE+TE+MFG)
Configuration management, data management, and quality assurance (CM, DM, QA)	0.07	0.10 (SW+HW+SE+TE+MFG)
Program management	0.18	Program management, financial management, clerical, cost engineering, measurement
Total	1.00	

Table 8-13. *Example of Top-Down Estimating Model*

simultaneous development of computer hardware and software. This set of estimating algorithms and proportions is an example (based on the experience of a large system developer), and you should develop your own set of algorithms and proportions based on experience. You will want a separate set for each type of development program and for each development environment.

To answer the questions posed at the beginning of this section, you must first convert the dollar amount for the total program to LM or LH using the dollars per LM or LH conversion value provided by your cost engineering organization or your financial organization. Next, you apply the appropriate proportions and estimating algorithms, such as shown in Table 8-13, to get the cost (effort) breakdown. Then you divide the estimated effort for software development by your software development overall unit cost value (e.g., LM/[LM/KSLOC]) to get the amount of software (KSLOC) that can be produced by the given effort.

Suppose that your project is to develop 500 KSLOC of new code with no associated computer hardware development or manufacturing. Starting with the given software proportion of 0.22, the proportion for computer hardware development will be 0.0; systems engineering will be 0.5 SW = 0.11; test and evaluation will be 0.5 SW = 0.11; manufacturing will be 0.0; logistics will be 0.09 of SW+SE+TE = 0.04; CM, DM, and QA will be 0.10 of SW+SE+TE = 0.04; and program management will be 0.18. The proportions add up to 0.69. The adjustment factor will be 1/0.69 = 1.45. You then use this adjustment factor to adjust each of the proportions up to a total of 1.00. These adjusted project proportions appear in Table 8-14.

You can estimate the software size by the methods in Chapter 7, and you can estimate the software costs by the methods in Sections 8.3 and 8.4. When you have estimated the software development and test costs, all other project costs will be proportional, as above,

Program Cost-Driver	Proportion	Cost (LM)
Software development	0.30	2,500
Computer hardware development	0.00	0
Systems engineering	0.16	1,333
Test and evaluation	0.16	1,333
Manufacturing	0.00	0
Product support	0.06	500
CM, DM, QA	0.06	500
Program management	0.26	2,167
Total	1.00	8,333

Table 8-14. Top-Down Cost Estimating Example

to the software development costs. The total of these costs will be the total system development costs.

For example, suppose that it costs 5.00 LM/KSLOC (corresponding to 200 SLOC/LM) for software development planning: preliminary and detailed design (systems engineering will provide the software requirements, and this example will not estimate that effort), development (coding and unit test), error correction support, and CSC integration. Also, assume that no computer hardware development or manufacturing is required. The software costs (for 500 KSLOC) will be (5.00)(500) = 2,500 LM. All other costs will be proportional to the software costs, as shown in Table 8-13.

As another example, suppose that $50,000,000 is available for a total system development program, including the development of computer hardware and software and all of the cost drivers shown in Table 8-13. How much software can you develop within this budget for this project? The relevant software activities include design, development, and integration testing. Assuming $10,000 per LM for labor and burden, 5,000 LM are available for the whole project. Using Table 8-13, 5,000(0.22) = 1,100 LM will be the software labor budget. At 5.00 LM/KSLOC (as in the example in the preceding paragraph) for the software development activities, you can develop 1,100/5.00 = 220 KSLOC.

8.9 HOW TO ESTIMATE COSTS OF SUPPORT TO SOFTWARE DEVELOPMENT

Table 8-15 lists the support costs for software development as additional percentages of the cost of software development that you might expect. You should use these figures only as examples and develop corresponding ones for your own organization's experience. For example, if the cost (design through CSC integration test) of a software product were 100

Activity	Percent Additional Cost
Quality assurance	5–10
Performance analysis and capacity planning	0.5–1.0
Buildings, libraries	8
Configuration management	1
Program management including financial management	13–15
Measurement	2–4
Clerical	2

Table 8-15. *Percent Additional Cost for Support to Software Development*

LM, then the measurement function would cost an additional 2 to 4 percent or 2 to 4 LM to provide estimation support and historical cost data.

These percentages indicate costs in addition to the software development costs and do not include the support costs for computer hardware development. Measurement activities include cost and size estimating, monitoring software costs, collecting data, and reporting. They do not include "front-end" measurement activities such as the initial establishment of a software experience database and cost proposal activities before the project officially begins. The data in Table 8-15 is (revised) from Cruickshank and Lesser (1982).

You should estimate the costs of supporting software development for every project. You should also realize that Sections 8.8 and 8.9 show how to estimate software effort or cost for two different situations. Section 8.8 presents a method for estimating software development effort (and size) from a given total program development effort or cost. Section 8.9 shows you how to estimate the costs of supporting software from a given software development cost. The two methods can be used as a rough cross-check on each other.

8.10 RISK IN ESTIMATES OF COST

It is important to have a quantitative measure of the variation inherent in an estimate of cost; this variation defines the risk. The cost estimate plus some multiple of the inherent variation represents the upside cost exposure to the software development project. If this upside potential exposure is so high that it might cause a serious cost overrun or if it might cause a decrease in the functionality delivered or a decrease in the product quality, your project is at risk, and you would have to increase your cost estimate and its associated budgets. You must be able to quantify this inherent variation to be able to make judgments about the upside and downside exposures.

You can treat an estimate of software cost in two ways, as a relative deviation from a target cost or as a probability of not achieving a target cost (say, corresponding to a budget imposed on you). You calculate the variation inherent in a cost estimate quite differently in each of these cases. This section presents these two methods of modeling and calculating the effect of this inherent variation. Throughout this section, the inherent variation in a software cost estimate is called "cost risk."

8.10.1 Point Estimates of Cost Risk

The point estimate of cost is the most common type of estimate. In this case, the percent cost risk is defined, for the unbiased point estimate of cost, by the relation:

$$\text{Risk} = \frac{(\text{Expected\_Cost}) - (\text{Dictated\_Cost})}{(\text{Dictated\_Cost})} \cdot 100$$

The Expected_Cost parameter is your estimate of costs without the influence of market or organizational pressures. The Dictated_Cost is a target cost and is the object established by market or organizational decisions. For example, the Dictated_Cost could be a proposed cost. With risk defined in this manner, a positive risk is a cost exposure, and a negative risk indicates cost protection. For example, if your software development organization produces an estimate of 750 LM for a software project and then management decides to propose 600 LM in the cost proposal, the cost risk, (150/600) S 100, is 25 percent.

8.10.2 Interval Estimates of Cost Risk

The method in Section 8.10.1 deals with, in statistical terms, a point estimate, i.e., just one estimate of cost (750 LM) out of an implied distribution of many possible estimates. In the previous example 750 LM is, to the estimator, the most likely point or value of cost. Much better cost risk estimates are possible if you know the distribution of possible costs because then you can make an interval estimate of cost, i.e., associating a probability with a range of possible costs.

Another more desirable method is to estimate a distribution of possible costs by assigning probabilities to the range or distribution of possible sizes and unit costs of the software product. Risk then becomes defined as a probability that the cost will exceed the dictated cost previously defined. This method of estimating cost risk is the equivalent of a statistical interval estimate.

To derive a distribution of possible costs, you must assign probabilities to the possible range of software product sizes in SLOC and to the possible range of unit costs in LM/KSLOC, i.e., the total LM divided by the total KSLOC. You can estimate the probabilities for size in KSLOC and unit cost in LM/KSLOC, as shown in Tables 8-16 and 8-17, using past experience as guidance. Alternatively, you can estimate the probabilities by surveying the software development managers and lead technical personnel to get their estimates of the probabilities then averaging these estimates to produce a set of probabilities (as in Tables 8-16 and 8-17). A method of obtaining a range of size estimates is suggested in Chapter 7.

You can estimate size using any of the techniques shown in Chapter 5, and you can build a range of possible values around the figures you develop by varying some of the assumptions underlying the estimate until you have covered the range of possible values of size. You divide the range of size values into intervals and, using experience as a guide, assign probabilities to them. You can generate unit cost probabilities in the same way.

Next, you cross-tabulate the unit cost values with the size values and create two values for each size—unit cost combination. The first value is the product of the size probability with the unit cost probability. This value indicates the probability of the occurrence of this size—unit cost pair, i.e., the probability of the associated cost. The second value is the

KSLOC	Probability
100	0.10
150	0.25
200	0.50
250	0.15
Total	1.00

Table 8-16. *Example of Size Probability Distribution*

LM/KSLOC	Probability
6.500	0.15
5.500	0.20
4.500	0.40
3.500	0.25
Total	1.00

Table 8-17. *Example of Unit Cost Probability Distribution*

product of size with unit cost and indicates the cost (in LM) associated with that pair. Then the two values generated for each size—unit cost combination (pair) are:

$$\text{Probability(Pair)} = \text{Probability(Size)} \cdot \text{Probability(Unit Cost)}$$
$$\text{COST(LM)} = \text{KSLOC} \cdot \text{LM/KSLOC}$$

In the case where the software system is composed of new and reused code, the size metric should be KESLOC, which you can determine using the methods in Chapter 7. For example, if reused code costs 30 percent of new code, then:

$$\text{KESLOC} = 1.0(\text{KSLOC}_{new}) + 0.30(\text{KSLOC}_{reused})$$

Table 8-18 shows the cross-tabulation and generation of the distribution probabilities with the LM cost estimates. The probabilities in Table 8-18 have been multiplied by 100 to express them as percentages of (the area under) the distribution.

Probability/Unit Cost	Probability/Size (KSLOC)			
(LM/KSLOC)	0.10	0.25	0.50	0.15
	100.00	150.00	200.00	250.00
0.150	1.50	3.75	7.50	2.25
6.500	650.00	975.00	1,300.00	1,625.00
0.200	2.00	5.00	10.00	3.00
5.500	550.00	825.00	1,100.00	1,375.00
0.400	4.00	10.00	20.00	6.00
4.500	450.00	675.00	900.00	1,125.00
0.250	2.50	6.25	12.50	3.75
3.500	350.00	525.00	700.00	875.00

Table 8-18. *Example of Derivation of Distribution of Costs*

Now, you can order the LM values with their associated probabilities of being realized, as shown in Table 8-19. You can compute risk by reference to a table of cost versus cumulative probability, such as Table 8-19. Risk is defined as the difference between the cumulative percent probability of any given target cost and 100. If management were to make a decision to propose the software at a target cost of 1,100 LM, the risk of attaining that figure would be 18.75 percent (see Table 8-19) in the example. You linearly interpolate the given target cost to calculate its probability. Conversely, if management were to ask, "What is the cost I should propose if I'm willing to live with a 20 percent risk?", interpreting the cumulative probability column of Table 8-19, we determine the answer to that question to be 1084 LM.

So, now you can say that there is "only" a probability of 0.5925 (by linear interpolation) that your expected cost estimate of 750 LM will be exceeded, while there is a 0.8500 probability (by linear interpolation) that the management-proposed cost value of 600 LM will be exceeded. The difference in these probabilities may cause the proposal value of cost to undergo further review. If a 20 percent risk is acceptable, the corresponding value by linear interpolation of 1,084.4 LM will be the software's new proposed cost value. Figure 8-1 shows this cost risk graphically.

The calculation of risk provides management with information it can employ as a rational basis for making business decisions about what is a good price to propose based on knowledge of the cost risk. The cost risk is one of several major factors involved in the development of a proposal price.

You should calculate cost risk for every software development project.

Cost (LM)	Probability (Percent)	Cumulative Probability
350	2.50	2.50
450	4.00	6.50
525	6.25	12.75
550	2.00	14.75
650	1.50	16.25
675	10.00	26.25
700	12.50	38.75
825	5.00	43.75
875	3.75	47.50
900	20.00	67.50
975	3.75	71.25
1,100	10.00	81.25
1,125	6.00	87.25
1,300	7.50	94.75
1,375	3.00	97.75
1,625	2.25	100.00

Table 8-19. Example of Distribution of Costs

8.10.3 Cost Risk Management Activities

The recommended sequence of estimation activities is to first estimate the size of the software product, then estimate the cost, and finally estimate the development schedule based on the size and the cost estimates. You can revise these estimates as often as available resources permit.

You use several cost-estimating methods (including size-estimating methods) whenever possible, because one method can serve as a useful cross-check on another. When the results do not agree to within 10 (or 20) percent, you should try to reconcile them by considering the nature of the assumptions underlying them.

It is important to realize that a cost estimate is not the same as a price, which in turn is not the same as a budget. A cost estimate is based on all the facts at hand. With this estimate, management may decide to take a cost risk and propose a different (usually lower)

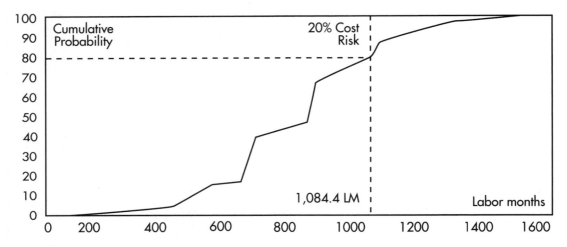

Figure 8-1. *Cumulative Distribution of Costs*

cost from which the price is computed. The proposed cost becomes the basis of negotiation with the customer. Emerging from these negotiations is a negotiated price including a profit. When you win the business, you establish budgets based on the negotiated price. These budgets are often lower than those derived from the negotiated price since it is standard procedure in many organizations to withhold 10 to 15 percent of every budget as a "management reserve." Thus, the cost corresponding to the negotiated price may be lower than the cost estimate, and the budget may be correspondingly lower also.

8.11 SOFTWARE MAINTENANCE COSTS

If the enhancements and the revisions to an existing software system are relatively large, the situation ceases to be maintenance of an existing system and becomes the development of a new version of the original system. In either case, the operations of adding, modifying, reusing, and removing code, as described in Chapter 6, are used. The process of developing a new version of an existing or "original" system (IEEE 1992) involves the process of deleting code from the original system, some of which is to be removed and some of which is to be modified for inclusion in the new version. This enhances the original system with new code that is added and with the modified code from the original system and reused code that was not deleted from the original system. Thus, the development of a new version of an existing system is the process of creating new code and combining it with reused code.

Software maintenance consists of relatively small-scale enhancements to the software system and the correction of errors (defects), often done in response to an engineering change proposal in the case of government contracts or as the result of market considerations in the case of commercial software development. You can view software maintenance as a form of software development. This guidebook treats defect correction and enhancements under a single category called "problems." Cruickshank (1988) reports that experience with a real-time operating system showed that there were 350 problems or defects in a 62 KSLOC operating system, or about 6.0 problems per KSLOC in the period after delivery, i.e., during maintenance. Other experience in software maintenance showed that each problem cost about 0.6 LM to fix. It is important that you develop maintenance cost data based on your organization's experience.

Estimates of defects per KSLOC existing at delivery, based on software design review and code inspection error data, show that you might expect man-rated (space) software to have about 0.02 defects/KSLOC at delivery. Ground-based software might have about 0.3 defects/KSLOC at delivery, and airborne and seaborne software can have about 0.7 to 1.0 defects/KSLOC at delivery. You can use these figures to estimate the costs of error correction or derive your own. Keep in mind that once you estimate the cost of maintenance and enhancements, the additional costs of support discussed in Section 8.9 also apply.

8.12 COSTS OF A MEASUREMENT PROGRAM

Experience shows that the activities inherent in a measurement/metrics program (see Chapter 3) costs an amount equal to about 2 to 4 percent of the software cost on average. However, this figure could be significantly larger depending upon the functions performed by the measurement program. This cost will vary as a function of various factors, including the number of metrics of the measurement program and the capability maturity level of the software development organization. When a software organization budgets for a development project, it should budget an additional amount equal to the percentage of the direct labor software budget (shown in Table 8-15) for the metrics program to support that software project. The cost of measurement activities should not be taken from the software budget because the software organization should not be in a position of sacrificing its own resources to support organizational measurement goals. Metrics and measurement should be budgeted separately.

8.13 SUMMARY OF RECOMMENDATIONS

The general recommendations presented in Chapter 8 are:
- Use LM or LH as the basis for the computation of software costs. Using these cost units facilitates cost comparisons. You can convert the LM or LH to dollars when appropriate.

- Have a defined and managed software development process for accurate cost estimation.

- Make estimates of software cost throughout the development cycle. The models you use to estimate cost will depend upon the process maturity level of your development organization. Generally, the lower maturity levels should use holistic models, and the higher maturity levels should use activity-based models.

- Cross-check cost estimates made by holistic and activity-based models whenever possible. The type of cross-checking depends on the process maturity level.

- Customize software costing models, metrics, and parameter values to your software development environment. The type of customization depends on the process maturity level.

- Consider the effect of an HOL and of product size on development costs.

- Use top-down models at the earliest stages of system conceptualization to estimate the allocation of resources (effort) to the general tasks to be accomplished.

- Estimate the costs of support to software development for every project.

- Make estimates of software development costs in parallel with an organization (such as measurements or cost engineering) that is independent of software development. Negotiate differences where they are substantial. If you cannot reconcile differences, then inform higher management.

- Estimate cost risk and cost exposure for every project. Use the information resulting from estimates made in parallel to provide estimates of cost risk and cost exposure.

Chapter
9

HOW TO ESTIMATE SCHEDULE

9.1 SCHEDULE ESTIMATION OVERVIEW

It is important to accurately estimate the calendar time required to develop a software product (schedule). It is also important to be able to create a staffing curve for the project development labor that you can use in project planning. Also, it is frequently useful to perform trade-offs between development effort and schedule during the project planning process.

This section provides methods that help you answer the following schedule-related questions:

- How long will the development take?

- What effect would a reduction in development schedule have on the development effort?

- What is the staffing profile (i.e., what is the profile of effort per month) over the project duration?

To address these questions, this section presents guidance on methods that tell you how to:

- Estimate a development schedule, given that you know (or have an estimate of) how much effort it will take to develop it.

- Make a trade-off between the length of the development schedule and the effort required to develop the product.

- Determine whether a schedule given to you is compatible with the size of a proposed product and the required effort estimated for its development.

- Develop a spread of software development labor over the development time (schedule) that you have estimated.

- Estimate the potential impact on the development schedule of incorporating reused code into the new software product that you are developing.

When planning the development of a new software product, you can make trade-offs among cost, schedule, and size. For example, if you want a lower cost, then you must reduce the product size. Schedule (the period of time for software development) is a key consideration in planning for a software development project. You should expect the effect of varying quality requirements to impact schedule and/or cost. Often, you can ensure higher quality software, in part, through more extensive testing. Sometimes this may increase the development effort and development time (schedule) over the time that would be required for a software product of a lower quality level.

9.2 ESTIMATING THE DEVELOPMENT SCHEDULE

This section tells you how to estimate the length of time, t_d, required to develop a software product, given that you know (or have estimated) its size (see Chapter 7) and how much, effort you will need to do so (see Chapter 8). To estimate t_d, use the formula (see Section 8.3.2.1, software development equation):

$$t_d = \left(\frac{S}{C \cdot K^p} \right)^{1/q}$$

where S is the software product size in SLOC (excluding comments) or ESLOC when reused code is involved (see Chapter 6 and Section 9.3). C is the technology constant that numerically represents both the complexity of the software to be developed and the sophistication of the development environment. The parameter C can be regarded as a generalized productivity measure since it includes the effects of project duration (schedule) and effort and size (together implying productivity). K is the development effort in labor years Finally, t_d is the development schedule (design through installation) in years. The parameters p and q have the values specified in Section 8.3.2, or ones based on the experience of your development organization.

You can also compute the schedule for this period plus that covering the creation of requirements using this formula, but with the figures for K and C adjusted accordingly.

This equation is based on the software development equation discussed in Chapter 8, which is:

$$S = C \cdot K^p \cdot t_d{}^q$$

Now consider an example application of the equation for estimating t_d. Suppose that C=6,000; S=300,000; K=166.7 labor years (equivalent to a development productivity of 150 SLOC/LM); p=0.6288; and q=0.5555. Solving for t_d and substituting the parameter values, you obtain:

$$t_d = \left(\frac{300,000}{6,000 \cdot 166.7^{0.6288}} \right)^{\frac{1.0}{0.5555}} = 3.5 \text{ years}$$

This equation only estimates the overall development schedule. You should not use it to estimate the length of time necessary to do each of the activities that compose the overall development process.

Alternatively, you might consider using an equation of the form $t_d = a \cdot sb$, where a and b are constraints derived from the experience of your software development organization. This is the form of the COCOMO schedule estimation equations provided in Section 8.3, covering holistic models.

9.3 SCHEDULE IMPACT OF REUSED OR COTS CODE

To examine the effect of code reuse (or COTS software) on your (estimated) development schedule, determine the size in KESLOC (as in Section 6.6) of your software system using the equation:

$$KESLOC = S_N + S_R (C_{VR}/C_{VN})$$

where S_N is the amount (in KSLOC) of new code in the application system, and S_R is the amount (in KSLOC) of reused code in the application system. C_{VN} is the unit cost (LM/KSLOC or LH/SLOC) of new code in your application system; C_{VR} is the unit cost of reused code in your application system.

To relate the lengths of the development schedule for a case in which the system consists of all new code to one that consists, in part, of reused code, let:

K_N	=	The effort (labor years) to develop an application system composed of all new code.
K_R	=	The effort to develop an application system consisting of both new and reused code.
P	=	The relative productivity enhancement to be found in developing the system when reuse is involved as compared with the case in which it is not.
t_{dn}	=	The development schedule (months or years) for an application system of size S KSLOC composed of all new code.
t_{dr}	=	The development schedule for an application system of size S KESLOC composed of both new and reused code.

R = The proportion of code reuse=$S_R/(S_N + S_R)$.

Gaffney and Durek (1991) give a formula that relates the schedule for developing a software system implemented with all new code to one required if the software system is implemented with a combination of new and reused code:

$$\frac{t_{dr}}{t_{dn}} = P^{\frac{(p-1)}{q}}$$

where:

$$\frac{K_R}{K_N} = \frac{1}{P} = \frac{C_{VN} \cdot (1-R) + C_{VR} \cdot R}{C_{VN}} = 1 + R \cdot \left(\frac{C_{VR}}{C_{VN}} - 1\right)$$

You may use the relation for K_R/K_N for various parametric "what-if" analyses to estimate the possible effect of various amounts of code reuse on the development schedule.

As an example, let C_{VN} = 5.0 LM/KSLOC, C_{VR} = 0.375 LM/KSLOC, and R = 0.9. Then 1/P=0.1675 and P = 5.97. Using the values of p = 0.6288 and q = 0.5555 given in Section 9.2:

$$\frac{t_{dr}}{t_{dn}} = P^{\frac{(p-1)}{q}} = P^{-0.6682} = 0.30$$

This means that the schedule to develop the software product containing new and reused code is only 30 percent as long as that to develop the same product with all new code.

Figure 9-1 shows the relative schedule reduction versus the relative productivity enhancement for two sets of values for the parameters p and q. The top line uses the parameter values developed by Putnam (1978) of p = 0.3333 and q = 1.3333. The bottom line uses more recent parameter values developed by Gaffney (1983) of p = 0.6288 and q = 0.5555. The thin shaded area between the lines shows that $P^{(p-1)/q}$ is relatively insensitive to a fairly wide range of p and q; therefore, it is a fairly robust estimator of t_{dr}/t_{dn}.

9.4 SCHEDULE/DEVELOPMENT EFFORT TRADE-OFF

Suppose that you used the software development equation of Section 9.2 to estimate that the "ideal" length of the schedule for your software product is t_0. This is based on size estimate (see Chapter 7) of S ESLOC and on a development labor effort of K_0 labor years with a technology constant of C. Now, suppose that you want to compute the amount of labor years required if you were to reduce the schedule from t_0 to t_1 (a figure that may have been

Relative
Schedule

$\dfrac{t_{dr}}{t_{dn}}$

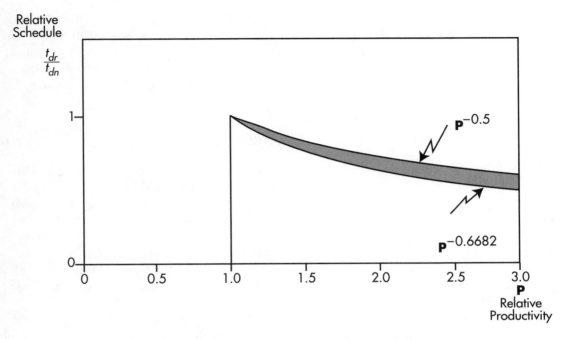

Figure 9-1. *Schedule Reduction Versus Productivity Enhancement*

imposed on you). The labor years required will increase to K_1, which is calculated using the equation:

$$K_1 = K_0 \cdot \left(\frac{t_0}{t_1}\right)^{q/p} = K_0 \cdot \left(\frac{t_0}{t_1}\right)^{0.8834}$$

with p=0.6288 and q=0.5555.

This equation is the schedule/development effort trade-off equation and is derived from the software development equation given above. A word of caution: use this equation only to estimate the effect of schedule compression on your development effort.

As an example, suppose there was a 20 percent schedule reduction. Then $t_0/t_1 = 1/.8 = 1.25$. Further, suppose that the originally estimated effort was $K_0 = 50$ labor years. Then, the effort for the case in which the schedule was reduced by 20 percent would be $K_1 = 60.9$ labor years or an increase of 22 percent. This calculation illustrates the effect of schedule compression on development effort that you can expect.

Make schedule/development effort trade-off studies for all software development projects and products. Trade-off methods should be part of your organization's software standards.

There are obviously limitations in the proportionate amount that the development schedule can be reduced. For example, if t_1 were to take the value of 0.1, i.e., a 90 percent reduction in the development schedule, the increase in effort would be about 7.6 times the original effort. But experience shows that no effort increase is likely to be able to overcome such a drastic schedule reduction to produce a product. Very large amounts of effort applied to software development in a very short time interval are not feasible.

9.5 SCHEDULE/EFFORT/SIZE COMPATIBILITY

Determine whether the figures (estimates or objectives) for schedule, size, and effort for your project are compatible. The customer or the marketplace may impose the length of time for development, or you may perceive a need to quickly get a new product out into the marketplace. Independent of such considerations, you may develop a size estimate of your intended software product (using one or more of the methods described in Chapter 7) and a productivity assessment and thence an estimate of the development labor required (using the methods described in Chapter 8). It is important to determine if these estimates for size (S), effort (K), and development period (t_d) are mutually compatible. You can determine their compatibility by using a test based on an application of the software development equation. First, you estimate the value of the technology constant C implied by the values of S, K, and t_d that you have been given or otherwise calculated. You calculate C from the equation:

$$C = \left(\frac{S}{t_d^{0.5555} \cdot K^{0.6288}} \right)$$

(p=0.6288 and q=0.5555)

You can use the same equation but with possibly different values of p and q based on the experience of your organization. On the basis of the value calculated for C, for this example, you can determine whether a given schedule is compatible with the size and effort (and hence, productivity) proposed for the project by using the process shown in Figure 9-2. That is, you compare the C that you have calculated (estimated for the project) with the C's for compatible complete projects.

9.6 SOFTWARE DEVELOPMENT LABOR PROFILES

This section provides a model that you can use to create an overall spread of labor months of development labor over the schedule of length t_d months. The model is based on the Rayleigh distribution (Norden 1958 and 1970). Putnam (1978) built on Norden's (1958 and 1970) work and showed that a Rayleigh curve represents, to a reasonable degree of approximation, the application of labor resources to the creation of a software product. The equation presented here is a variant of the Putnam (1978) representation. The method does not take into consideration the individual activities that constitute the development project you are planning (as described in Chapter 8) nor does it take into consideration the nature of the technology your organization uses for the project in question. You can use this model to provide a first approximation to the software profile. The one finally used in your software development plan should be based on a more detailed consideration of the activities that compose your development process.

Obviously, the relatively simple staffing model presented here cannot reflect the effects various factors could have on your selection of a staffing profile appropriate to your particular software development situation. Clearly, it is preferable for you to develop a staffing profile based on your organization's experience. That experience might cause a different emphasis, such as greater front loading, than the profile estimate based on the Rayleigh model as described here.

You should use a two-step process to develop a staffing profile. First, make an estimate based on the Rayleigh model. Next, look at the spread the Rayleigh model provides and decide if it looks reasonable, based on whatever experience your organization has. Your evaluation of the profile may lead you to modify it, perhaps adding more effort (i.e., a faster buildup) to the initial portion of the spread. Several modification cycles may be required, depending upon your expectations.

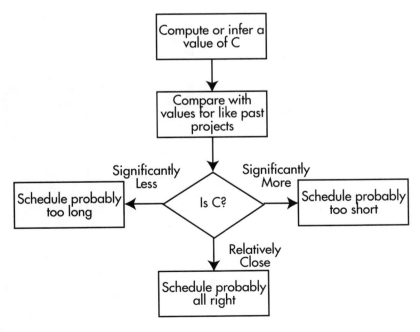

Figure 9-2. *Schedule Compatibility Testing Process*

9.6.1 Basic Rayleigh Model

The "instantaneous" or density form of the Rayleigh distribution is:

$$y(t) = \frac{E}{t_p^2} \cdot t \cdot e^{-\frac{t^2}{2t_p^2}}$$

The cumulative form is:

$$Y(t) = E \cdot \left(1 - e^{-\frac{t^2}{2t_p^2}}\right)$$

Note that t is the time, E is the total area under the curve to infinity, and Y(t) is the area under the curve to time t. Since your software development project will not run to infinity, this model has to be adjusted to represent a practical staffing profile. You replace E by K/X, where K is the total labor expended from t = 0 to t = t_d, the time of delivery, and X is a factor, the determination of which is described later in this section. Note that Y(t_d) = K. Also note that the parameter t_p in the Rayleigh model is the location of the peak of the instantaneous curve y(t).

9.6.2 Practical, Discrete Rayleigh Model

Your software project staffing will be done in terms of discrete intervals of time (months in the examples shown here; the method applies to weeks or other convenient intervals as well, however). Consequently, we now indicate the nature of the more practical discrete model that you should use and illustrate its application with an example.

The instantaneous form of the staffing curve is given by:

$$y(t) = \frac{K/X}{t_p^2} \cdot t \cdot e^{-\frac{t^2}{2t_p^2}}$$

The cumulative form of the staffing curve is given by:

$$Y(t) = \frac{K}{X} \cdot \left(1 - e^{-\frac{t^2}{2t_p^2}}\right)$$

You should use the discrete form of this method to develop your (initial estimate of the) staffing profile. It gives you the effort, F(t), for each one-month interval in the t_d months that compose your software development period. Note that t extends from time equal to t-1 to time equal to t. F(t) is given by the equation:

$$F(t) = Y(t) - Y(t-1) = \frac{K}{X} \cdot \left(e^{\frac{(t-1)^2}{2t_p^2}} - e^{\frac{t^2}{2t_p^2}} \right)$$

where K is the total development effort equal to $K(t_d)$ as explained above. Note that K = XE, where E is the area under the curve from 0 to infinity. Note that t is the interval or month number and that there are N = $t_d/12$ one-month intervals in a development period of t_d months.

Now, we consider how you should select the value of X that you should use. You can fix the ratio of y(td), the approximate staffing level at the end of the development process, relative to the approximate peak staffing level, y(tp). This ratio is the definition of the parameter R. X is fixed by selecting a value of R. This selection also establishes the ratio, $r = t_d/t_p$, the number of schedule months relative to the month in which the peak staffing occurs. Table 9-1 shows some values R, r, and X. Section 9.6.3 shows you how to compute the values of these parameters.

If you do not want to select a value for X, you can use X = 0.999 to obtain a first-pass staffing profile estimate.

9.6.3 Formulas Relating X, r, t_d, and t_p

Recognize that:

$$X = 1 - e^{\frac{-t_d^2}{2t_p^2}}$$

R = y(t_d)/y(t_p)	r = t_d/t_p	X
0.8029	1.5000	0.6754
0.4463	2.0000	0.8647
0.1810	2.5000	0.9561
0.0916	2.8000	0.9802
0.0549	3.0000	0.9889
0.0061	3.7169	0.9990

Table 9-1. *Relative Staffing Levels and Schedules*

and that

$$r = t_d/t_p$$

Thus, you can write

$$X = 1 - e^{-\frac{t^2}{2}}$$

Therefore, $r = (-2 \cdot LN(1 - X))^{1/2}$, where LN means the natural logarithm. Note the minus sign. This is O.K. The expression LN(1–X) will be negative because $1 - X$ is less than 1.

Also, $t_p = (-t_d^2/(2 \cdot LN(1 - X)))$.

You can calculate values for $R = y(t_d)/y(t_p)$ by substituting into the expression given earlier for y(t) the instantaneous Rayleigh staffing profile.

9.6.4 Procedure for Calculating Staffing Profile

You should use the following steps to calculate the values of a Rayleigh staffing profile estimate:

- Select the value of t_d, the number of months of development schedule. Determine this figure using the methodology presented earlier in this section.

- Calculate the value of X based on the value of r, the approximate ratio of the staffing level at the peak of the staffing profile relative to that upon delivery. You can use your organizational experience, expert opinion, or detailed planning for the project, as the basis for your selection of r, and hence X.

- Calculate the value of t_p, the number of months into development at which the peak staffing is estimated to occur. Use the formula given above to do so. Round to the nearest number of whole months.

- Select the value of K, the number of LM effort required to develop the software. Use the methodology presented in Chapter 8 to do so.

- Calculate Y(t), for all integer values of t from t=1 to t=t_d.

$$Y(t) = \frac{K}{X} \cdot \left(1 - e^{-\frac{t^2}{2t_p^2}} \right)$$

- Calculate the month-by-month values of the staffing profile F(T), for all integer values of t from t=1 to t=t_d.

9.6.5 An Example of Rayleigh Staffing Profiles

Now, we apply the methodology described above to the development of two alternative staffing profiles for a software development project. The two profiles differ with respect to the value of R, and hence, of X used. The first profile, Case A, reflects a situation in which there is relatively early peaking and build down during the development period. The second, Case B, represents the situation in which the staffing level is not reduced to such a great degree after the peak, which also occurs later in the development period. Case B may be reflective of a less mature development organization.

The example development project has been estimated to require 1000 LM of effort and to require 20 months for completion. Table 9-2 presents the values of R that were selected, and the values of r, etc., that correspond to them.

The staffing profiles for Cases A and B are provided in Figures 9-3 and 9-4.

Case	R	r	$t_p = t_d/r$	X	K/X	$1/(2.t_p^2)$
A	0.0549	3.00	6.667	0.9889	1011.22	0.0112
B	0.4463	2.00	10.00	0.8647	1156.47	0.0050

Table 9-2. *Example Values of R, etc.*

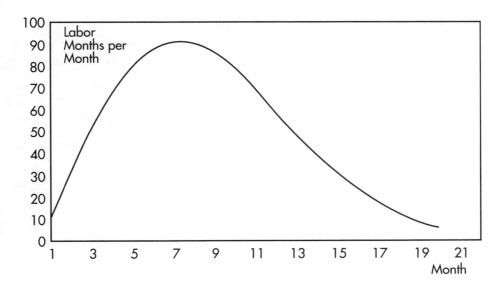

Figure 9-3. *Case A, Labor Months Per Month*

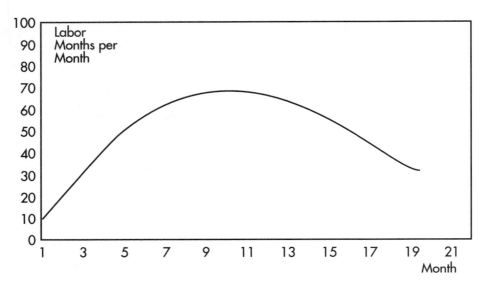

Figure 9-4. *Case B, Labor Months Per Month*

9.7 SUMMARY OF RECOMMENDATIONS

The recommendations on schedule estimation presented in Chapter 9 are:

- Always keep in mind the basis for what you are doing when you are developing an estimate. You are trying to develop an estimate that uses all of the information available to you (which may be principally expert opinion and well-considered experience) and put it together in a rational manner.

- Estimate the schedule for every product.

- Use a Rayleigh distribution to develop an initial estimate of the overall software product development staffing profile.

- Recognize that methods for schedule estimation, compatibility testing, and trade-offs should be part of your software standards.

- Test the estimated schedule for compatibility with the size and estimated development effort.

- Generate a labor profile for every software product.

- Make schedule/development effort trade-off studies for every product.

- Reestimate schedule and redo your staffing profile several times during development as data on actual project performance becomes available to you.

- Develop and use an experience database to aid in schedule estimation.

- Do trade-off studies between schedule and effort.

- Reuse code, if possible, to reduce the schedule.

- Test for compatibility of schedule, effort, and size.

Chapter
10

SOFTWARE QUALITY MEASUREMENT

10.1 OVERVIEW

"Quality" may be viewed as the degree to which the requirements for a software process or the product it produces are satisfied (IEEE 1990). Measuring the quality of the software process and/or the products it creates is a very important aspect of the MDSM process (see Chapter 2). Quality measurements are taken of the degree of compliance of a process and/or the products it produces with the requirements they are supposed to satisfy. The measurements are to be used as the basis for modifying the process or product to minimize its degree of deviance from the established requirements. Such use of software metrics is a primary attribute of attaining the highest levels of (SEI) process maturity (as described in Chapter 3).

This section shows ways in which you can define and measure software quality as well as some aspects of system quality. It is sometimes difficult to distinguish between the quality of a system and that of the software which is a component of it. The measurement of quality is complementary to the establishment of requirements. Chapter 5 shows how to quantify requirements. This chapter complements Chapter 5 by showing how to specify measurements of the degree of requirements attainment. Thus, such measurements quantify quality. This chapter also deals with requirements that are expressed as quality factors, such as usability (see Section 10.4.2).

There are two primary categories of software quality. The first category is concerned with discrepancies in functional requirements. The second category is concerned with discrepancies in other nonfunctional types of requirements. The nonfunctional category includes process requirements (e.g., a requirement to produce a product within 10 percent of budget) and product requirements (e.g., a requirement that a product must attain certain measures of usability, see Section 10.4.2). Currently, there is a greater emphasis on the functionality-oriented view of software quality than the nonfunctionality-oriented view. Indeed, "a popular viewpoint about software quality concerns the detection and removal of errors from executing code" (Deutsch and Willis 1988). The nonfunctional quality attributes, generally speaking, deal with the "goodness" of a software development process or a software product. One difficulty with these quality attributes is that there are no generally agreed upon measures for them. However, they have the potential to be very useful as a means of clarifying the meaning of software process or product qualities of interest. Section 10.4 shows you how to select metrics for software or systems nonfunctional quality attributes using the GQM paradigm (see Chapter 6).

A primary purpose of this section is to show how to measure the discrepancies of a software product or process (defects) from the requirements imposed on it. The fundamental objective of your software process is to minimize making errors that result in such defects. The goal of various software organizations is "zero defects." Such a goal is not often realized. Quality goals should be based in part on considerations of cost-effectiveness. Always try to determine where in the process each error that resulted in a discrepancy was committed. You should use such information as a basis for process modification/improvement. Such action will help to minimize the likely number of defects in future products.

The methodologies presented here have been found to be useful in measuring and estimating the number of errors or defects in a software product. Defects are defined as discrepancies in a product with respect to its requirements specification. This chapter describes several approaches for making projections of defect content in software upon completion of development, i.e., in postdelivery operations. Considerations in the estimation of availability are also presented.

The section also describes the nature of statistical quality and process control, and shows how it may be applied to defects or problem discovery in the software system (e.g., preliminary design, detailed design, code, etc.) that are created by the various activities of the software development process (see Chapter 4). It also states what your software development organization should be doing about defect data collection and analysis to be certifiable at various levels of (SEI) software process maturity. Further, this chapter shows the connection between software process maturity levels and quality assessment.

10.2 THE NATURE OF SOFTWARE QUALITY

This section provides some definitions of quality as applicable to software, to systems containing software, and to the software development process. The section also describes where quantitative quality assessment fits into the software development process.

10.2.1 Some Definitions of Quality

As stated in Section 10.1, there are two principal categories of software product quality measurement: functional and nonfunctional. Several definitions from industry and government standards are presented. A recent one from the March 1992 draft of MIL-STD-2168 A (Department of Defense 1992) is:

> *Software quality. The conformance to explicitly stated functional and performance requirements, explicitly documented development standards, and implicit characteristics, such as maintainability and modularity.*

This definition is a generalization of the relatively simple one given by Crosby (1979):

> *Quality is conformance to requirements.*

It is important to note that both definitions cited cover products and the processes that create them. They also cover the functional (defect- or error count–based) and the nonfunctional categories of quality measures. You should observe several important points about these definitions. First, quality should be defined and measured according to some basis, some standard. Second, there are different aspects or types of quality, including the functional and the nonfunctional aspects of a software system (noted as "performance" types in the definition quoted and in the DoD source referenced). Third, the nonfunctional aspects can include standards applicable to all, or a subset of, the software products produced by a development organization. Product defects (functional discrepancies), in preliminary design, detailed design, or the actual code, should be noted. For example, defects in the detailed design are identified with respect to the preliminary design or to the requirements statement. Both of them are higher level or more abstract representations of the software. Also, such defects are identified according to general standards that apply to all software products developed by the organization. For example, the two-way conditional (If-Then-Else) structure might be forbidden, and a CASE structure must always be employed when you develop a software system. Such a standard design requirement might be an explicit standard (see the DoD definition above) to facilitate the achievement of product "adaptability."

Two other definitions (IEEE 1990) of quality are:

- The degree to which a system, component, or process meets specified requirements.

- The degree to which a system, component, or process meets customer or user needs or expectations.

The first definition is preferred to the second. You should develop a system to satisfy stated requirements. If a user has a need or "expectation" not stated in the requirements document in such a manner that it can be verified, it should not be viewed as a requirement. Unfortunately, there is a difference between what a customer needs or wants (or believes he is going to get) and what he actually gets, even if that product or system meets the specification imposed on it. Software is a "component" of a system as defined above. A system consists of hardware, software, and procedures for operating it. The focus of Chapter 10 is software quality. However, keep in mind that if you are concerned with software quality issues (and measures), you will also have to be concerned with system quality issues (and measures). This is because the software is a component of a *system*, generally containing hardware also. One such measure is availability. Software is neither available nor unavailable; however, the system that includes software is described that way (see Section 10.6.3).

10.2.2 On the Role of Quality in the Software Development Process

You should measure the quality of your software process and the product it is creating to determine their degree of compliance with the requirements. This is an important aspect to implementing the MDSM view of the software development process (see Chapter 2).

Chapter 5 tells you to develop requirements that are incrementally verifiable. Chapter 4 shows that each activity of the software development process includes a verification step. In this step, the quality of the output of that activity (a product it creates) is assessed. For example, you should not wait until code has been written to determine whether the software system under development satisfies the functional specifications imposed upon it. Rather, you should check for compliance at intermediate steps in the creation of the code. One way to do this is to determine if the defect discovery profile is within the bounds established for it (see Section 10.8 on statistical quality and process control).

Think of software quality management as an aspect of MDSM, in which you should:

- Incrementally measure the quality aspects (as described in Chapter 10) of your product and process.

- Use the measurements to determine, with some degree of confidence (verify), whether the goals are being realized or will have been realized at the completion of the development process.

- Estimate the risk of not attaining your goals at each phase of the development process.

- Take (corrective) action appropriate to the results of your verification (including measurement) process.

10.2.3 Users

The nature of software quality depends on your viewpoint. For example, the hands-on user of a software product might have a rather different perception of software quality than the developers of that product (Deutsch and Willis 1988). When you refer to the "user" of a software product, be careful to specify whom you mean. There are (at least) five different categories of users. Each of these groups may have its own, possibly unique, perception of what constitutes software product quality. Table 10-1 provides five categories of users

User Group	Principal Software Quality Objective
End User Management	Specifications support business goals
Hands-On End User	Product helps me do my job better, faster, easier
Buyer	Product meets the specifications
Developer	Product is defect-free when installed
Maintainer	Product is understandable, modifiable, testable

Table 10-1. *User Group Quality Objectives*

together with their principal quality objectives. Note that the items of importance can be called "goals" in the sense of the GQM paradigm (described in Chapter 6 and Section 10.4.3). It is never a certainty that a product meets specifications and/or is defect-free. Rather, a cost-effective amount of verification is done, and some degree of confidence is realized that the product does what is specified for it to do. Deutsch and Willis (1988) identified the last four categories listed in Table 10-1.

10.3 QUALITY AND QUALITY FACTORS

This section describes the nature of software quality factors. Software quality factors relate to those aspects of quality that interest a particular set of users and reflect their particular concerns. As shown subsequently, metrics, such as for usability (see Section 10.4.2), can be devised to dimension the specific concerns of a user or group of users.

10.3.1 The Nature of Software Quality Factors

Quality can be defined as "the degree to which a system, component, or process meets customer or user needs" (IEEE 1990). Software quality factors (SQFs) are attributes that a specific group of users believe a specific software system should possess (Bowen, Wigle, and Tsai 1985). That is, an SQF is a user-oriented view of an aspect of software product quality (Department of Transportation, Federal Aviation Administration 1991). In fact, one or more sets of SQFs may constitute a subset of the requirements for a software product. Following the view expressed in Chapter 5, any such requirements should be quantifiable. As this section shows, various SQFs do not appear to be quantifiable, at least in terms that a significant body of software engineers would agree with. McCall (1979) identified a number of SQFs (defined below). A number of SQFs are associated with one or more metrics.

10.3.2 Some Software Quality Factors

The SQFs identified by McCall (1979) and their definitions, as stated by Gaffney (1981), are given in Table 10-2. Bowen, Wigle, and Tsai (1985) developed metrics for each of these factors, and they are given in the column labeled "Metric" in Table 10-2, with the word "fault" substituted for the word "error." The USAF Rome Laboratory, through the Software Quality

SQF No.	Software Quality Factor	Definition	Metric
1	Correctness	The extent to which a program satisfies its specifications and fulfills the user's mission objectives	1–(faults/lines of code) Faults relative to requirements and standards
2	Efficiency	The amount of computing resources and code required by a program to support a function	1–(actual utilization/allocated utilization)
3	Flexibility	The effort required to modify an operational program	1–0.05 (avg. labor days to change)
4	Integrity	The extent to which access to software or data by unauthorized persons can be controlled	1–(faults/lines) Faults relative to security
5	Interoperability	The effort required to couple one system with another	1–(effort to couple/effort to develop)
6	Maintainability	The effort required to locate and fix a defect in an operational program	1–0.1(avg. labor days to fix)
7	Portability	The effort required to transfer a program from one hardware configuration and/or software system environment to another	1–(effort to transport/effort to develop)
8	Reliability	The extent to which a program can be expected to perform its intended function with required precision	1–(faults/lines of code)
9	Reusability	The extent to which a program can be used in other applications	1–(effort to convert/effort to develop)
10	Verifiability (called Testability by McCall)	The effort required to test a program to ensure that it performs its intended function	1–(effort to verify/effort to develop)
11	Usability	The effort required for one to: learn, operate, prepare input for, and interpret the output of a program	1–(labor days to use/labor days to develop)

Table 10-2. *Software Quality Factors*

Technology Transfer Consortium, has taken these software quality factors/attributes and created models and a methodology termed the "Rome Laboratory Software Quality Framework" (Chruscicki 1992a). The items in the "Metric" column of Table 10-2 are as in (Chruscicki 1992a) and (Bowen, Wigle, and Tsai 1985) except that the former uses the term "fault" instead of the term "error." Observe that correctness and reliability have the same definition which tends to minimize their usefulness.

The maintainability metric is defined as mean time to fix as opposed to 1–0.1 (average labor days to fix) for the attribute given in Table 10-2. The Software Quality Technology Transfer Consortium's current quality metric focus is defect-oriented, that is, on measures related to compliance of a software product with the functional requirements imposed upon it.

10.3.3 Interaction among Software Quality Factors

The users of a software system may wish to have a number of the software quality factors indicated in Table 10-2 satisfied simultaneously. Unfortunately, a given subset of these factors cannot necessarily be defined and imposed on the development team independently because the factors may not be independent. Consequently, a metrics analyst and/or a member of the software development team may have to conduct a trade-off study to clarify the relationships among the software quality factors and to help the interested users understand the limitation that one quality factor may impose on another. An example of potentially conflicting demands among reliability, efficiency, and flexibility is found in Bowen, Wigle, and Tsai (1985). Its essence is that an embedded software system may have to be very reliable. Yet, it may have to be efficient because of limitations imposed on the target processor and memory resources. Also, an embedded software system may need to be flexible to accommodate a variety of missions and/or varieties of aircraft versions for which it is being developed. Unfortunately, highly efficient code is likely to be tightly written assembly code and may not be as reliable or as flexible (amenable to change) as code written in a higher order language. An increasing degree of flexibility for code tends to be associated with increasing ease of maintainability but a lesser degree of efficiency.

10.3.4 Some Other Software Quality Factors

This section presents additional SQFs to those provided in Table 10-2. One or more metrics are presented for each of them and are described more fully in Section 6.10.

The first two SQFs given in Table 10-3 relate to the structure of the software unit or product to which they refer, especially to the interconnections among the elements that compose it. All four metrics associated with these two SQFs have been found empirically to be associated with "error-proneness." "Error-proneness" is the likelihood that a unit of code

Software Quality Factor	Metric
Control Complexity	McCabe Metric (=number of two-way conditional jumps plus 1); also termed cyclomatic complexity
Design Goodness	1. Halstead's "difficulty" metric [see chapter 6.10] 2. Coupling and strength [see chapter 6.10] 3. Data bindings [see chapter 6.10]
Defect (Error) Discovery Efficiency	1− (number of latent defects/number of life-cycle defects injected during development) [see chapter 10.6.4]

Table 10-3. *Additional Software Quality Factors*

contains a large number of defects. Strictly speaking of course, a unit is not "prone" to have (some level of) defects; it either does or does not have this level. However, this term is relatively common, so it is employed here as well.

The third SQF given in Table 10-3 relates to the discovery of software defects during the software development process. The number of latent defects that factor in the metric is an estimated value of the number of defects remaining in the software product when it is shipped. See Section 10.6 for mathematical definitions of these terms.

10.3.5 Software Quality Factors and Product and Process Quality

A particular SQF and associated metric, such as one of those given in Table 10-2 or Table 10-3, may relate to a software product or to the process that created it or to both the process and the product. Examples are:

- Maintainability and expandability relate to the product.

- Complexity and design goodness relate to both the process and the product.

- Defect (Error) discovery efficiency relates to process. However, it is derived from measures taken of the product as shown in Section 10.6.

10.4 USING THE GOAL-QUESTION-METRIC PARADIGM IN THE SELECTION OF QUALITY METRICS

Use the GQM paradigm to select the metric or set of metrics that matches your users' view of quality (see Table 10-1) expected from your software product. It is important to keep in mind that different user groups are likely to have substantially different perceptions of quality for the same product or process that you intend to deliver to them. Two examples of applying the GQM paradigm in the selection of quality metrics are in correctness and usability. Usability is considerably more detailed than correctness; therefore, use the second example as the basis for selecting quality metrics for your software system or process.

10.4.1 An Example of Quality Metrics Selection: Correctness

Suppose a buyer's goal for the product is that it meets its specification. The buyer might ask the question, "Does the product meet its specification?" Essentially, he is expressing interest in the correctness quality factor (see Table 10-2). One metric that might be used to provide an answer for this question is the number of defects discovered during the development process (probably the normalized value, defects/KSLOC, rather than the absolute value, defects). Another metric might be the (estimated) number of latent defects remaining in the software when it is delivered (presumably the same as when shipped) to the end-user.

10.4.2 An Example of Quality Metrics Selection: Usability

This section provides a more detailed example of the selection of a set of metrics for a SQF. Two approaches are provided. This is to demonstrate that there is often more than one way to define the attributes of a SQF and the metrics used to quantify them. Table 10-2 provides one definition for SQF. Now, we reconsider it and show how to develop a set of metrics that can be employed to quantify "usability" as applied to a specific product. It is important to note that a universal or unique set of aspects (or corresponding metrics) to characterize "usability" does not exist. The metrics you should use to characterize usability depend on the questions you ask about the product. Basically, you ask the question, "How usable is this product?" This question is not specific enough for you to select a set of metrics for the usability software quality factor. Therefore, you must develop more specific questions that are dependent on the prospective use of the specific product. You should select the metrics for "usability" according to the needs of a specific user set for the product.

It is unlikely that metrics of general applicability across all possible products can be developed for usability or for any other SQF. Rather, you will need to select specific metrics that are tailored to the set of users involved, based on what usability means to them.

Consider the example of identifying a set of metrics that characterize a text editor's degree of usability. First, you select the goal(s) for the metrics you will identify. In this example, the goal is that a prospective text editor be usable by the people for whom it is to be developed. Bailey (1984) defined three aspects of usability for text editors: ease of learning, efficiency, and operational error-proneness. From these, you can develop the questions your prospective metrics must answer. Consider each of these aspects in terms of the editor's performance on a set of benchmark tests for either of two user groups: novice or expert software engineers. This approach to defining usability is analogous to benchmarking a computer system's performance. Learning is considered from the novice user's point of view and is defined as the number of benchmark tests completed per unit time. Efficiency is defined as the time required by an expert user to successfully complete the entire set of benchmark tests. Finally, error-proneness is defined as the time an expert user spends correcting errors divided by the time to conduct the benchmark tests (including the correction of errors). This measure of error-proneness is analogous to the unavailability of a system (see Section 10.6.3.2). Table 10-4 gives you three questions and their associated metrics that you might choose.

Clearly, aspects of usability other than ease of learning, efficiency, and error-proneness can be selected as a basis for quantizing usability. Boehm (1978) defined one possible alternative set of aspects in which he states that there are two principal aspects of usability, product-related and user-related. The product-related category includes notions of product adaptability and the ease of modifying the product to meet new requirements. A question that addresses the product-related aspect is, "Can this product be used in other situations (environments)?" A corresponding metric can be the number of environments in which the editor is designed to operate divided by some agreed upon target number, such as 3. In this case, the corresponding metric ranges from 0.33 (for the case of only one environment) to >1 (for the case in which there are more than three environments). By convention, set values >1 are considered to equal 1. The user-related category includes ease of use by all target classes of users or of a particular class. A question that addresses the user-related aspect of usability could be, "Are the functions well-commented?" This question is not specific enough to be the basis for an evaluation (verification) as to whether the quality objective "well-commented" was achieved or not. This question can be rephrased into, "Does the editor provide comments for each of the functions?" A corresponding metric can be the proportion of functions for which there are comments. This metric would range from 0 to 1.

This section shows you two alternative ways that you can apply the GQM paradigm to select practical metrics for the usability software quality factor. You can employ a similar approach to select a set of metrics more appropriate to your situation for usability or for

Question	Metric
How easy is it to learn to operate this editor?(relates to learning)	Number of benchmarks completed per hour (average for a sample set of novice users)
How efficient is this editor?(relates to efficiency)	Number of hours required to successfully complete the set of benchmarks (average for a sample set of expert users)
How error-prone is the operation of this editor?(relates to error-proneness)	Number of hours correcting errors divided by number of hours required to successfully complete the set of benchmarks. The figures used are the averages for a sample set of expert users

Table 10-4. *Example Questions and Metrics for Usability*

another SQF. The example illustrates several very important points that you must keep in mind when you select software quality metrics:

- There are no universally accepted metrics for any software quality factor, such as usability.

- Apply the GQM paradigm when selecting quality metrics. Do not just pull a set of metrics "out of thin air." Select them according to the needs of the set of users identified for your process or product.

- Base the metrics on questions that relate to specific, quantifiable, and verifiable characteristics of a process or product.

- Base the metrics on measurable aspects (see Chapter 6) of the process or product to which they refer, i.e., they should be operational and repeatable on an objective scale.

10.4.3 Quality Factors and the Goal-Question-Metric Paradigm

Although the literature does not suggest that the SQFs were selected using the GQM paradigm, this is possible, as illustrated by the previous examples. The process of establishing such metrics complements the establishment of quantitative requirements or goals for a process or product, as described in Chapter 5.

10.5 SOME DEFINITIONS FOR DEVIATIONS FROM REQUIREMENTS

This section gives you several definitions for the deviations of a software product from its requirements. There is often confusion about their meaning because they are not used consistently. Some important terms and definitions are:

- *Defect:* A software product anomaly (IEEE 1988); the evidence of the existence of a fault (Conte, Dunsmore, and Shen 1986). Examples include such things as omissions and imperfections found during early life-cycle phases and faults contained in software sufficiently mature for test or operation.

- *Fault:* A manifestation of an error in software (IEEE 1988); an incorrect step, process, or data definition (IEEE 1990). Commonly, the terms bug and error are used (IEEE 1990). An accidental condition that causes a functional unit to fail to perform its required function. A fault may cause a failure.

- *Error:* Human action that results in software containing a fault (IEEE 1988). Examples include omission or misinterpretation of user requirements in a software specification and incorrect translation or omission of a requirement in the design specification.

- ***Failure:*** A manifestation of an error in software (IEEE 1988); an incorrect result (IEEE 1990). (1) The termination of the ability of a functional unit to perform its required function. (2) An event in which a system or system component does not perform a required function within specified limits. A failure may be produced when a fault is encountered.

You can relate these various terms as follows. An error is what the programmer does in creating a fault or a defect in software. The manifestation of a fault is a failure. Often, the terms error, defect, and bug are used interchangeably. As noted in IEEE (1990), for example, an error model (see Section 10.6) is used "...to predict the number of remaining faults." Also, the SEI process maturity model questions related to quality use the term "error" synonymously with "defects," "faults," and "failures."

A fault can exist in any unit of software—requirements, design, or code. Its existence is noted on the basis of a disagreement with a higher authority. For example, a fault exists in the detailed design of a software system if it is not derivable from the preliminary design for that system. Also, a fault may exist in the detailed design if an aspect of the preliminary design is not manifested appropriately in the detailed design. Thus, there are faults due to both "commissions" and "omissions." A fault also exists in the detailed design if the design is not properly expressed according to the syntax of the design language standard for that project.

A fault in the design and code is defined with respect to either the requirements (which is a higher level representation of the software system) or to some standard or common practice (e.g., that you may not have a loop that does not terminate). A fault in the requirements document can only exist with respect to some standard (for example, one that might mandate that a requirements document be consistent and complete). One possible definition says that a requirements document is erroneous if it does not represent what the customer/user wants. Unfortunately, defining a fault in a requirements document in this manner might be difficult.

10.6 DEFECT OR ERROR MODELS

Section 10.6 provides an overview of various mathematical models used for estimating the defect or error content of a software system or unit. This section uses the terms error and defect interchangeably (in keeping with common engineering usage) to cover failures, faults, errors, and defects. Section 10.5 provides definitions of these terms. The subject of Section 10.6 is software error models. As noted in IEEE (1990) an error model is defined as "a model used to estimate or predict the number of remaining faults, required test time, and similar characteristics [such as mean time between outages and availability]." Note that the terms error and fault are treated as synonymous here even though strictly speaking, they are not. However, you should know what you really mean when using a term such as error or fault.

These models are used for three principal purposes: prediction (of error or defect discovery, availability, etc.); comparative analysis (to help you answer a question such as, "How does my product compare with others?"); and product development control (part of statistical process control described in Section 10.8).

10.6.1 Purpose of Software Error Models

Software error models use information about software failures to make projections (estimates) of such items as:

- The number of failures that will be found during some time period in the future.

- How much time will be required to detect a certain number of failures.

- What is the mean time between failure detections.

These models are probabilistic, not deterministic. The error models presented later in Section 10.6 provide expected values for defect discovery rates, not exact predictions. You can use the outputs of these models to infer the number of faults from the number of failures predicted provided that you know the relationship of faults to failures. Remember, a failure is the manifestation of a fault (see Section 10.5). There are several factors to consider here, including the number of locations in the code required, on average, per failure to be fixed and the degree of masking a failure. Masking relates to the fact that the logical structure of a system, composed of hardware and software, might be such that some faults are masked. This is an aspect of "fault tolerance": they are not detectable (from an external view of the system). You can get around this problem by focusing on the failures that are observed and not on the number of faults. Based on the experience of your organization, you can estimate the number of instructions that need to be fixed, on average, per (unmasked) failure observed. This figure is the effective number of faults per failure.

Most of the work on error models that has been reported in the literature is based on hardware reliability theory. Hardware fails for physical reasons (due to such causes as alpha particles injuring a computer chip). However, software does not fail in the same sense as hardware. Software can only fail when operating in a computer. Always keep this in mind when working with software error models.

10.6.2 Overview of Software Error Models

This section provides an overview of software error models and the primary assumptions underlying these models. This section also briefly describes the two principal types of these models: time-based and phase- or activity-based.

10.6.2.1 Primary Assumptions

There are many software error models such as those constructed by Musa, Goel, Jelinski, and Moranda, and Schick and Wolverton as described in Goel (1980 and 1985); Shooman (1983); Musa, Iannino, and Okumoto (1987); Cho (1987); Conte, Dunsmore, and Shen (1986); Gaffney and Davis (1988); Gaffney (1984a); Gaffney and Pietrolewicz (1990); and many other sources. Most of these models share some characteristics, including:

- Data about the incidents of software unit failures or system failures attributed to the software is fit to an equation. Estimates of the software's future behavior are based on the values of the fitting equation parameters.

- The defect in a piece of software can be counted (or inferred from the count of software failure to perform per the requirements specification imposed upon it).

- The number of defects remaining in a piece of software can be projected from the number discovered to date (and equation for the rate of discovery).

- Defects can be removed one by one; this is done before the software continues to run and data is collected concerning its performance.

- No new defects are introduced in the software as errors that have been identified are removed. This assumption is sometimes modified, and a factor for the injection of additional errors is included in the model.

- The stimulation of software during the time interval that defect data is collected has the same characteristics as the stimulation that is expected during the interval for which the projection is made.

The last point is of particular importance and may not be noticed by those who are overly focused on the "elegance" of the error models' mathematics they are using. Projections about the software's performance in operation are frequently made during the testing period, before the software has been delivered to users and put into operation. The validity of a projection is based on the assumption that the nature of the tests, the stimulation to the software, statistically represents what will be experienced in the operational environment during the period for which the projections are made.

10.6.2.2 Principal Error Model Types

The two principal types of software error models, time-based and activity- or phase-based, are differentiated by the nature of the principal independent variable that they employ to represent the passage through the development process or part of it. In time-based models, either calendar time or processor-on time (often referred to as central processing unit [CPU] time) is used. The latter is preferred. Some models use a combination of calendar time and processor-on time. This type of model cannot be used until the code is operating (albeit in a test stage of development). Time-based models are presented in Section 10.6.3.

In activity- or phase-based models, the independent variable is a number indicative of the major activities of the development process. The idea is to fit an equation for defect discovery as a function of a number indicative of the activity in which it is delivered. The activities are ordered in the principal sequence in which they are executed (e.g., preliminary design, detailed design, code and unit test, CSC integration test, and CSCI test in the case of projects adhering to DOD-STD-2167A). The term phase or development phase is used here to represent this sequence (or corresponding ones if other names, such as top-level design, are used). Phase-based models are presented in Section 10.6.4.

10.6.3 Time-Based Error Models and Availability and Reliability

This section presents two time-based error models. One is based on the use of the "decaying exponential" equation, and the other uses the Rayleigh equation. The former is described in Section 10.6.3.3 and the latter is presented in Section 10.6.3.4. Both of these models use equations that represent the incidence rate of defect discovery as a function of time. The values of a time-based model's parameters are calculated by using regression or other mathematical techniques to fit the equation to error or defect (actually failure) data. The data used for the fit is obtained from tests conducted during development as soon as the coding effort has been completed.

10.6.3.1 Software Stimulation and Model Time Bases

Typically, data obtained during the testing operation is used to make projections (estimates) about how the software, or the system, will behave in the future. In order for these projections to have any validity, the environment and the time base (duty cycle) must match the operational situation. The environment category relates to the nature of the stimulation of the software. The testing inputs should represent what will be expected in operation.

The time variable used in these models is CPU time, calendar time, or a combination of the two. CPU time, or a surrogate for it, is preferred. This is necessary in order for projections using the models to be valid. The reason for this is that the models assume that defects are discovered as a function of the actual time that the software is stimulated. For example, software stimulated only during one 8-hour shift over a one-day period (33.3 percent duty cycle) will not be as likely to fail if it has been stimulated on a continuous basis during that (24-hour) period, a 100 percent duty cycle.

10.6.3.2 Reliability and Availability

The time based models are used in connection with the estimation of reliability and availability. These terms are defined as:

- *Reliability.* "Software reliability is the probability that the program performs successfully [in compliance with its specification] for a given time period." (Shooman 1983). That is, it is the probability that there are no failures in the time interval 0-t. Another definition is that software reliability is "the ability of a system or a component to perform its required functions under stated conditions for a specified period of time." (IEEE 1990)

- *Availability.* "Software availability is the probability that the program (software) is performing successfully (meeting requirements), according to specification, at a given point in time." (Shooman 1983)

Availability is used more often than reliability. Frequently, the term reliability is used when availability is meant. The method for computing availability comes from hardware experience. A formula for computing it is:

$$\text{Availability} = A = (MTBF)/(MTBF + MTTR)$$

where:

MTBF= mean time between failures

MTTR= mean time to repair

The MTBF is the inverse of the failure incidence rate obtained from an error or defect model. The error model provides the metric "errors/unit time," while the metric MTBF means "time/errors." (You should expect that nominally the MTBF for software will increase over time, provided that the defects are removed from the software as their effects [failures] are observed.) Consequently, the error density should decrease over time and the intervals between their discovery (the expected value of which is the MTBF) should correspondingly increase over time. Note that this is not necessarily what occurs with hardware. Hardware failures typically occur due to physical deterioration (although they can occur due to design flaws as in the case of software), and thus the MTBF for a hardware unit may decrease over time. For software, A, the availability, would increase over time, provided that the MTTR either remains constant or decreases over time. The term "availability growth" can be used to express this concept. In the case of software, it is more appropriate to define MTTR as "the mean time to restore service." This is due to the fact that the system can often continue operating after a failure caused by software, and the software is typically "repaired" off-line.

Another view of availability is that it is the proportion of time that the software is successfully operating. The corresponding formula is:

$$\text{Availability} = A = \text{Up\_Time}/(\text{Up\_Time}+\text{Down\_Time}) = \text{Up\_Time}/\text{Total\_Time}$$

The down time is equal to the number of failures over the (total) time interval times the MTTR.

The corresponding formula for unavailability is:

$$\text{Unavailability} = (1-\text{Availability}) = 1-A = U = (\text{Down\_Time}/\text{Total\_Time})$$

Apply these formulas for calculating availability and unavailability to an example. Let:

$$\text{MTTR} = 0.00278 \text{ hours (10 seconds)}$$
$$\text{MTBF} = 1752 \text{ hours}$$

This figure is based on using an error model that projects 5 failures over a 1-year (8,760 hours) period: 1,752=8,760/5. This is based on 100 percent duty cycle (24-hours-per-day operation).

$$A = 1,752/(1,752 + 0.00278) = (8,760 - (5S0.00278))/8,760 = 0.9999984$$
$$U = 1 - A = 0.0000016$$

10.6.3.3 Decaying Exponential Time-Based Error Models

The most basic error model (of defect discovery) is shown in Figure 10-1. Goel (1985) has stated that the rate of defect discovery, r(t), can be approximated by the equation:

$$r(t) = EBe^{-Bt}$$

This model is usually applied after the code unit test phase or later in the development cycle. An important feature of this model is that it assumes that no new defects are being injected (no new errors being committed). Hence, the rate of defect discovery will decline

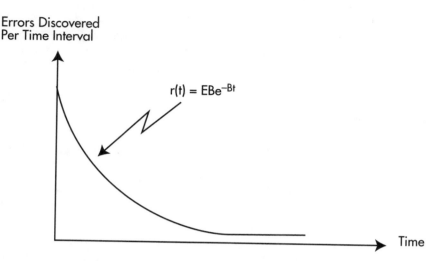

Errors Discovered
Per Time Interval

$r(t) = EBe^{-Bt}$

Time

Figure 10-1. *Decaying Exponential Error Model*

with time. The model holds to a lesser degree of accuracy if this assumption does not hold. The decaying exponential function is a simple model of this situation. The model has two parameters: E and B, where

E = Total number of defects in the software at the beginning of the test phase (or at whatever point the time on the time scale of the discovery plot is 0).

B = $1/t_d$

t_d = The time at which 63.2 percent of the defects, i.e., 0.632E have been discovered.

The number of defects discovered over the interval 0-t, N(t), is given by the expression:

$$N(t) = E(1 - e^{-Bt})$$

You can use regression techniques (Graybill 1961) to estimate the parameters of this model based on experience data. Note that the model is continuous. Strictly speaking, this is not a completely correct representation of the defect discovery process (although it is a reasonable approximation). Actually, the data you fit to an error model is discrete. Gaffney and Davis (1988) provide an alternative decaying exponential error model that provides a discrete fit to the data.

Note that you can normalize the parameter E to represent defect density as defects per KSLOC. This can facilitate your comparison of the discovery profiles for different-sized software products.

10.6.3.4 Rayleigh Time-Based Error Model

Another time-based model uses the Rayleigh equation to represent the rate of defect discovery as a function of time. Figure 10-2 represents the Rayleigh error model.

The Rayleigh model represents the rate of defect discovery, r(t), by the expression:

$$r(t) = \frac{E}{t_p^2} \cdot te^{-bt2}$$

The number of defects discovered over the interval 0-t, N(t), given by the expression:

$$N(t) = E \left[1 - e^{-bt^2} \right]$$

where

$r(t)$ = the number of errors generated during a particular interval

E = total lifetime errors

t_p = peak of the rate curve, the point at which 39 percent of E total defects have been injected into the software

b = shape parameter of the curve, $b=1/(2t_p^2)$

t = interval number (i.e., interval 1)

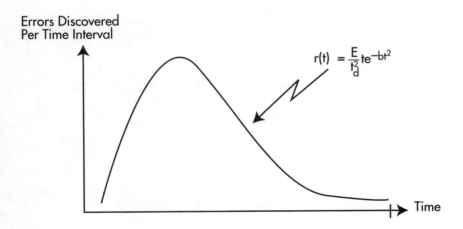

Figure 10-2. *Rayleigh Distribution Error Model*

You can use regression techniques (Graybill 1961) to estimate the parameters of this model based on experience data.

Note that you can interpret the parameter E to represent defect density as defects per KSLOC rather than the total number of defects. This facilitates your comparison of the discovery profiles for different-sized software products.

10.6.4 Rayleigh Phase or Activity-Based Model

You can also use the Rayleigh equation to model defect discovery data on an activity-by-activity basis. Using this model enables you to employ valuable data from inspections and other verification mechanisms obtained before the code is executing. This cannot be done with the time-based models described in Section 10.6.3 (Gaffney 1984a; Gaffney and Pietrolewicz 1990). The equations provided in Figure 10-3 summarize this model.

The independent variable t, in Figure 10-3, represents "error discovery activity index" values for the case of six error discovery phases, where a "phase" is one or more activities grouped together to apply the model and performing estimates. In this model, there are six phases. The incremental (phase) form of this model is:

$$\Delta V_t = E\left[e^{B(t-1)^2} - e^{-Bt^2}\right]$$

where ΔV_t = the number of defects (or defects per KSLOC) discovered during development activity t.

The number of latent defects, L, the number of defects or defect/KSLOC remaining at the conclusion of the development process, is given by the expression:

$$L = Ee^{-BM^2}$$

where M is the number of defect discovery phases in the development process. If M= 6, then:

$$L = Ee^{-36B}$$

One may define the "efficiency" of the defect discovery process as:

$$EFF = \frac{(E - L)}{E} \times 100$$

Thus:

$$EFF = 1 - e^{-36B}$$

Higher efficiency processes have larger values of B or smaller values of t_p. The earlier in the development the peak is reached, the higher the efficiency of the error discovery process. It is interesting to note that the two parameters of the Rayleigh phase-based model shown in Figure 10-3—the location of the peak (t_p) and the area under the curve (E), respectively—correspond to mutually exclusive aspects of software error discovery. E corresponds to the "goodness" of the development process, which relates directly to the area under the curve. Poorer processes produce (inject) more errors and have higher values of E. Poor verification methods let more of the injected defects "leak" into later phases, resulting in higher values of t_p, the location of the peak.

10.7 THE EFFECT OF REUSE ON SOFTWARE QUALITY

This section describes the impact of software reuse on the quality of the software product. It shows that greater amounts of reuse generally result in a lower number of latent defects. What is said about "reuse" and quality in this section applies to "COTS" and quality as well, because the use of COTS software is just a particular form of reuse.

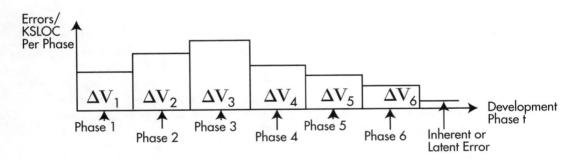

Rayleigh Curve Fit: $\Delta V_t = E\left[e^{B(t-1)^2} - e^{-Bt^2} \right]$

E = Total lifetime error rate (errors per KSLOC)

$B = \dfrac{1}{2t_p^2}$; t_p = Defect discovery phase constant, the location of the "peak" in a continuous fit to the data.

Rayleigh Curve, Cumulative Form: $V_t = E\left(1 - e^{-Bt^2}\right)$

Figure 10-3. *Activity-Based Rayleigh Model*

10.7.1 Reuse and Quality, Overview

If a software system is composed, in part, of reused code, its quality will probably be greater than if it were composed entirely of new code. Here, higher quality means fewer defects remaining undiscovered when a software system is shipped to its users. Reuse enhances the quality of a software product principally because of the increased opportunity it provides for defect discovery. Each time reusable code is used in a new application software system, it passes through the integration and system test processes again. Thus, an additional opportunity is provided for defect discovery and removal. This section focuses on the effect on quality (defined in terms of defect content) due to code reuse and, implicitly, due to the reuse of the requirements and the design from which it came as well.

10.7.2 Model of Effect of Reuse on Software Quality

This section develops a model showing the effect of code reuse on software product quality. The model shows the increase in product quality (fewer defects) due to reuse (relative to the quality of the product if it were all new code). This model reflects the fact that multiple uses of the same code affords more opportunities for discovering errors or defects than if that element of code were employed for the first time in the software product.

Assume that the code to be reused in a new software system has gone through the complete development process (whether it is provided from a library or taken from a prior system). Then, this code is presumed to go through integration and system test again during the development of the new application system. However, it is assumed the code does not go through the defect discovery steps of design and code inspections and unit test again.

Let D_{VR} be the latent error density (see Section 11.6) of some (reused) code to be incorporated into a new software system. Let D_{VN} be the latent error density of the new code portion of the new software system. Let both D_{VN} and D_{VR} be measured in errors per KSLOC.

Then, the expression for D_{Ri}, the latent defect density in the new software product which includes the ith use of the "reused" code:

$$D_{Ri} = D_{VN} \cdot (1 - R) + D_{VR} \cdot R \cdot p^{i-1}$$

where R is the proportion of code reused (on the average over the N planned uses of the reused code). Let:

$$p = 1 - \frac{\text{Defects discovered and removed during the integration and system test process}}{\text{Total number of lifetime defects}}$$

Further, note that $D_{VR} = p \cdot D_{VN}$.

In the case of the first reuse after the creation of the reusable software, $i = 1$, and:

$$D_{Ri} = D_{R1} = D_{VN} \cdot (1 - R) + D_{VR} \cdot R$$

In the case of the second reuse:

$$D_{Ri} = D_{R2} = D_{VN} \cdot (1 - R) + D_{VR} \cdot R \cdot p^1$$

An example value of p can be derived from data in Gaffney (1984a) that is presented in Table 10-5.

Phase/Activity	Percent of Lifetime Errors
High-Level (Preliminary) Design Inspections	7.69
Detailed Design Inspections	19.70
Code Inspections	23.93
Unit Test	20.88
Integration Test	14.27
System Test	7.92
Latent Error Content	5.61
Total	100.00

Table 10-5. Example Values of Error Discovery Percentages

In this case:

$$p = 1 - \frac{14.27 + 7.92}{100} = 1 - 0.2219 = 0.7781$$

The thinking behind the factor $p^{i-1} \cdot D_{VR}$ in the expression for D_{Ri} is as follows. After the reusable code has been developed for the library or for use in some prior application system, it still has some of the defects (such as 5.61 percent of the errors indicated in the example situation in Table 10-5) that were injected during the development process. Upon the first of N reuses, the code to be reused goes through integration and system tests again, thus removing a proportion of the defects remaining upon the completion of its development (latent defect content) given by:

$$\frac{14.27 + 7.92}{100} = 0.2219$$

and leaving a proportion of $1.0 - 0.2219 = 0.7781 = p$ times the latent defect content of the code after it was developed and put into the library. Thus, the same relative percentage of error reduction occurs when going from the first reuse to the second reuse, and so on.

Let L be the latent error content of a software product composed of both new and reused components, relative to one composed entirely of new code. Thus, for a product having no reused components, $L = 1$. In general, $0 \leq L \leq 1$. Thus for the ith instance of reuse out of N:

$$L_i = D_R i / D_{VN},$$
and
$$L_i = (1 - R) + \frac{D_{VR}}{D_{VN}} \cdot R \cdot p^{i-1}$$

Now, if you assume that the defect discovery profile shown in Table 10-5 applies to both the new code created for an application system and the reused code, then $D_{VR} = p \cdot D_{VN}$. In this case, the equation for L_i can be written as:

$$L_i = (1 - R) + R \cdot p^i$$

L, the average latent error reduction over the N usage instances, is given by the expression:

$$L = \left(\sum_{i=1}^{N} L_i \right) / N$$

And:

$$L = (1 - R) \cdot \frac{N}{N} + \frac{R}{N} \left(\sum_{i=1}^{N} p^i \right)$$

This expression for L can be simplified to (Cruickshank and Gaffney 1991a):

$$L = (1 - R) + p \cdot \frac{R}{N} \cdot \left(\frac{1-p^N}{1-p}\right)$$

As N gets larger, L tends to a limit of (1–R).
   Consider the following example in Table 10-6 in which p = 0.7781.

L	N
1-0.222R	1
1-0.308R	2
1-0.382R	3
1-0.445R	4
1-0.499R	5
1-0.678R	10

Table 10-6. *Sample Values of L for p=0.20*

   L tends asymptotically to (1-R) as N increases. Figure 10-4 presents plots of L as a function of N for p = 0.7781 for three values of R. The model holds under the important assumption that the errors detected during the various discovery stages are removed, more or less, concurrently with their discovery.
   You can use the formula given here for L to estimate the impact of extensive reuse in an application system. First, the latent defect or error content of new software is estimated, based on past experience with similar kinds of code. Then, this number is reduced by the factor L, and it is computed as described above.

10.8 STATISTICAL PROCESS AND QUALITY CONTROL

You can use software defect data collected during the development of your software product to help assess and manage its quality. Here, quality means the degree to which the software meets its requirements. You can also use the defect data to help determine the effectiveness of the defect discovery process (see Section 10.6.4). Section 10.8 outlines how you can do so. Taking these product measurements should be viewed as an important part of the process improvement activity of your software development organization. This section defines the nature of statistical process and quality control and shows you how to apply it to monitor and better control software quality.

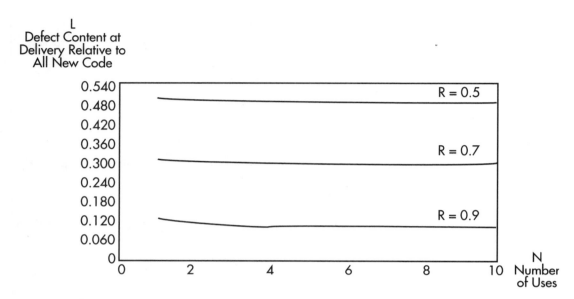

Figure 10-4. Average Relative Defect Content Versus Number of Uses (p=0.20)

10.8.1 Statistical Process and Quality Control Definitions

A prime objective of statistical process control (SPC) is to enhance the predictability of a process. This is also a primary requisite for a software organization to be certifiable at the higher levels of software process maturity (see Chapter 3). SPC uses products measurements to monitor and support the control of the production process that creates them by predicting future quality based on past experience (Rock and Guerin 1992). Quality control is "...the act of directing, influencing, verifying, and correcting [software and/or the software process] to ensure the conformance of a specific product to a design or specification" (Cho 1987).

10.8.2 Quality Control Charts

This section describes the concept of a control chart. Control charts have been applied in the manufacturing industries for many years. Control charts serve three general purposes (Rock and Guerin 1992):

- They define a standard form variable to be tracked. This variable is an indicator of the quality of the product to which it applies, i.e., a measure of the degree to which the unit meets some specific requirement.

- They provide information for process feedback that may be dynamically applied for process modification. In the case of software (see Section 10.8.3), this requires a development organization to be assessable at the highest levels of process maturity.

- They indicate the status of a process.

Figure 10-5 illustrates the concept of a control chart. The example is an assembly line for paint can tops. The diameter of each paint can top produced on the line is measured. Acceptable tops are those whose diameters lie within a range called a "control band" (see Figure 10-5). Those tops whose diameters lie outside the control band are rejected. The top diameters are monitored over a period of time, corresponding to the horizontal axis in the figure. Divergences from the planned goal, the middle line in the control band, indicate potential trouble. The nearer to the maximum or the minimum acceptable lines, the greater the level of trouble. If the product track (i.e., the dotted curve in Figure 10-5) is consistently situated in the section of the control band between the planned goal and the maximum acceptable value, this indicates that the process should be reevaluated. Clearly, something needs to be done because the planned goal is not being achieved for any can top produced. As you can see, the measure of the product can be used to indicate something about the production process and about the quality of the individual product.

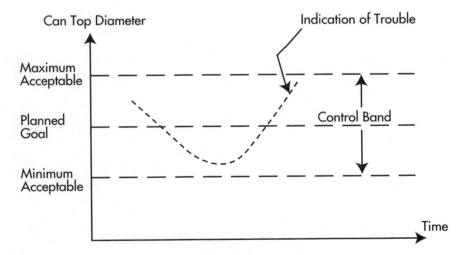

Figure 10-5. *Control Chart for Paint Can Top Diameter*

10.8.3 Applying Quality Control Charts to Software

You can apply the concept of a quality control as described for a physical product such as a paint can top to software as well. This section shows how this is done. The idea is to use a technique similar to the one presented in Section 10.8.2. You define goals for defect discovery for the software development activity (e.g., preliminary design, detailed design, etc.) of a software development process. These activities are analogous to the stations of a manufacturing process.

The basic concept of the methodology is to plot and monitor defect discovery versus development activity or phase number. You can make a control chart (Figure 10-6) where you define a control band. This control band prescribes a tolerance range of acceptable values for the number of defects/KSLOC to be found in the defect discovery (verification stages) of each development activity, such as preliminary design. These tolerance range values relate to the **control limits** that you must establish for your quality control process. You use control bands to establish acceptable departures from a base or satisfactory quality level of behavior. Sections 10.8.5 and 10.8.6 tell you how to establish a control band.

You use the defect data obtained from one or a number of products to make inferences about the process used to develop them. Thereby, you can use product monitoring as an input to process control. You can see that this process is viewed as an implementation of MDSM (as described in Chapter 2) in which you establish a goal, you monitor its degree of realization, and you take corrective action, as appropriate. The corrective action can be, for example, to recycle your software back through detailed design if too many defects are

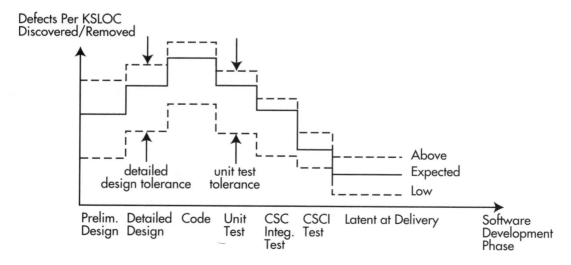

Figure 10-6. *Software Defect/Error Statistical Quality Control Chart*

being discovered during the verification portion of the coding activity. You should collect defect data and use it to monitor the quality level of your products and also to make inferences about the quality of the process used to create them. One measure of the process quality is the efficiency of the defect discovery process (see Section 10.6.4). You can use the data as input to a decision process and action strategy to modify the process or product.

10.8.4 Using a Software Defect Statistical Quality Control Chart

This section describes how you might use a software defect/error statistical quality control chart. The chart in Figure 10-6 shows a sequence of activities in an order generally followed in software development. It shows the expected value for defect discovery and the acceptable range of values. In an actual case, you would plot the defect counts (the actual value or the values normalized with respect to KSLOC) on the graph. Then, you would see if the plot stays within the tolerance range. If not, you would take appropriate action. You should expect the defect profiles for a set of products produced by your development process to lie within the tolerance band. Depending on how the profiles were grouped, you might wish to take action to change your process. For example, if the plots were consistently above the middle of the tolerance range, this could indicate that your process needs to adopt an improved methodology for verification and defect removal. Conversely, if the plots were consistently below the middle of the tolerance range this could indicate that the process was injecting, but not detecting, existing defects. Or, if the process were a new process, lower defect detection levels could indicate that the process was an improved process.

10.8.5 Establishing Control Bands for Software Quality Control Charts

Using a software statistical quality control chart, you can establish objectives for defect discovery (and removal) during the defect discovery phases (the verification portions of the activities constituting your software development process described in Chapter 4). You should establish a desired goal defect discovery profile pattern and two tolerance profiles related to that profile pattern (the upper and lower profiles). They define the tolerance band for defect discovery during the development process. For example, the range of error discovery bounded by the tolerance profiles for preliminary design corresponds to an "acceptable" range for the defects found in preliminary design. It is called the defect tolerance range. The range relates to the control limits of your software quality control process.

You use the established phase-by-phase control limits to indicate departures from satisfactory or "quality level" behavior and to anticipate/help forecast them. Doing this will enable you to take earlier, more cost-effective action to rectify problems that will otherwise not be found until later in the development process. You should view the establishment of defect discovery goals, and their tracking or monitoring the degree of compliance realized during the development process, as a fundamental aspect of MDSM. The establishment of discovery goals is equally important to the establishment and monitoring of cost, schedule, and size objectives.

There are a number of ways you can establish the total defect injection and latent defect content values for the (Rayleigh) goal error discovery profile. One way is to base them on previous experience. You determine that you are now using a better process than the one employed to develop a previous product. Hence, you may be willing to establish smaller values of both E (the total estimated/injected error content) and t_p (the location of the peak of the defect profile) as a goal. Refer to Section 10.6.4 for a discussion of the Rayleigh fit to phase-based defect discovery profiles. E can be reduced by the use of better design methods that result in the introduction of fewer defect than preceding development efforts. The value of t_p can be reduced (moved to the left) due to the use of improved verification methods.

Alternatively, you can establish the parameter values of the goal defect discovery profile based on the reliability requirements that the product is to satisfy. For example, the software product may have less than some value of latent defect content in order for it to be plausibly characterized as meeting some reliability objective. The tolerance band about the goal profile could correspond to its ability to satisfy your customer's reliability requirement and/or to the degree to which you believe your process can control the level of defect introduced into your software. Another alternative for selecting the defect discovery goal profile is a combination of customer requirements and general process improvement (including verification) objectives that have been established for your organization.

Thus, using the defect discovery profile graphics and the analysis support they provide, you can employ software product data to make inferences about the development process being used to create the product (during development or after it has been completed). By monitoring the product, you can improve control of the software development process. Such data can be used in your decision process and action strategy to support modifying the product under production while you are creating it or the process you employ to produce it (or, if post facto analysis is employed, after you have created it). This approach provides developers with data in a timely manner to aid them in discovering departures from the development process and supports returning it to control. You use the information displayed in graphs (such as Figure 10-6) to prompt corrective action.

10.8.6 Applying Taguchi Quality Control Concepts to Software

An alternative method for establishing tolerance profiles is based on work done by Dr. Genichi Taguchi (Barker 1990). Taguchi has focused on improving the quality of measuring systems and measuring procedures by introducing the concept of sensitivity

(Cherng, Fathy, and Lumsdaine 1989). Taguchi suggests using the concept of signal-to-noise ratio to evaluate the sensitivity of a measuring system. So far, there is no report of these ideas being applied to software. Electrical engineers widely apply the concept of signal-to-noise ratio. The basic concept is if there is a desired signal value, G, and it is imbedded in noise whose power is $\sigma 2$ (corresponding to statistical variance), then S, the signal-to-noise ratio, is equal to G/σ. The inverse of this value is known to statisticians as the "coefficient of variation," when G is taken as the expected value of a random variable. Larger values of signal-to-noise ratio correspond to smaller values of the defect tolerance range.

You can apply the Taguchi concept to establish a defect discovery pattern goal and the tolerance patterns above and below it as now described.

Two ways to establish the goal defect discovery profile pattern are to select:
    1. The total defect content (total injected), E, and the latent defect content, L; or

    2. The total defect content (total injected), E, and the location of peak defect discovery, t_p.

Two ways to establish the (optional) tolerance profile patterns are to select:
    1. The percent upper tolerance level, p_U, and the percent lower tolerance level, p_L; or

    2. The value of the signal-to-noise ratio, S.

The equation for the goal defect profile (G_t) value for phase t is:

$$G_t = E\left[e^{-B(t-1)^2} - e^{-Bt^2} \right]$$

In the first case, the equations for the upper (U_t) and lower (L_t) error profile values for phase t are: $U_t = E (1 + p_U \cdot 0.01) \cdot$ phase multiplier and $L_t = E (1 - p_L \cdot 0.01) \cdot$ phase multiplier. The "phase multiplier" is given by the expression:

$$\left[e^{-B(t-1)^2} - e^{-Bt^2} \right]$$

In the second case, you establish the signal-to-noise value, S, let $p_U = p_L = p$, and establish $p = 100/S$. Then, $U_t = E (S + 1)/S \cdot$ phase multiplier and $L_t = E (S - 1)/S \cdot$ phase multiplier. Note that S must be greater than 1 for these equations to hold.

See Section 10.6.4 for more details about the Rayleigh phase-based model of defect discovery.

10.9 SUMMARY AND RECOMMENDATIONS

This section provides an overview of software quality. It indicates that "quality" refers to both your process and the products resulting from it. It indicates the great importance of quality management techniques to your organization. Also, you should realize that "quality" is concerned with more than the detection and removal of errors from code. Fewer defects in a software product clearly indicates "higher quality." However, the term "quality" does not mean just "defect content." There are other attributes of software quality, such as usability. The degree to which your software system realizes these attributes can be tracked throughout the development process.

This section also indicates that:

- Software quality measurement is key to both project control and process improvement.

- You need to:
  - Know where you are now.
  - Monitor progress toward your goals.
  - Have a database of quality metrics for your process and products to help you set goals for your new products and expectations of process change results.

- Quantify the quality goals for process and product and then monitor metrics indicative of their degrees of realization.

- View quality measurement as part of the MDSM process.

- View defect injection and discovery in the context of MDSM.

- Predict the number of defects expected to be left in the product before the code is running.

- Use defect discovery as input to software process evaluation.

- Recognize that various types of defect data collection and analysis are key requisites to attaining higher levels of process maturity.

Chapter

11

MANAGEMENT INDICATORS FOR TRACKING AND MONITORING

11.1 MANAGEMENT AND MEASUREMENT

This section presents quantitative methods and procedures for tracking the product and the progress of a software development project. Project management personnel routinely determine progress; compare results to estimates, commitments, and plans; analyze reasons for discrepancies; adjust the commitment and plans; and develop corrective action if needed. These management actions require a continuing process of measurement in order to be done well. Establishing quantitative objectives, monitoring project status, and evaluating product and process quality all involve measurement of some kind. This section discusses how to measure the status of a software development project and how to use measurements to make judgments about a project (such as a possible recycle back through the development process in order to rectify errors and thus to improve the product).

11.1.1 Software Development Project Tracking and Monitoring

This section describes the nature of quantitative software project tracking and monitoring.

11.1.1.1 Status Tracking

The effective management of a software project requires quantitative information to support decisions about the achievement of project objectives both during development and at the completion of the project. The process of producing this information begins with defining quantitative project objectives, continues with status tracking during the software development project, and ends with the recording of project performance in the experi-ence database. Managing to achieve project goals requires quantitative information about project status and the degree of achievement of goals at various points in the development process. Some of the metrics used for this are from the set discussed in Chapter 6. Others are unique to the process of status tracking. The metrics discussed in this chapter are called "management indicators" because they indicate the project status relative to size, cost, schedule, quality, stability, and computer resources. The process of using these indi-cators to support managing a software development project is called "tracking" or "monitoring." (This section uses the terms "tracking"and "monitoring" interchangeably.) The tracking process consists of periodically collecting data, calculating indicator metrics from that data, and creating reports that indicate the status of the project.

The goals of software project tracking and monitoring (Paulk, Curtis, and Chrissis 1991) are:

- Track the actual results and performance of the software project against plans and commitment.

- Take corrective actions when the results and performance of the project devi-ate significantly from the plans.

- Understand and agree to commitment changes by all affected parties.

Tracking and monitoring metrics should be such as to alert management to potential or actual problems that could prevent project goals from being achieved. For example, if the effort to date plus the projected effort to complete the project (when compared with the budget) indicates a possible budgetary overrun, the management has to take some action such as increasing the budget or decreasing the amount of testing (while preserving quali-ty). The metrics should also provide information about how to solve or mitigate any problem discovered. In the example, if the ongoing analysis of product defects discovered during development (a quality metric) shows that high quality is being achieved, then per-haps the amount of testing can be reduced and the projected costs decreased.

11.1.1.2 Measurement and Status Tracking

The principal rules to follow in selecting and using tracking metrics are:

- Select the metrics to be used based on the questions management wants to be able to answer. Select the corresponding measurements to be collected in advance of the start of the effort. The measurement function should work with software and project management to define and quantize project goals and the metrics needed to indicate project and product status. Use the GQM paradigm (see Chapter 6) to aid in the definition of tracking metrics that sup-port the achievement of the project goals.

- Relate the metrics selected to action that you can take to rectify problems (or at least limit the damage).

- Collect measurements during the project. Do not reconstruct them after the fact. This is very important.

- Collect an appropriate set of measurements to aid you in setting realistic goals for the future, to enable you to determine the degree of improvement, and to provide input into your estimating algorithm.

- Ensure the validity of the measures you collect (Basili and Weiss 1984).

The measurement function defines the data collection methods; indicator construction; and software development planning, tracking, and monitoring procedures in its software development standards and policies. Management should not have to be concerned with the technical details of data collection or the construction of the indicator metrics since the measurement function (however organized) performs the data collection and analysis. However, management should understand what the indicators are revealing about the project. Then, management will be able to take the appropriate actions to solve any problems indicated by the tracking indicators.

11.1.1.3 Tracking Activities

The following lists the top-level activities for tracking and monitoring a software development process (Paulk, Curtis, and Chrissis 1991):

- Use the documented software development plans for tracking and monitoring the software activities and communicating status.

- Ensure that senior management reviews and approves all commitments and commitment changes made to all parties external to the software development organization.

- Communicate approved changes to software commitments to software development, software-related organizations, and the customer.

- Track project size, cost, and schedule and take corrective actions.

- Track project-critical target-computer resources and take corrective actions.

- Track project product quality and take corrective actions.

- Track software engineering technical activities and take corrective actions.

- Track the software technical, cost, resource, schedule, and quality risks throughout the project development life cycle.

- Track software project and replanning measurement and metrics and recode for use by the technical staff and management.

- Ensure that the software staff and managers conduct regular reviews to track status, plans, performance, and issues against the software development plan.

- Conduct formal reviews of accomplishments at selected milestones and at the beginning and the end of selected stages of the software project.

11.1.2 Project Monitoring and Process Maturity Levels

In order to be capable of being assessable at capability maturity Level 4 (SEI assessment question 2.3.1) (Paulk, Curtis, and Chrissis 1991), your organization needs to have a database for process metrics/measurement data. Chapter 6 of this guidebook presents process and product measurement/metrics data (size, cost, schedule, quality, etc.) that should be in such a database. You can use this quantitative information to help you improve your process and products in the long term, i.e., in future development projects.

There is, however, another aspect to data collection. Chapter 6 discusses the collection of "actuals" at the project's completion for historical analysis and both process and product improvement. You also should develop metrics to track the project during development. This data can be fed back to the ongoing project to make short-term adjustments to mitigate problems by improving the process and to aid in achieving project process and product objectives. You must collect data during the project development for process and product improvement while in development. You should keep this data in your software experience database or in a separate database. This chapter discusses the analysis of this "in process" data and how you can use it to determine project status.

You should begin data collection and analysis for both historical and project monitoring purposes as soon as possible. There is no need to wait until your organization is at capability Level 3 or equivalent to do so. The organization at Level 1 or 2 should be able to feed back the experience data for incremental process and product improvement, whether historical or immediate. The quantitative monitoring of a software development project by tracking progress, process, and product during development through data collection, analysis, and management action is characteristic of a Level 4 or 5 or equivalent organization.

11.2 MANAGEMENT INDICATORS

Many sets of software management indicators have been used and/or published. Some of the sets may include hundreds of metrics. Obviously, you cannot perform effective tracking with hundreds of indicators, so you must select a set of manageable size. You can find extensive discussions of indicators in Grady (1992), Grady and Caswell (1987), Schultz (1988), Air Force Systems Command (1986), Army Materiel Command (1987), National Aeronautics and Space Administration (1990), Paulk, Curtis, and Chrissis (1991), and Carleton et al. (1992). This guidebook presents 38 metrics that you can use to track a software development project. Many of these indicator metrics have been taken from these references. Many of them have been redefined to be more precise.

It is important to recognize that a management indicator can have several alternative metrics associated with it. For example, you can measure the cost-to-date indicator in LM, LH, or dollars. If your software standards do not specify cost units, your measurement function should decide how best to measure the cost-to-date indicator. You can select either LH, LM or dollars, or all three.

Table 11-1 presents some management indicators for your guidance. You should view this table as a "menu" from which you can select indicator metrics for tracking and monitoring. Select and define the indicators by using the GQM paradigm relative to your project's goals. The indicators that you require for a particular project may not be in this table, and hence, you may have to design indicators according to the needs of the project. Effective tracking depends on selecting a set of indicators small enough to be manageable, but large enough to provide all of the information needed.

Many of the size, cost, schedule, and quality indicators and metrics are the same as those useful for project control, listed in Chapter 6. An important difference is that the indicators and metrics in Table 11-1 are based on intermediate measurements made for tracking during the development of the software (i.e., during project execution) and thus are labeled "...to date" or "...elapsed." The Chapter 6 metrics for project control have the same intent and direction as the corresponding indicator metrics in Table 11-1, but they are not discussed in the specific climate of tracking and monitoring.

Table 11-1 also contains some metrics that have no corresponding metrics in Chapter 6, such as the project stability indicators and the earned value indicator. These indicator metrics are important and specific to the tracking and monitoring process, but they have less value once the project has been completed.

Use the data collected during the development process for tracking product and for determining project status. Feed back the collected data to incrementally optimize the software development process. In addition, you should use at least the minimum data set for project tracking purposes. Your enterprise will define its own data set for tracking.

You can develop the indicators in Table 11-1 as functions of time and graphically and numerically present them. You can track the actual measurements or metrics instead of the percentages if so desired.

11.3 HOW TO SELECT MANAGEMENT INDICATORS

This section describes how to select metrics that support project goals.

Number	Measurement Category	Indicator	Metrics
1	Software product size	Current estimate or count	New, reused, and total KSLOC (or function points)
2	Software product size	Current estimate or count	KESLOC
3	Software product size	Percent current estimate is of estimate at initiation	(Current/initial)100
4	Software cost	Cost to date	LM
5	Software cost	Cost to date	LH
6	Software cost	Cost to date	Dollars ($)
7	Software cost	Percent of budget spent to date	Percent LM
8	Software cost	Percent of budget spent to date	Percent LH
9	Software cost	Percent of budget spent to date	Percent $
10	Development schedule	Elapsed development time	Elapsed months
11	Development schedule	Percent of schedule elapsed	(Elapsed months/schedule months)100
12	Project technical stability	ECPs	Count ECPs
13	Project technical stability	Percent requirements undefined (expected major subsystems undefined)	(Requirements to be defined/total requirements)100
14	Project technical stability	Number of software action items (SAIs)	Count SAIs
15	Project technical stability	Percent SAIs closed to date	(SAIs closed/total SAIs)100
16	Project technical stability	Authorized positions staffed	Count people
17	Project technical stability	Percent planned positions staffed to date	(Staffed/planned)100
18	Project status	Percent requirements designed	(Requirements designed/total requirements)100
19	Project status	Percent requirements coded	(Requirements coded/total requirements)100
20	Project status	Percent requirements tested	(Requirements tested/total requirements)100
21	Project status	Percent tests passed	(Tests passed/total tests)100
22	Project status	Percent measurement units (KSLOC, function points, CSUs, or CSCs) designed to date	(Units designed/total units)100

Table 11-1. *Software Management Indicators and Metrics*

Number	Measurement Category	Indicator	Metrics
23	Project status	Percent measurement units (KSLOC, function points, CSUs, or CSCs) coded (including CSU test) to date	(Units coded/total units)100
24	Project status	Percent measurement units (KSLOC, function points, CSUs, or CSCs) tested (including CSC test) to date	(Units tested/total units)100
25	Project status	Percent measurement units (KSLOC, function points, CSUs, CSCs, or CSCIs) integrated (including CSCI test)	(Units integrated/total units)100
26	Quality indicators	Number of defects per KSLOC in preliminary design reviews and detailed design reviews	Defects or errors in preliminary design reviews/KSLOC, defects or errors in detailed design reviews/KSLOC (use actual or estimated KSLOC)
27	Quality indicators	Number of defects per KSLOC in code inspections	Defects or errors in code inspections/KSLOC (use actual or estimated KSLOC)
28	Quality indicators	Design quality	Complexity, error discovery efficiency, strength, coupling
29	Quality indicators	Number of (valid) PTRs opened	Count (valid) PTRs
30	Quality indicators	Percent of PTRs closed to date	(PTRs closed/total PTRs)100
31	Quality indicators	PTRs per KSLOC in CSC test	PTRs/KSLOC
32	Quality indicators	PTRs per KSLOC in CSCI test	PTRs/KSLOC
33	Quality indicators	PTRs per KSLOC in system test	PTRs/KSLOC
34	Quality indicators	Predicted defects/KSLOC at delivery	Predicted defects/KSLOC at delivery
35	Earned value	Overall proportion of software (in KSLOC, function points, etc.) complete	See Chapter 11
36	Computer resources	Target CPU processing speed (for standard functions)	(Target mips/host mips) x ((function size in millions of inst.)/(host processing speed in seconds)) = estimated target mips for standard function
37	Computer resources	Proportion of memory utilization (words, bytes, characters, or bits)	CPU used/CPU available or mass storage used/mass storage available
38	Computer resources	Proportion of software I/O capacity utilized	(Message length)(arrival rate)/(processing speed)

Table 11-1. *Software Management Indicators and Metrics, continued*

11.3.1 Goal-Question-Metric Paradigm

Use the GQM paradigm to select the metrics that you track. The goals and questions will determine the metrics to be used for tracking. As an example, suppose your project goals are as follows:

- Productivity for the activities of preliminary design through CSCI test should be at least 200 SLOC/LM.

- Do not begin designing until all requirements are defined.

- Without changing the review and inspection process, hold the total defects/KSLOC injected in the development process at less than 25.

- Deliver software with an estimated latent defect density of no more than 1.0 defects/KSLOC.

- Complete the project within budget and planned schedule.

The questions and metrics (i.e., management indicators from Table 11-1) associated with these goals are shown in Table 11-2.

11.3.2 Incremental Improvement

If you find that the indicator metrics you are using have revealed a problem, such as not meeting a project goal, it may be necessary for management to change the software development process. As the tracking and monitoring procedures are applied and reapplied throughout the software development cycle, many such decisions will probably have to be

Goal	Questions	Metrics (Management Indicators)
1	What is the estimated overall productivity?	1,4,35
2	What is the number of requirements? What percent of requirements are undefined?	12,18 13,22
3	What is our current total defect density?	26,27
4	What is our current estimate of latent defect density?	1,26,27,31–34
5	What is the current budget status? What is the current schedule status? What is the development status? What problems remain?	4–9 10,11 18–25,35 12–15

Table 11-2. Example of Goal-Question-Metric Paradigm for Tracking

made. In each case, the management indicator metrics might not only indicate the possibility of a problem, but also provide information on what adjustment to make in the process. Therefore, try to select metrics that give you indications of problems in the development cycle as early as possible so that you can minimize the cost and scheduling impact to rectify them or to reduce their effect.

11.3.2.1 Feedback

The value of the management indicator metrics at any stage in the development process is that they not only show that a problem exists but also provide information useful in improving your software development process. For example, consider the project goals stated in Section 11.3.1. Assume that 100 KSLOC of software are to be developed and that this software is currently in the coding activity, having been completely designed. At this point, the tracking and monitoring process discovers that the current total defect density is already 30 defects/KSLOC, thus exceeding the third project goal of 25 defects/KSLOC. A problem has been shown to exist.

It seems that, in this case, the error discovery process, especially with respect to design reviews, is working well. However, too many design errors are being generated. Since the coding cannot begin until the requirements are complete (the fourth project goal), it seems that the high design defect rate is not from undefined requirements. Therefore, the software product is not being designed correctly the first time through, i.e., before the design reviews. You could redesign the software at this point. If you don't, you will have to relax the defect density goal. In the long term, future projects may change to structured methods, for example, and use a program design language. Or perhaps better training is needed for the designers. All of these actions help to incrementally improve the development process by feeding the metrics information back to the process through management over a longer term.

11.3.2.2 Corrective Action

The example discussed in Section 11.3.2.1 suggested corrective actions that could be taken to improve the development process in the long term, i.e., future development efforts. Often, management can take short-term actions to solve or at least minimize the effect of a problem. Consider the set of project goals stated in Section 11.3.1 as an example. Suppose you have discovered that when the software was almost completely coded the project effort had spent 10 percent over the design, code, and unit test budget of 355 LM, and that there is a high probability of your not meeting the fifth project goal. Management could decide to try to make up those $(0.10)(355)=35.5$ LM by trying to make the test process more efficient. If the total budget is 500 LM (100,000 SLOC/200 SLOC/LM), then 35.5 LM has to come out of the remaining budget of 500–355=145 LM. Management may decide to institute a two-tier testing procedure for CSC integration in which all of the program units that are critical or error-prone are extensively tested while noncritical and stable units are tested less intensively. Also, the CSCI test can be made more cost-efficient (but perhaps reducing its effectiveness) by forgoing stress testing near or at the performance boundaries of the software function. Such a process improvement might save 20 to 25 percent of the testing budget and make up for most, if not all, of the design and coding overrun. Before cost reduction decisions such as those described here are taken, the risk in taking them (e.g., not finding all the errors that more testing would have found) should be evaluated.

11.4 HOW TO COMPUTE MANAGEMENT INDICATORS

This section defines a set of metrics for software project tracking and monitoring that you might use.

11.4.1 Software Product Size Indicators

You should track the size of a software system using indicator 1 or indicators 2 and 3 because the delivered size is almost always larger than the initial estimate. Also, there are often memory or CPU processor constraints that restrict program size, and these restrictions can become critical in the later stages of development. Monitor the size of the software product (i.e., the new and the total [new plus reused] KSLOC) through the full development schedule. You can also monitor the number of function points as an indicator, if you use them. If estimates of the software product size are available, track revised estimates during the project as they are developed. If actual code counts are available, track the actual code counts. While the software product is in design, you can still track the estimated KSLOC by converting the counts of SLOD or process bubbles to KSLOC estimates. The past experience of the enterprise design process, as recorded in the enterprise software experience database, will reveal the SLOC-to-SLOD ratio. You can also continually track function points and counts of externals or other indicators of the ultimate size of your software product throughout the development process.

11.4.2 Software Cost Indicators

Indicators 4 through 9 relate to development cost. You should monitor dollars and either LH or LM, relative to the budget. You should track software development costs in LH or LM but track expenses, such as computer support and equipment, in terms of dollars. You should track subcontractors effort in LM or LH, if possible. However, since subcontractor billing is usually done in dollars, you may have to track dollars expended. Also, you should track total dollars spent to date. When you place the data in your software experience database, you should annotate this data with the date on which it was incurred so that you can relate or compare it with similar experiences on other projects at different times.

11.4.3 Development Schedule Indicators

Schedule tracking should be standard practice on every software development project. Schedule tracking, as in indicator 10, is usually in terms of months. The percent of schedule elapsed, as in indicator 11, may be helpful in comparing time resources spent (for example) to financial resources spent.

11.4.4 Project Technical Stability Indicators

Project technical stability is an indication of the extent to which the requirements of the software development are undefined from the time of the project's initiation. This lack of definition is principally manifested in incomplete and contradictory technical requirements and in insufficient human resources. Insufficient schedule and budgets are also related to technical instability, but these situations are covered by other management indicators.

Technical stability of the software development project, as shown by indicators 12 through 17, is important since stability is often the prime determinant of whether or not the project is completed within the required cost, schedule, and quality requirements. The volume of engineering change proposals and the percent of undefined requirements are key indicators that you should track. It is often difficult to find a sufficient number of qualified software development personnel. A shortage of such people can severely impact the schedule. You should closely monitor the number of unfilled software development positions.

11.4.5 Project Status Indicators

You can monitor the status (the degree of project completion) and the earned value (the amount of work done in terms of product actually complete) by measuring the degree of implementation of the requirements analysis activity through the CSCI testing activity (shown by indicators 18 through 20). You should express the project status in terms of the percentage of measurement units that have been completed at each of the development activities (shown by indicators 21 through 25). Measurement units can be SLOC, function points, CSUs, CSCs, or even CSCIs.

11.4.6 Quality Indicators

The data records you normally keep as part of design reviews and code inspections should provide the data for the quality indicators 26 and 27. You can use these indicators, together with quality indicators 31 through 33, as input to methodologies. Gaffney and Pietrolewicz (1990) predict software defects per KSLOC at delivery.

Indicator 28, design quality, has many facets that are listed in Table 11-1 and defined in Chapter 5. You may want to track some or all of these metrics; however, they are not part of the minimum set.

11.4.7 Computer Resources Indicators

Sometimes you track computer resources, as shown by indicators 36 through 38, especially when you have doubts about the existence of sufficient computer resources. The software specification sometimes requires that the software to be developed or a specific software function must execute at a minimum speed on a CPU that is specified but is not yet developed or is otherwise unavailable. To approximate and monitor target processing speed (as shown by indicator 36) when the target CPU is unavailable, you must first identify the key software functions that have the potential to impose major constraints on the speed of application processing. These functions may be frequently used routines or modules that have (perhaps) some difficulty in handling the information flow. Examples include fast Fourier transforms, Kalman filtering, message handling, or input/output (I/O) routines.

For any of these functions, the ratio of the specified target CPU speed in millions of instructions per second (mips) to the host (development) CPU speed in mips represents the ratio of processing speeds for these particular functions or for the developmental software in general, whatever the specification requires. If you divide the software function size in millions of instructions by the number of seconds it takes the host CPU to process the software function (or multiple iterations of the function), you obtain the software function host execution speed in mips. You can multiply this host execution speed by the ratio of processing speeds to yield an estimate of the target CPU software processing speed in mips.

This CPU processing speed indicator, or estimates of it, can be monitored as you develop the software function(s). The early software versions may indicate a target processing under the specification; but as you develop and optimize the software with respect to speed (among other factors), the estimated target process speed should approach the value in the software product specification.

You calculate indicator 37, memory utilization, by dividing the CPU utilization by the CPU available capacity. You can measure memory in words, bytes, characters, or bits. You can calculate the proportion of mass storage utilization by dividing mass storage utilization by mass storage available. In addition, you can use tracks and cylinders as measures of memory for disk units.

Indicator 38, I/O facility utilization, requires knowledge of the statistical distribution of message length in which messages are the units of information that the I/O software processes. With knowledge of this distribution, you select a high message length of about three standard deviations above the mean. You convert this message length (which you express in characters, words, or bytes) to the number of bits per message. Multiply this length in bits by the arrival rate of the messages (in or out) in messages per second. Then divide this product by the processing capacity in bits or bytes per second of the I/O software that prepares and sends messages to or receives messages from the hardware channel. These calculations result in the proportion of I/O software capacity used. You can monitor this proportion (i.e., you can calculate and compare it with the specification) as you develop and optimize the software that is concerned with message handling capacity.

11.5 OVERALL PROPORTION COMPLETE AND EARNED VALUE

This section describes how you can estimate the overall proportion complete (OPC) and the earned value (EV) of a software development project. Earned value is a very important quantity that you should track during software development. Unfortunately, it often is not tracked because of a lack of knowledge about how to use the applicable metrics. It measures the degree of project completion. The measured degree of a project or product completion is not the same as a measurement of labor or dollars expended to date. It is possible for you to expend more effort and resources with very little useful work (product development) to show for it. EV is a measure of the actual work that you have accomplished to date as distinct from the amount of effort expended to date.

EV is calculated from the more fundamental measure, the OPC. You calculate EV in terms of useful work completed. The expenditure of effort does not necessarily mean that you have accomplished any actual work in terms of product developed (e.g., design completed or code written). The EV metric shows what actual work, i.e., the degree of product completion, you have actually accomplished. This metric is based on the degree of completion of each of the activities in the development process. From this EV metric, it is relatively easy to show how much additional effort you will require to complete product development.

Estimating the degree of completion, i.e., the overall proportion complete, of a software development project is difficult because many elements of the software products being developed are in different activities and have different degrees of completion, i.e., may be at any point during the development life cycle. Figure 11-1 illustrates the overlapping and very complex nature of the cumulative percent complete of software development activities. Avoid measuring the overall degree of completion by merely guessing or grossly estimating the percent complete of the software product without using any detailed completion measurement data and without the aid of any quantitative methods. This section provides quantitative algorithms to accurately calculate the EV using detailed completion data.

The steps in computing OPC and EV are:

1. Characterize each activity in the development process by a unit cost or a labor rate in LM/KSLOC or equivalent units. The unit cost for activity i is designated as C_i.

2. Determine the proportion of the output planned for an activity, measured in SLOC or other designated measurement units, that is complete for each activity. You may be able to obtain status data from a software status report. The proportion of software that is complete through activity i is defined as:

$$P_i = \frac{\text{units\_through\_activity\_i}}{\text{total\_number\_of\_units\_required}}$$

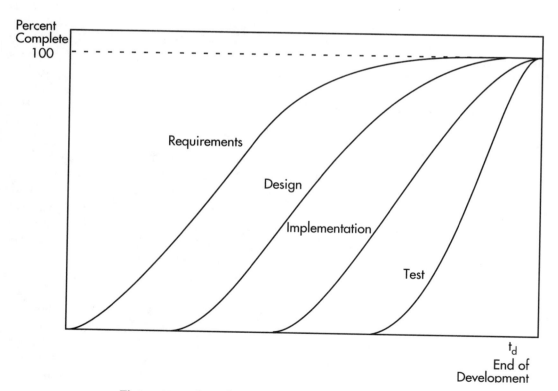

Figure 11-1. *Cumulative Patterns of Activity Completion*

where the units of size can be measured in CSUs (modules), SLOC, SLOD, function points, etc. The examples in this guidebook measure code size in SLOC.

3. Compute the OPC for the software product as indicated in the formula below for each activity in your software product.

The development process of a software component is composed of activities 1 through p with corresponding unit costs for each of the P activities of software development, C_1 through C_p, and with a total unit cost of ΣC_i. Unit cost is in LM/KSLOC and size is in KSLOC. Alternatively, you can use LH/SLOC and SLOC. Let each activity's proportion of completion be P_1, P_2, ... P_p, where $P_1 \geq P_2 \geq \ldots \geq P_p$. Then the OPC of the software product is:

$$OPC = \frac{\sum_{i=1}^{p} C_i P_i}{\sum_{i=1}^{p} C_i}$$

You can use the OPC metric to track the progress of the development of your software product. The progress of the ith activity is given by P_i as a function of time (see Figure 11-1). A program manager could also look at the OPC metric as a function of time and compare a plot of the actual OPC values over time with the corresponding planned OPC time profile in the software development plan. If the actual (overall) progress falls below the planned figure, the manager can look at each of the individual activities (as illustrated in Figure 11-1) in the development process.

4. Multiply the OPC for each CSC or CSCI by the corresponding (estimate of) SLOC (or other unit) to obtain the EV in terms of the designated measurement units such as LM or LH. You can add the EVs over all of the CSCs or CSCIs to obtain the total earned value.

The units of the estimated size, S, used in the EV calculations are in terms of KESLOC or ESLOC. The user must choose which of these units is appropriate for his situation. KESLOC and ESLOC are used here because they are the general representations of size. If you calculate EV for a project that involves developing only new code, the units of size should be KSLOC or SLOC. But if you calculate EV for a project involving both new and reused code, use KESLOC or ESLOC.

$$KESLOC \text{ (or } ESLOC) = S_N + w \cdot S_R$$

where S_N and S_R are in the appropriate units of KSLOC or ESLOC. Other size units, such as function or feature points, can be used in EV calculations where they meet user needs.

As an example of the calculation and application of the EV metric, suppose that a software product (i.e., a CSCI) has a development process and present status, as described in Table 11-3. Assume that 60 percent of the code (KESLOC) is through preliminary and detailed design, 45 percent is through code and CSU test, and 10 percent is through CSC integration. Also assume that the product size is not increasing: there is no code growth.

Using the previous formula, the OPC for new code is:

$$
\begin{aligned}
\text{OPC} &= [0.52(0.60)+0.82(0.60)+2.21(0.45)+0.74(0.10)+0.73(0.0)]/5.02 \\
&= 1.8725/5.02 \\
&= 0.373
\end{aligned}
$$

If, for example, there are 75 KESLOCs in the CSCI, the EV is:

$$\text{EV} = 75(5.02)(.373) = 140.4 \text{ LM}$$

11.6 THE ESTIMATE AT COMPLETION

The estimate at completion (EAC) is an estimate of the completed cost of the software product, a prediction of the actual cost. At the beginning of development, the EAC is equal to the estimated actual cost of the software product. However, during development, the EAC is composed of the inception to date (ITD) cost (the actual cost to date, also known as cost to date) and the estimate to complete (ETC) (the current estimate of the actual additional cost to complete the remaining development of the software product). In equation form, this is:

$$\text{EAC} = \text{ITD} + \text{ETC}$$

i	Activity Complete	Ci(LM/KESLOC)	Pi (Proportion through i)
1	Preliminary design	0.52	0.600
2	Detailed design	0.82	0.600
3	Code and CSU test	2.21	0.450
4	CSC integration test	0.74	0.100
5	CSCI test	0.73	0.000
	Total	5.02	

Table 11-3. Product Completion Indicator Calculation

The ETC for the software development project is (in generalized form):

$$ETC = S \cdot \left(\sum_{i=1}^{p} C_i \right) \cdot (1 - OPC)$$

$$ETC = 75 \cdot 5.02 \cdot (1 - .373) = 236.1 \text{ LM}$$

Suppose that you have expended 180 LMs ITD. Therefore, the EAC is:

$$EAC = ITD + ETC = 180.0 + 236.1 = 416.1 \text{ LM}$$

This estimate may be compared with the initial cost estimate using the total labor rates from Table 11-3. The initial (before development began) EAC was:

$$EAC = 5.02(75.0) = 376.5 \text{ LM}$$

It appears from this result that the project will exceed the initially estimated cost.

The current estimated final product unit cost is considerably higher than the initially planned unit cost of 5.02 LM/KSLOC. This final product unit cost is calculated as:

$$\frac{ITD}{S \cdot OPC} = \frac{180}{75 \cdot 0.373} = 6.43 \text{ LM/KSLOC}$$

You should note that this calculation depends on your estimate of the size, S. The ratio of unit costs, 6.43/5.02=1.28, indicates that the actual development to date is 28 percent more costly than the planned development. You can adjust the ETC to reflect this more costly process if you think that the project completion will continue in the higher cost mode.

$$EAC = ITD + ETC_{adjusted} = 180.0 + 236.1 \cdot 1.28 = 180.0 + 302.2 = 482.2 \text{ LM}$$

This EAC of 482.2 LM is much larger than the initially planned EAC of 376.5 LM. The (adjusted) EAC could also be calculated as:

$$EAC = \frac{ITD}{OPC} = \frac{180}{0.373} = 482.6 \text{ LM}$$

It appears that the project is likely to exceed the initial estimate of cost.

11.7 ALTERNATIVE METHOD FOR COMPUTING OPC AND EAC

This section presents an alternative method for computing the OPC and EAC metrics for your software project. You may find that these formulas provide an advantage relative to the others presented in preceding sections of Chapter 11 because they do not require you to use a priori estimates of the cost structure of the development process (the C_i, as defined and described earlier) or of the expected size, S (say, in KSLOC), of the product under development. Rather, these formulas rely solely upon data obtained during the development process.

Work completed status information (EAC and OPC) is often currently computed based on an a priori, an assumed, effort distribution amongst the activities that compose the development process. Also, often such estimates require the assumption of some size, S, for the product under development. Use of such a priori information does not enable the status calculation to recognize that changes may have taken place in the actual allocation of effort across the development activities on this particular job, as compared with the original estimate or with prior jobs. Thus, you might find it useful to take another approach to estimating OPC and EAC in which the effort distribution is determined empirically during the course of the development project. Doing so would enable changes since the original estimate, such as in the sizes of the CSCIs, the functionality to be developed, and/or the actual development costs and their allocation among the development activities, to be reflected more accurately in the determination of project status. An approach to doing so is now described.

11.7.1 EAC, Effort Distribution, and OPC Metrics

The proportion of the product complete (where the product is a CSCI or the overall software system) is designated as OPC, where

$$OPC = \sum_{i=1}^{p} P_i \cdot C_i$$

where P_i is the proportion complete of development activity i, and C_i is the proportion of the development cost attributable to activity i.

You can develop an empirical estimate for each of the C_i factors, $1 \leq i \geq p$ (for each of the p activities that compose your software development process) by using the equation:

$$C_i = \frac{EAC_i}{EAC}$$

where EAC_i (estimate at completion for activity i) and EAC are given by the expressions:

$$EAC_i = \frac{ITD_i}{P_i}$$

$$EAC = \sum_{i=1}^{p} EAC_i$$

Thus, the distribution of the development effort is given by the set of metrics $\{C_i\}$. Therefore, the percent of the development effort in activity i is equal to $C_i \bullet 100$.

ITD_i is the inception to date effort for development activity i, and P_i is the proportion of activity i completed to date. If little or none of activity i has been completed to date, the estimate for EAC_i can be determined in one of several ways. The first is to set EAC_i equal to the original estimate of the effort required to accomplish activity i. A second, and perhaps somewhat more accurate, estimate for EAC_i would be to raise or lower the original estimate in proportion to the average percent increase or decrease for the actuals of the costs of the other activities relative to the original estimates for them.

Thus, one can estimate the EAC and/or the OPC without using any a priori assumptions about either the cost structure or the size of the product. This is valuable, because the size may have changed from the original estimate and/or the cost structure may have changed from that originally thought to be the case, say, at the beginning of the project.

The formulas presented above have one implicit assumption of note: that the cost structure is homogeneous; the cost to complete activity i will be at the same rate as for this activity to date. If desired, this assumption can be avoided. In such a case, it could be assumed that the cost for the remainder of the work of activity i (to complete the proportion $1 - P_i$ of the work of activity i remaining) would be conducted at a rate different than that for the proportion P_i that has been completed. This effect would be represented in the formulas given above by replacing P_i with $A_i \bullet P_i$. Thus, if the remaining work of activity i was expected to cost more than the portion of it done to date, the factor A_i would be set to be somewhat less than 1. Similarly, if it was expected to cost somewhat less than the completed portion of the work, then A_i would be somewhat greater than 1. The following formula for EAC_i shows where the factor A_i is placed.

$$EAC_i = \frac{ITD_i}{A_i \bullet P_i}$$

11.8 THE EFFECT OF SOFTWARE PRODUCT SIZE GROWTH

Code growth often occurs when optimistic estimates of product size are made at the time of project planning and proposal submission or when the estimator does not fully understand the number and extent of the requirements. As you make successive estimates of software product size using the increasingly better information available as the development life cycle progresses, your estimates of size become more realistic. The most current estimates of size are almost always larger than the initial estimates. Section 7.7 gives some quantitative experience with code growth.

The proportion of code growth can be defined as:

$$\text{Code Growth} = \frac{(\text{Latest Size Estimate}) - (\text{Initial Size Estimate})}{(\text{Initial Size Estimate})}$$

Code growth occurs in two situations. It can occur when there is no increase in requirements, i.e., no increase in function. For example, as the software product moves through the development life cycle, more and better information about the software product becomes available, and thus more precise estimates of size are possible. These more precise estimates are usually larger than the initial size estimates because the initial estimates are almost always very optimistic. Code growth can also occur when there is an increase in the number of requirements, i.e., an increase in the amount of function. Often, both types of code growth may occur simultaneously. This section discusses the effect of both types of code growth on the ETC.

11.8.1 Code Growth with No Function Growth

The developer reestimates the size at some point during the development life cycle and discovers that it is considerably larger than the initial estimate. Even though the amount of function to be developed remains the same, the amount of code required to implement the functionality is now larger than originally estimated.

You may first detect code growth during the code and CSU test activity. This activity is when you make the first actual code counts and when code growth is first indicated. The situation results from the requirements and the design causing more code (KESLOC) to be generated than was originally estimated. This is a very common phenomenon. You also may have a hint that there is going to be more code than originally estimated if you find that there is more design (SLOD, etc.) than had originally been estimated.

The development work actually accomplished will still exist since it is assumed that the discovery of increased size will not affect the work that you have done to date. But the proportions of work through code and CSU test and the following phases will decrease. The method for calculating the EV, considering increased software product size, assumes that you have calculated an ETC just before you discovered the increased size; therefore, you can compare this ETC with the new, more costly ETC based on code growth.

Consider the previous example of 75 KESLOC. Assume that during the code and CSU test activity and immediately after the last ETC of 236.1 LM (as in the previous example), the latest size estimate is 33 percent larger than the original estimate, increasing to 100 KSLOC for the same required function with no change in the process. Then, the proportion of code through the code and CSU test, the CSC integration, and the CSCI test activities will be 1/1.33 = 0.75 as large as previously calculated because the work has not been completed yet. However, the completed proportions for the design activities have not changed because the work has been finished in these activities. This situation is shown in Table 11-4.

Using the previous formula, the OPC is:

$$OPC=[0.52(0.60)+0.82(0.60)+2.21(0.34)+0.74(0.075)+0.73(0.0)](1/5.02)=1.611/5.02=0.321$$

The earned value now is:

$$EV = 100(5.02)(0.321) = 161.1 \text{ LM}$$

The ETC is:

$$ETC = 100(5.02)(1 - 0.321) = 340.9 \text{ LM}$$

where the OPC and KESLOC are the values associated with the increased size.

The reduced OPC and the increased KESLOC combine to significantly increase the ETC from 236.1 LM to 340.9 LM. Note that the code growth has the expected effect of decreas-

i	Activity/Phase Complete	C_i (LM/KESLOC)	P_i (Proportion through i)
1	Preliminary design	0.52	0.600
2	Detailed design	0.82	0.600
3	Code and CSU test	2.21	0.340
4	CSC integration test	0.74	0.075
5	CSCI test	0.73	0.000
Total	5.02		

Table 11-4. Example of Code Growth with No Function Growth

ing the OPC and increasing the ETC. An unexpected effect of the code growth is the increase in the EV from 140.4 to 161.1 LM. This increase is due to the fact that more work was done than originally estimated because of (equivalent) code growth.

11.8.2 Code Growth with Function Growth

Code growth also occurs when the requirements and, therefore, the amount of required function increases. When the amount of function to be implemented increases relative to the original estimate, you should immediately make a new estimate of software product size so that you can estimate the costs of implementing the additional code.

The development work actually accomplished will still exist since the discovery of increased size is assumed not to affect the work that has been done to date. But the EV should not be expected to substantially change in cases where the additional requirement (function) has no effect on the existing requirements because the work completed is still finished even after the additional requirements (function) are added to the project. As in the case of code growth but no function growth, the method for calculating the EV, considering increased software product size due to function growth, assumes that you have calculated an ETC and EAC just before you discovered the increased size. Therefore, you can compare the ETC and the EAC with the more costly ETC and EAC based on code growth.

The additional code (the excess of the newly discovered [estimated] code over the previous estimate of code) will have to go through the whole development process, so the previously estimated values of the proportion of development complete will actually decrease. Then you can handle the calculation of the OPC, EV, and ETC for the case of code growth with function growth in exactly the same way as the case of code growth with no function growth. In other words, the cause of code growth does not matter in a procedural sense because the computations are the same (with different values of proportions through activities) in either case.

Consider the example of 75 KESLOC previously discussed. Assume that immediately after the original ETC of 236.1 LM additional requirements are placed on the development thus causing function growth. Now, assume that this function growth causes the estimated size of the code to increase 33 percent from 75 to 100 KESLOC. As before, there is no change in the process; then the proportion of code through all phases will be $1/1.33 = 0.75$ as large. Table 11-5 shows this situation with the complete proportion of all activities being decreased by the presence of new requirements that have not been addressed.

Using the previous formula, the OPC for new code is:

$$OPC=[0.52(0.45)+0.82(0.45)+2.21(0.34)+0.74(0.075)+0.73(0.0)](1/5.02)=1.410/5.02=0.281$$

i	Activity/Phase Complete	C$_i$(LM/KESLOC)	P$_i$ (Proportion Through i)
1	Preliminary design	0.52	0.450
2	Detailed design	0.82	0.450
30	Code and CSU test	2.21	0.340
4	CSC integration test	0.74	0.075
5	CSCI test	.73	0.000
	Total	5.02	

Tabe 11-5. *Example of Code Growth with Function Growth*

And the EV is:

$$EV = 100(5.02)(0.281) = 141.1 \text{ LM}$$

The ETC is:

$$ETC = 100(5.02)(1 - 0.281) = 360.9 \text{ LM}$$

Code growth, for whatever reason, always causes a decrease in the OPC and an increase in the ETC versus the case of no code growth. Code growth with no function growth always decreases the OPC and increases the ETC. But code growth with no function growth actually causes an increase in the EV because code growth awards additional credit for product development for activities already completed. Therefore, *OPC is a better measure of product status than EV.*

Code growth, if caused by function growth, has little effect on the EV. In the example above, the code growth with function growth caused only a very small increase in the EV over the original no growth EV. The OPC metric gives more information about project status than the EV metric does. You should *use the OPC metric is the prime indicator of status.*

11.9 THE PROJECT STATUS ASSESSMENT

The implementation of tracking and monitoring procedures is really a continuous process of quantitatively assessing the product and process; comparing those measurements and metrics with the quantitative goals and limits set by the project plans; and taking corrective action when the performance falls outside the preset limits or falls short of the preset goals. Figure 11-2 illustrates this monitoring and control process as a flow chart.

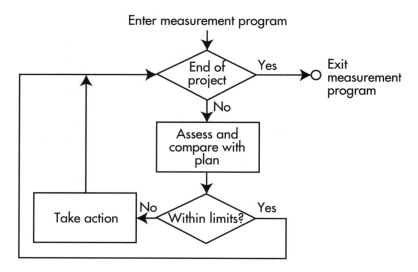

Figure 11-2. *The Monitoring and Control Process*

A typical series of the actions required to perform the project status assessment is presented here. This is not the only way to proceed, but it is an approach that has been successfully used in industry.

11.9.1 Activities for Project Status Assessment

1. Collect the data:

   a. Number and status of requirements.

   b. Size and status of design. Total number of design modules, number of SLOD, number of design modules through preliminary design inspection (reviews) through PDR, number of design modules through detailed design inspection (reviews) through CDR.

   c. Size and status of software code. Total number of software modules and SLOC counts, number of modules through code inspection.

   d. Size and status of integration test. Number of software modules through CSC integration test, total number of integration test procedure steps, and number of integration test procedure steps completed.

e. Size and status of system (CSCI) test. Number of software modules through CSCI system (product) test, total number of system test procedure steps, and number of system test procedure steps completed.

f. Cost of project. All applicable cost accounts in the work breakdown structure (WBS). Collect budgeted LH or LM, actual LH or LM, and actual development computer dollars.

g. Quality. Number of defects discovered during design reviews and code inspections categorized by major and minor and type of error, and number of program trouble reports (PTRs) by category.

h. Project cost and schedule status reports.

i. Project organization charts.

2. Analyze the data for each CSCI or software product:

a. Status of design. Calculate preliminary and detailed design percent complete using CSUs, SLOD, or other available units.

b. Size and status of code and unit test. Calculate code percent complete using SLOC data.

c. Size and status of integration test. Calculate percent complete by module and/or any test steps.

d. Size and status of system test. Calculate percent complete by module and/or by number of test steps.

e. Cost of project. Summarize and total budgeted LH or LM and inception to date (ITD) LH or LM by activity and by CSCI and/or by CSC. Calculate the percent budget expended. Calculate earned value (EV), estimate to complete (ETC), and estimate at completion (EAC). Compare EAC to budget for each software product.

f. Quality. Calculate defect density by development activity. Project defect densities to product delivery. Compare with project objectives.

g. Calculate project stability, productivity, and other appropriate management indicators.

h. Calculate the project risks.

3. Prepare the Project Status Assessment Report.

11.9.2 The Project Status Assessment Report

A project status assessment contains the measurements and management indicators that are vital to the MDSM process. They must be made readily available to project management for use in basing project control decisions. It is, therefore, absolutely necessary to present the results of the analysis in the form of a highly communicative report. The following is an outline of a project status assessment report that has been used successfully in industry.

- *Objective—General Discussion.* State the general objective of the report, which is to provide a status assessment, as of a certain date, of the size, cost, schedule, and quality of the project. Other report objectives are to provide the proportion of the work completed and a projection (estimate) of the cost to completion. An analysis of the product quality and projection (estimate) of the quality at delivery should also be provided.

  Include a brief discussion of any unusual or extraordinary circumstances surrounding the creation of this report or the nature of the project reported upon. State that this is a scheduled assessment. If it is unscheduled, the reason for creating the report should be documented.

- *Ground Rules and Assumptions.* A reference to the organization standards can be placed here. Reasons for collecting data that may not have been according to standard should be noted. Note any extraordinary procedures in the process, special support tools, or personnel that affect the projections. Note any estimating models that require adjustment factors.

- *Approach.* You may state methods of data collection. Note whether the data was personally collected by the analyst or provided by some automated mechanism or other project personnel. Briefly discuss methods of analysis. Explain the calculation of metrics not directly measurable, such as productivity, or reference a standard.

- *Summary of Status Assessment.* This is the boiled down result of the project status assessment. It should include the project size, cost, schedule, and quality summaries. The summaries may be tabular or graphical results only; do not include analytical information. Include risk exposure shown by the analysis in this section. The information can be presented in the context of information from prior reports for comparison and progress indication.

- *Analyses.* Analysis is the process of reducing the raw data to meaningful information in the form of management indicators. This section can contain the spreadsheets used to develop the detailed listings of the organized data and the summaries of the derived information. This section shows the use of the estimating models and the projections developed from the models. All calculations are shown for derivation of the overall proportion completed and the estimate to complete and any other management indicators.

- **Recommendations.** The project status assessment almost always uncovers certain facts that were not apparent prior to the analysis. At times, there will be indications of problems with the product or process. These problems may exist or may be of a potential nature. It is the analyst's responsibility to bring these perceived problems to the attention of management and, if possible, recommend a course of action to avoid a potential risk or problem or mitigate an existing one.

   Once a draft of the analysis report is completed, the measurement function should show the software project management and staff the results to get their input. There may be some errors or undefined areas in the report that must be changed. The project personnel may or may not agree with the conclusions contained in the report. If the project personnel disagrees, the measurement function should not necessarily feel that the results of the analysis must be changed. However, the project personnel should feel that the report is fair and accurate. Since they may have contributed data, they should see the results of the analysis. This communication is also a good way for you to build support for the measurement function. After discussion with the project staff, the analyst may wish to revise the report.

- **Appendix.** This section is not distributed with the report. It is only included for the benefit of the analyst. All the raw data is saved here.

11.9.3 Cost and Schedule Performance Reporting for Tracking

Some organizations use different terminology in reporting cost and schedule for project tracking. Table 11-6 compares the cost and schedule terms used for many Department of Defense projects (Department of the Army, Communications-Electronics Command 1991) with those discussed in this guidebook. An entry of "none" indicates that the particular term was not discussed in the corresponding document.

Table 11-7 shows the equivalent estimation formulas for cost and schedule status reporting for tracking software development projects given by the Department of Defense (Department of the Army, Communications-Electronics Command 1991) and this guidebook.

Several differences between the Department of Defense reporting system discussed here and the methods presented in this guidebook are:

- BCWP is sometimes submitted by the reporting organization rather than computed during the tracking process as an EV.

- The Department of Defense ETC computation includes a factor (1/CPI) that adjusts the ETC (and therefore the EAC) for cost performance to date.

The Department of the Army, Communications-Electronics Command (1991) gives an example of status reporting using actual data and formats.

Department of Defense	Software Measurement Guidebook
Budget at completion (BAC)	Budget (BUD)
Actual cost of work performed (ACWP)	Inception to date (ITD)
Budgeted cost of work performed (BCWP)	Earned value (EV)
(none)	Estimate to completion (ETC)
Estimate at completion (EAC)	Estimate at completion (EAC)
Budgeted cost of work scheduled (BCWS)	(none)
(none)	Overall proportion complete (OPC)

Table 11-6. *Comparison of Cost and Schedule Reporting Terms*

Department of Defense	Software Measurement Guidebook
Budget at completion: BAC	BUD=S (size) • EUC (estimated unit cost)
BCWP (submitted by reporting organization)	EV=BUD • OPC
Cost performance index: CPI = BCWP/ACWP	EV/ITD
(BAC − BCWP)/CPI	$ETC_{adj} = (BUD - EV)(ITD/EV)=(1 - OPC)(ITD/OPC)$
EAC = ACWP + (BAC − BCWP)/CPI	$EAC_{adj} = ITD + ETC_{adj} = ITD/OPC$
Schedule performance index: SPI = BCWP/BCWS	EV/BUD (to date)
Current cost performance: BCWP − ACWP	EV − ITD
Current schedule performance: BCWP − BCWS	EV − BUD (to date)
Variance at completion: EAC − BAC	$EAC_{adj} - BUD$

Table 11-7. *Equivalent Estimation Formulas*

11.10 GRAPHICAL METHODS OF MONITORING AND CONTROL

This section shows some selected examples of presenting tracking and monitoring information graphically.

11.10.1 Graphical Methods of Earned Value Monitoring

This section provides several graphical methods for EV monitoring. Figure 11-3 illustrates the relationships among EV, budgeted value, and the total budget for the development of the software product. The budgeted value is the planned value of the product as it is developed, i.e., the planned value of the resources spent through time. The EV approximates the budgeted value as the product is developed; and they both converge in the total budget at the end of development, assuming no overruns or schedule slippage. Values are stated in LM, and the total initial budget is 245 LM.

Figure 11-4 illustrates the effects of two types of changes to the EV: in the budgeted value and in the total budget. Case A assumes an initial budget of 245 LM for development. This case illustrates the effect of code growth with no function growth. With the discovery of increased size, there is a corresponding decrease in earned value at the time of discovery, time A. There could be a possible increase in budget to accommodate the code growth. Case B also assumes the same initial budget. This case illustrates the effect of an increase in the estimated size of the software product due to an increase in requirements and function at time B. This increase in requirements causes a corresponding increase of 30 LM in the total budget, as shown in the figure.

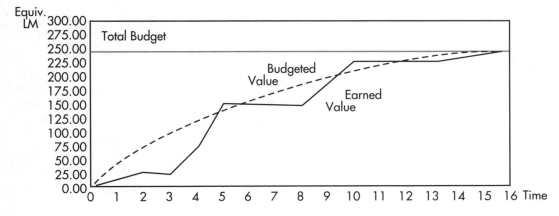

Figure 11-3. *Earned Value and Budgeted Value*

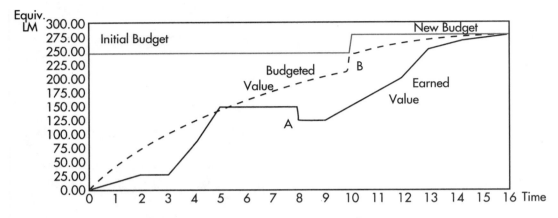

Figure 11-4. *Changes in Earned and Budgeted Value*

11.10.2 Graphical Methods of Project Monitoring

Figures 11-5 through 11-10 are examples of using graphical methods of project monitoring. These illustrations were suggested by similar graphical techniques shown in Air Force Systems Command (1986). Figure 11-5 illustrates a graphical method of monitoring the total defects per KSLOC of a software development project. If the level of defects is at a level that exceeds the maximum acceptable limit, then perhaps the software process is inserting too many errors. It may be necessary to manage the risk by revising the process.

You can also track project status in terms of the proportion complete by the graphical method shown in Figure 11-6.

Figure 11-7 shows the pattern of the cumulative number of program trouble reports (PTRs) opened minus the number of PTRs closed over time. You should expect that at the early stages of testing the rate of PTR opening to be high and increasing and the rate of PTR closing to be low, lagging behind the rate of opening. At some point in time, the rates will be equal and the process will peak. As the testing progresses, expect that the rate of opening will decrease and the rate of closing will increase. An indicator that this project is under control and that the product is approaching readiness to be released is why the difference between the total number of PTRs opened and closed decreases as a function of time.

Figure 11-8 graphically shows a situation of new code growth together with the disappearance of the amount of reused code (Carleton et al. 1992) expected in the software product. This causes cost growth over the development cycle due to the fact that more new code was developed than originally estimated.

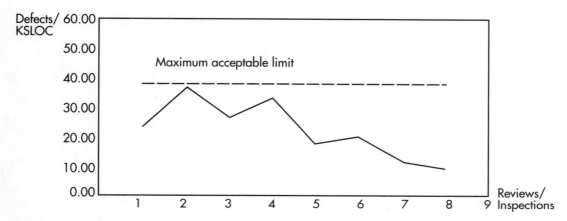

Figure 11-5. *Example of Monitoring Defects Per Thousand Source Lines of Code by Review or Inspection*

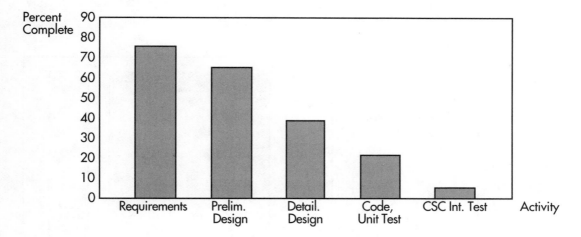

Figure 11-6. *Example of Status Tracking*

Figure 11-9 shows the monitoring of a computer resources indicator where there are both upper and lower control limits.

Figure 11-10 shows graphically the distribution of engineering hours by development activity (Grady 1992) for applications software. You should compare a similar graph of your effort performance to date with the planned distribution of effort in your software development plan.

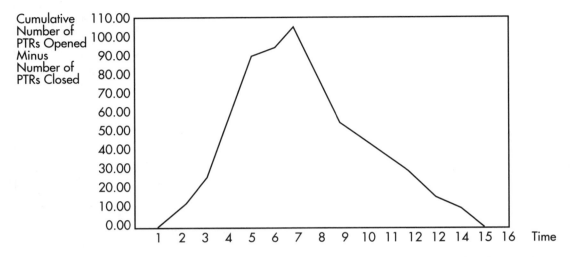

Figure 11-7. *Problem Trouble Reports Opened Minus Problem Trouble Reports Closed Over Time*

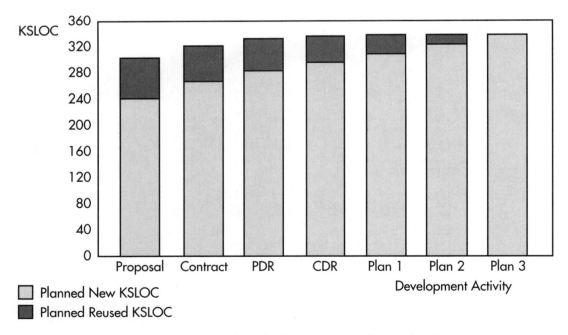

☐ Planned New KSLOC
■ Planned Reused KSLOC

Figure 11-8. *Cost Growth–Disappearance of Reused Code*

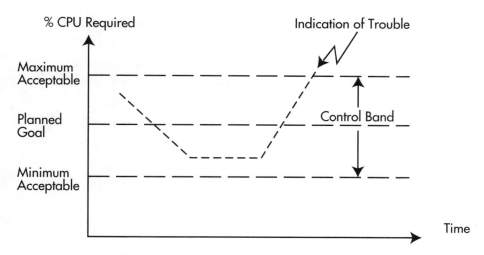

Figure 11-9. *Example of Computer Resource Monitoring and Control*

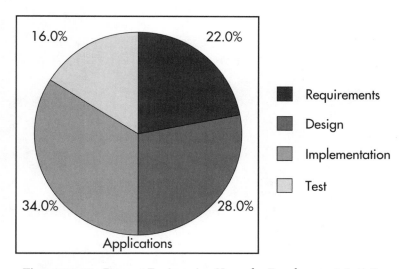

Figure 11-10. *Percent Engineering Hours by Development Activity*

11.11 SUMMARY OF RECOMMENDATIONS

The recommendations on project tracking and monitoring presented in Chapter 11 are:

- Use the GQM paradigm to select indicator metrics.

- Define data collection methods and project tracking and monitoring procedures in your software standards and policies.

- Track the status of software development projects for your organization. Your organization should define procedures for deciding what projects are to be tracked.

- Use the minimum data set for software project tracking.

- Begin data collection for tracking at the earliest possible time, regardless of process maturity level.

- Feed back data to improve the process and the products it produces.

Chapter
12

EXPERIENCE DATABASES AND DATA COLLECTION

12.1 OVERVIEW

This section presents ways of collecting and organizing software development experience data to aid you in achieving higher levels of performance and in making dependable plans for the future. You can use data about the performance of your organization on past projects to enhance the predictability of its performance on future projects. It is important that an organization preserve and learn from its software development experience. The acquisition of new business requires you to make accurate estimates of cost and schedule. Process improvement is based on quantitative knowledge of process history. The activities of the software development process can be quantitatively characterized. Experience data is vitally necessary for the software development organization to be able to achieve higher performance levels of process improvement, project control, and product quality.

12.2 THE SOFTWARE EXPERIENCE DATABASE

Every organization concerned with software development should establish and maintain a repository of its software development experience. The database used for this purpose should contain measurements, metrics, and other important information (such as product and development environment descriptions) that can be used to support software project control and software process improvement, both short and long term. The establishment and maintenance of a software experience database should be mandated by and supported at the highest organizational level since the data collected and the metrics derived from that data will be used in the organization's business to form the basis of software standards, estimate costs, evaluate product quality, and improve the development process.

Various projects and organizations will contribute information to the experience database. Software development, systems engineering, system test, quality engineering, measurement, cost engineering, finance, configuration management, product support (logistics), and project management are among the organizational functions that will contribute to the database and will benefit from the software information it contains. All of the organizations concerned with software development and/or maintenance should be familiar with the database. The experience database should not become the exclusive property of the group that maintains it. All organizations should be encouraged to contribute to it and to use it.

Use your software experience database both to preserve software measurement and metrics information and to feed back the data about the organization's past performance to help:

- Improve the software development and support processes.

- Make cost and schedule more manageable.

- Control development projects.

- Manage risk better.

- Improve software quality.

- Develop productivity guidelines.

- Determine size and unit costs of software.

- Develop and refine estimation models.

- Raise process maturity levels.

- Develop and refine software standards.

- Improve the planning and proposal processes.

A software experience database is an important component of the management-driven software management process. It is a powerful tool for improving organizational performance. Every organization concerned with software development should establish such a database.

12.3 DATABASE MANAGEMENT SYSTEMS

A database, under control of a database management system (DBMS), is the conventional mode of data storage. Emerging measurement organizations may elect to begin their data storage gradually with a microcomputer application, or the decision may be made to permanently maintain the database on a microcomputer. An advantage of this system is that diskettes containing the database can be easily copied on many microcomputers throughout the organization. Such an arrangement allows a wide range of the staff to become familiar with the database.

Where the resources are available, a networked workstation or a mainframe DBMS may be used. Any of the alternatives is acceptable. A small DBMS on a microcomputer can handle up to a billion records. Most development organization collections will not exceed a few thousand records per year. The mainframe, on the other hand, usually offers the advantage of centralized maintenance and control and wide access.

The DBMS will manipulate the data in the database but the database structure has to serve the organization's development projects. These organizations, as well as the measurement function, should have an influence on the structure and contents of the database. Assuming the measurements to be stored have been selected, they should be organized according to database theory into entities, relationships, and attributes in the form of a data model. Consider normalizing the model to third normal form to prevent excessive use of storage space and loss of integrity through data redundancy. Also, doing so will enhance ease of information retrieval. Even if database implementation requires outside consultation, the recommendation stands, for its acquisition is a worthwhile investment.

12.4 MEASUREMENTS AND METRICS DATA COLLECTION

You need to use measurement data to support the software development process. This section describes several approaches to the collection of that data.

12.4.1 Definition

Data collection (for any purpose) may be defined as the activities of locating, gathering, organizing, and archiving information at a level consistent with the intent of the measurement goal that it is designed (or selected) to satisfy. In other words, you collect data at the highest organizational level consistent with the goal it satisfies. This definition means that you do not collect metrics data, for example, on a software development effort from individual time cards. Instead, you collect effort data from accounting records, which conglomerate effort data from the time cards and/or other sources in labor months or labor hours at the appropriate process or product level. In addition, you do not collect the size of a CSCI by visually counting individual source statements. Rather, you obtain the overall count from the code-counting facility built into the software development environment. The capacity to automatically count code should be one of the capabilities of the software development environment and should be used by the organization's configuration management organization as part of its normal way of doing business.

12.4.2 Organization and Activities

The data collection activity involves a "hands-on" approach. The organization with software metrics data collection responsibility should not simply send out forms and expect to receive data with any degree of reliability. The data collection function must follow up and support the filling out of forms. With the proactive support of the measurement analyst, if the forms are filled out at all, the data will probably be incomplete, inaccurate, and biased toward making the project performance look good. Often, project personnel will provide "actuals" that are not actual and that reflect project performance objectives rather than actual cost, schedule, and quality accomplishments. Therefore, you need to personally assure yourself that the data you have acquired has, in fact, been properly collected. The organization that has the responsibility for the software experience database, which in all probability is the metrics or measurement function, must collect actual performance data at the end of the project by personally reviewing project and accounting records. You should keep in mind that it is difficult to collect actuals at the end of the project if the project has not been tracked during its execution. Both the tracking of ongoing projects and the collection of actual project performance metrics data are measurement activities, regardless of what organizational function actually performs them. In all probability, it will be the measurement function, but it may be software development, systems engineering, or some other functional organization. In fact, the measurement function may be part of these organizations.

You should collect the metrics data in real time, i.e., at the planned time during the project and immediately upon completion of the project. It is a mistake to try to reconstruct measurement after the fact when the project records may be gone. Also, it is very difficult to collect the proper metrics data at the end of a project if the metrics group has not been tracking the project during the development. The tracking and monitoring effort provides the measurement personnel with a basic familiarity of the processes, products, and problems of the development project. This enables efficient and precise data collection.

The group with the data collection responsibility should take pains to reassure project personnel, both technical and management, that they are collecting the data to determine status and anticipate problems, not to evaluate personnel performance. They should reassure, whenever necessary, project personnel that the data does not affect their performance appraisals. To reinforce this statement, do not label the data with the names of any project personnel. Project personnel should be made to feel that they are participating in process and project improvement.

Most software development environments include a code-counting ability. You should use this ability to count source statements. Count both logical and physical lines. Count all source statements, not just executables, and count comments separately from the source statements. Also, be sure that you count statements that result in instructions as well as statements that result in data. Chapter 6 discusses code counting in more detail.

The software organization, together with the accounting organization, should establish a policy such that, for each software development project, the WBS must reflect the software product and process. There should be a separate cost account for every development activity, and development activities should be at least at the DOD-STD-2167A levels of preliminary design, detailed design, code and unit test, CSC integration test, and CSCI test or equivalent. You should use additional activities and a more detailed breakdown if possible. The activity cost accounts should tier up to the total cost account for the corresponding CSCI (or software product if there is only one CSCI or equivalent unit). There should be a separate tiering structure for every CSCI or major size software unit. Such a WBS makes the collection of cost (effort) data efficient, precise, and much easier.

12.5 DATA SOURCES

An organization that develops complex systems will have many information sources that it can use for software development tracking. Table 12-1 shows some metrics data and its probable sources.

12.6 WORK BREAKDOWN STRUCTURES

Figure 12-1 shows an example of a partial WBS for software as a subsystem, i.e., an organization for financial reporting in which the various major (developmental) hardware components and the various major (developmental) software components each have their own tiering structure (Department of Defense 1991b). The system or platform is at Level 1, the highest level of the tiering structure and the level that contains the cost account(s) for total (developmental) costs. Major subsystems are at Level 2, and major components of the subsystems are at Level 3. The Level 2 WBS in Figure 12-1 shows a structure for application software. The Level 2 structure could also show a structure for system software (e.g., executive or operating systems) and/or for support software (logistics software, test scenarios, diagnostics, etc.).

Often the software and systems engineering organizations will work in tandem on the same system or subsystem. The software organization may have the software development responsibility from (software) design through CSC integration test as Level 4 activities. The software organization may have (as usual) responsibility for user documentation such as user and operator manuals and version description documents. The software organization may also have the responsibility for doing software builds (often called configuration management) for software system test and for maintaining the library of software components; but in the WBS in Figure 12-1, the systems engineering (test) organization has this responsibility. The systems engineering organization may have the requirements analysis responsibility and the test planning responsibility for both the developmental hardware (if any) and software as Level 4 activities. In addition, the systems engineering organization may have the system test responsibility (CSCI test) as shown in the partial WBS example in Figure 12-1.

The defects found by the test organization will cause code rework and perhaps design rework. These rework activities should have separate cost accounts. Also, it is desirable that the cost of each iteration through design or code for rework should be recorded within those cost accounts. Retest cost or effort in CSC integration testing can be recorded as part of the code rework cost account. The cost or effort data for each rework iteration will prove valuable in estimating the effectiveness of risk management efforts.

Measurement Category	Indicator Group	Organization	Data Sources
Size	Current estimate or count of size	Software development (library) or configuration management	1. Software development plan 2. Count from programming environment or CASE tool 3. Configuration management reports 4. Software library
Cost	Cost	Finance	Accounting reports
Schedule	Elapsed time	Software development	Software development plan
Stability	Engineering change proposals (ECPs)	Systems engineering (change control) or project management	1. ECP status report 2. Program management reports
	Undefined requirements Satisfied requirements	Systems engineering (change control)	1. Requirements analysis reports 2. Requirements traceability matrix
	Software action items (SAIs) Project staffing	Software development Software development	Software status report Software status report
Status	Software progress	Software development	Software status report
Quality	Current and predicted defects (reviews and inspections) Program trouble reports (PTRs)	Software quality engineering (assurance) Software quality engineering or system test	1. Software quality plan 2. Software quality status report PTR status report
Earned value	Overall proportion complete (OPC) or Earned value (EV)	Software development	Software status report
Computer resources	Computer resources	Software development or systems engineering	Software and system development plans

Table 12-1. *Data Sources*

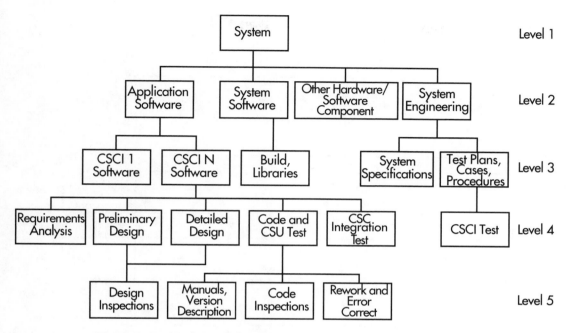

Figure 12-1. *Work Breakdown Structure for Software as a Subsystem*

Figure 12-2 shows an alternative WBS with software as a subcomponent. In this structure, costs are gathered by component. All of the cost accounts are one level lower than in the previous WBS because the structure tiers up to a subsystem rather than a system. It is very important that the WBS provide "slots" for all of the activities for which you wish to collect labor and other cost data.

12.7 METRICS FOR MANAGING SOFTWARE SUBCONTRACTORS

A contractor needs to require the same size, cost, schedule, and quality measurements and metrics from the software subcontractor as he requires from his own software development projects. He needs to collect experience data at the completion of the contract at least to the extent of the minimum experience data set. But since the contractor, in most cases, will not have direct access to the subcontractor's data sources, it will be necessary to get the subcontractor to report the data. This means that the contractor must validate the reported data to a considerable extent. But if he has required data reports from the subcontractor at planned intervals during the contract execution, validation of the final actuals should be fairly straightforward. Note that it is necessary to make all software data reporting require-

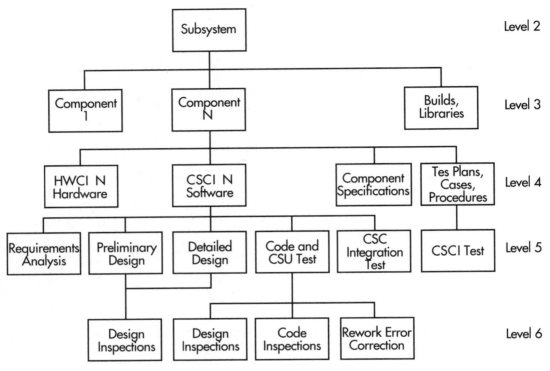

Figure 12-2. *Work Breakdown Structure for Software as a Subcomponent*

ments a part of any subcontract. If this is not done, it is a virtual certainty that you will not be able to get the data from a subcontractor.

The requirement that the subcontractor report software metrics data during the contract execution should be recognized as very important. The subcontractor should also report tracking and monitoring data at least to the extent of the minimum data set for tracking and monitoring. The contractor should always monitor software subcontractors; and he should plan to assign managerial, technical, and financial personnel to this monitoring function.

The contractor should apply the same (or equivalent) software standards to the subcontractor that govern the contractor. The subcontractor WBS should be to the same level of detail that the contractor must use.

Often the subcontractor will report effort expended in terms of dollars and not LM or LH. This format often appears in the monthly bill that the subcontractor submits. The contractor will need to get an overall (for the contract) average dollars/LM or dollars/LH metric from the subcontractor so that he can convert this information to LM or LH.

12.8 DATA VALIDATION

Collected data is not necessarily validated data. It is quite possible that development project personnel can record or transmit inaccurate or otherwise "wrong" data to the measurements/metrics function. It is also possible that the measurement group (i.e., the data collection agency) will misunderstand the information that it is given and will again record "wrong" data. So, it is always necessary to validate or test the data for accuracy before you use it in an analysis (Basili and Weiss 1984).

One method to validate data is to use a general reasonableness check approach. For example, if the reported total cost of a software development project is 430 LM and you have observed approximately 20 developers working for 20 months (400 LM), then the observed and reported effort are reasonably close; within 20 to 25 percent of each other will satisfy the test. However, if you are told that the overall development labor rate is 5.125 LM/KSLOC and your investigation reveals that 125 LM was used to develop a (counted) 50 KSLOC (2.500 LM/KSLOC), then the reported and observed values are far apart, and the data values are thus highly suspect.

You can test size and schedule measurables in similar ways. For example, if it is reported that the size of a delivered software product is 142 KSLOC and that investigation reveals that similar products have been at least 210 KSLOC, then additional investigation is required. Perhaps the code was counted by very different methods for the product in question. Perhaps some program units were inadvertently excluded from the latest product size count. Another possibility is that data statements were not counted.

Another method of validating cost or effort data is to use the top-down estimation methods discussed in Section 6.7 to check the cost or effort allocation that is reported. For example, suppose that a project involves software development but no hardware development, and suppose you find in the accounting records that the total cost of software development was 100 LM and that the cost of product logistical support was 50 LM. Chapter 6 suggests that the ratio of software development to logistical support should be about 5 to 1, certainly not 2 to 1 as in this scenario with software development but no hardware development. Thoroughly investigate this apparent discrepancy. There may be plausible reasons for the high product support cost, which you should record.

You should also validate the metrics data collected to ensure that it really accomplishes the purpose that it was designed to accomplish. Use the GQM paradigm to select the metric used. Metrics thus selected should fulfill that purpose since the GQM paradigm forces the metric to correspond to a specific project goal. The GQM paradigm is itself a method for validating metrics data.

Data validation is based on experience tempered by common sense. It frequently involves using data from various sources and comparing them, or it may involve checking the reported data against some standard or rule of thumb. You can validate data for reasonableness without much trouble, but it is very difficult to establish the precision of reported data.

12.9 SUMMARY OF RECOMMENDATIONS

The recommendations on data collection and validation presented in this section are:

- Begin data collection as soon as you institute a measurements program, regardless of process maturity level.

- Collect at least the minimum data set (or the equivalent as defined by your organization).

- Arrange for management, with the help of the metrics group, to define the measurements data to be collected. You should use the GQM paradigm to help select metrics.

- Ensure that the software standards and policies define the data collection methods, indicator construction, metrics definition, and project monitoring procedures.

- Feed data back to those responsible in order to improve the process and the products it produces.

- Plan for the metrics group to collect experience data (actuals) at the end of each software development project.

- Ensure that the metrics group maintains a software experience database.

- Arrange for the software project WBS to gather cost data down to the level of the development activities within each CSCI.

- Establish a software experience database to aid in deriving software metrics and in estimating. This database should contain the "actuals" (actual costs, counted sizes, etc.) from the process and product aspects of the project collected upon completion of the project.

- Save metrics for use in process improvement, for increasing product quality, and for refining standards and estimating algorithms.

- Encourage project personnel to feel that, in contributing data, they are part of process improvement. Reassure them that their personal performance is not being audited.

- Record LM or LH as well as dollars for cost performance. LM and LH should include overtime, even if unpaid.

- Establish separate WBS cost accounts for each CSCI. Establish separate CSCI-specific cost accounts for each development activity that tier up to each total CSCI cost account.

Chapter
13

INTEGRATED EXAMPLE

13.1 OVERVIEW

This section presents an integrated example that covers the estimation of software product size, cost, and schedule, and of cost and schedule risk. The purpose of the example is to help you apply some of the quantitative methods presented in other sections of this book in a comprehensive manner. You should estimate not only software product size, cost, and schedule, but also the degree of risk or exposure that your organization should expect to face in attempting to meet cost and schedule goals that have been established (say, by management and marketing).

This section considers the example of estimating for the development of an embedded software product from scratch (i.e., no reuse). The software is to be coded in Ada. You are going to estimate the size of the system, the cost of software development (no estimate of CM, systems engineering, etc., is required), and the duration of the development process (i.e., development schedule). In addition, you are going to estimate the cost (equated with effort, here) and the corresponding schedule, which reflects a 20% risk (or a 0.2 probability) of being exceeded during development.

13.2 ESTIMATION OF SOFTWARE PRODUCT SIZE

In a typical software development situation, you must estimate the size of the software product before you estimate the effort and schedule. This is because size is the primary determiner of cost and schedule (and of the defect content of the software, as well). Now, we consider a specific example. You apply the statistical method presented in Section 7.4 to the example of the four-function software product also shown there. As indicated in Table 7-1, reproduced here for your convenience as Table 13-1, the software project will consist of the development of four software functions that you have estimated to have an overall expected size of 51.51 KSLOC.

Since this estimate has some uncertainty associated with it (as all such estimates do), you should develop an approximate distribution of the range of the total size of your prospective four-function product. You should select a number of values for the size metric and ascribe a probability to each of them. They are to be interpreted as interval estimates. When ascribing a probability to a particular value of size, you are signifying that that probability applies to a range about that size figure. The range of the size values you select should cover the possibilities that might be expected. It is often appropriate in such cases to ascribe a probability of 0.50 (50%) to the "expected value" derived from a statistical estimation procedure, such as shown in Section 7.4, the results of which are summarized in Table 13-1. Further, you might identify the most "optimistic" (typically, the smallest) size that might be anticipated. This might correspond to what the marketing people feel is a "winning" figure. Correspondingly, at the other end of the range of possible sizes, you also might ascribe a relatively low probability to some large value for the size of the four-function product of our example. You should thus select three or four values to cover the range of sizes that you expect for your prospective software product.

Consider the statistical size estimate that you developed that is summarized in Table 13-1. You will use the information summarized in this table plus available expert opinion and experience (yours and others, ideally at least partially captured in your organization's software experience database) to develop this distribution based in part on the figures in this table and/or derivable from it. It is reasonable for you to ascribe a probability of 0.50 to the expected value of the size of the product, seen to be 51.51 KSLOC in Table 13-1. Further, suppose that experience and expert opinion suggests that there is only a 0.20 probability that the total size of the project is in the vicinity of the total of the smallest sizes estimated for the four functions, i.e., 5.83 + 9.375 + 6.3 + 5.875 = 27.38 KSLOC (per Table 13-1). Further, you come to feel (backed up by consultation with those skilled in the application area to be

Function	Smallest	Most Likely	Largest	Expected*	Standard Deviation*
A	5,830	8,962	17,750	9,905	1,987
B	9,375	14,625	28,000	15,979	3,104
C	6,300	13,700	36,250	16,225	4,992
D	5,875	8,975	14,625	9,400	1,458
Overall			E_{tot}=51,509	σ_{tot} =6,374	

*Using PERT-size formulas as shown in Section 7.4.

***Table 13-1.** Size Estimation Table Example*

addressed by the new software system and by the experienced software people who will lead its development) that there is a nontrivial possibility that the size of the software system will be substantially larger than the expected value given in the table. After some thought, you ascribe a probability of 0.25 to the size value, 70.63 KSLOC (equal to 51.51 KSLOC, the expected value, plus 3 times the standard deviation of 6.374 KSLOC). Finally, you have come to believe that there is a very slim possibility that the size of the prospective software system could be as large as 100 KSLOC. Therefore, you decide to ascribe a probability of 0.05 to a product size of 100.0 KSLOC (Table 13.2). It is very important that you normalize the probabilities assigned to the estimates of size that you derive by consultation with experts as described above. You must ensure that the probabilities of the alternative sizes that you determine, such as those shown in Table 13-2, sum to 1.00. This is because the alternative possible sizes that you identify in your estimation process must cover the entire range of possible size of your new software product.

Remember to be careful in your selection of the range of estimates that you use. Do not use rose-colored glasses! If you really think that there is a possibility of the prospective system's being very large, say, even 2 or more times its "expected value" per an analysis such as that summarized in Table 13-1, then do include that figure in the range of sizes that you report. Of course, you also have to assign some probability to it.

You can combine the set of size estimates shown in Table 13-2 to produce a weighted average, or "expected value," of the size of your product (as stated in Section 7.8). This is 53.89 KSLOC (= (27.38.0.20) + (51.51 $\times$ 0.50) + ...). If you are asked for the (one or your best) estimate of the size of the new software product, this is the value you should cite.

Always keep in mind the basis for what you are doing when you are developing an estimate. You are trying to develop an estimate that uses all of the information available to you (which may be principally expert opinion and well-considered experience) and put it together in a rational manner.

KSLOC	Probability
27.38	0.20
51.51	0.50
70.63	0.25
100.00	0.05
Total	1.00

Table 13-2. *Example Size Probability Distribution*

13.3 ESTIMATION OF SOFTWARE DEVELOPMENT UNIT COST AND PRODUCTIVITY

The next step for you to take is to estimate the overall unit cost of developing the software for your prospective four-function software product. You are going to use an activity-based model (as described in Section 8.4). The general form of such a model is:

$$cost = unit\ cost \times size$$

Here, "cost" is expressed in LM (could be in LH, if you prefer); "unit cost" is expressed in LM/KSLOC; and "size" is expressed in KSLOC. Recall that productivity, P, is defined as P=1,000/U, where U= unit cost. Thus, if the (overall) unit cost for software development is 10 LM/KSLOC, then the corresponding productivity is 100 SLOC/LM (=1,000/10).

As Chapter 8 described, you determine the unit cost for the overall software development process by adding the unit costs (in LM or LH per KSLOC) for each of the activities that compose the software development process. In the present case, you determine from talking with the software manager for the project that the software process will be composed of the following activities: requirements analysis, preliminary design, detailed design, code and unit test, CSC integration test, and CSCI test. Your organization has a set of baseline unit costs for these activities, based on its recent Ada development experience for software products reasonably similar to the prospective software product for which you are developing this estimate. They are shown in Table 13-3, below. Note that the unit costs in this table are identical to those in Table 8-10.

You now estimate the value of unit cost for the new software development project. You use an approach analogous to that which you employed for estimating the size of your software product, as described in Section 13.2. That is, you make several estimates that you

Ada Model Activity	LM/KSLOC	Percent
Requirements Analysis	0.74	7.4
Preliminary Design	1.67	16.7
Detailed Design	2.22	22.2
Code and Unit Test	2.22	22.2
CSC Integration Test	1.60	16.0
CSCI Test	1.55	15.5
Total	10.00	100.0

Table 13-3. Baseline Ada Development Unit Costs

believe will cover the range of possibilities that you foresee. Each of these estimates is based on a different set of assumptions. You assign a probability to each one.

You now consider how the new software development process is expected to differ from the ones on which the Ada unit cost data in your database (as shown in Table 13-3) is based. You learn from the software development manager that some new software tools are going to be used during development. You estimate, based on consultation with various members of the software development staff and tempered by your own experience, that the effect of these tools is expected to increase preliminary design costs by 10 percent and to decrease detailed design costs by 20 percent. Now, you estimate these effects on the baseline unit costs (in Table 13-3). You apply the 10 percent and 20 percent figures just cited as follows. You expect the unit cost for preliminary design will be 1.84 LM/KSLOC (= 1.67 × 1.10) and that the unit cost for detailed design will be 1.78 LM/KSLOC (= 2.22 × 0.80).

Assuming all other unit costs for development activities remain as shown in Table 13-3, the estimated overall unit cost of development, if the tools are used, is expected to be 9.73 LM/KSLOC. These calculations are shown in Table 13-4. After some reflection and discussion with the software development manager and some other people, you decide to assign a probability of occurrence of 0.40 to the unit cost of 9.73 LM/KSLOC.

Upon some reflection, you decide to cover in your estimates, the possibility that the unit cost will be significantly larger than past experience suggests. You do this just to "cover your bets" and to reflect the (estimated to be) very slim possibility that the new application could be found to be much more difficult to develop than the software systems in your database (whose overall average unit cost is 10.00 LM/KSLOC). You believe that the corresponding (high) unit cost would be 15.00 LM/KSLOC in such a case (50 percent greater than your baseline unit cost figure). Because you believe that this is a rather unlikely situation, you ascribe a probability of 0.10 to it.

Ada Model Activity	LM/KSLOC	Percent
Requirements Analysis	0.74	7.6
Preliminary Design	1.84(=1.67x1.1)	18.9
Detailed Design	1.78(=2.22x0.80)	18.3
Code and Unit Test	2.22	22.8
CSC Integration Test	1.60	16.5
CSCI Test	1.55	15.9
Total	9.73	100.0

Table 13-4. *Example Unit Cost Probability Distribution*

The three alternative values of unit labor (cost) that you have estimated, as described above, are tallied in Table 13-5. As in the case of the alternative size estimates (see Table 13-2), the probabilities of the alternative labor unit costs must sum to 1.0. This is because the alternative possible unit costs that you identify in your estimation process must cover the entire range of possible unit costs of your new software product.

Combine the set of unit cost estimates shown in Table 13-5 to produce a weighted average, or "expected value," of the unit cost of your product in a manner similar to what was done for size (see the end of Section 13.2). The weighted average unit cost is 10.39 LM/KSLOC (= (9.73 × 0.40) + (10.00 × 0.50) + ...). If you are asked for the (one or your best) estimate of the unit cost of the new software product, this is the value you should cite. The productivity corresponding to this unit cost figure is 96 SLOC/LM ((1000/10.39)=96.25).

13.4 ESTIMATES OF POSSIBLE COST VALUES, THEIR DISTRIBUTION, AND COST RISK

Now, you develop a range of costs (in LM), based on the range of sizes and of unit costs that you have estimated. You develop one (estimated) value of cost for each size of unit cost pair, using the formula (given earlier):

$$cost = unit\ cost \times size$$

Since you have estimated four values of size and three values of unit cost, you compute twelve values of cost. Further, you compute the probability of occurrence of each of these twelve values. Each of these probabilities is computed using the formula:

$$prob(cost) = prob(unit\ cost) \times prob(size)$$

It is convenient to arrange your calculations as shown in Table 13-6.

LM/KSLOC	Probability
9.73	0.40
10.00	0.50
15.00	0.10
Total	1.00

Table 13-5. *Example Unit Cost Probability Distribution*

Probability x 10^{-2}/Unit Cost (LM/KSLOC)	Probability x 10^{-2}/Size (KSLOC)			
	0.20	0.50	0.25	0.05
	27.38	51.51	70.63	100.00
0.100	2.00	5.00	2.50	0.50
15.000	410.70	772.65	1,059.45	1,500.00
0.500	10.00	25.00	12.50	2.50
10.000	273.80	515.10	706.30	1,000.00
0.400	8.00	20.00	10.00	2.00
9.730	266.41	501.19	687.23	973.00

Table 13-6. *Example Distribution of Labor Months and Their Probabilities*

Next, you should rewrite the data in this table in order of increasing costs, commencing with the smallest estimated value, 266.41 LM. The results of doing so are shown in Table 13-7.

You should interpret the cumulative probabilities given in Table 13-7 as now described with reference to an example. The table indicates that there is a 0.97 probability that the cost for the development will be less than or equal to 1,000 LM (and 0.03 that it will be greater than that figure).

You can combine the set of cost estimates shown in Table 13-7 to produce a weighted average, or "expected value," of the cost of your product in a manner similar to what was done for size and unit cost. The weighted average cost is 560.0 LM (= (266.41 × 0.08) + (273.80 × 0.10) + ...). If you are asked for the (one or your best) estimate of the cost of the new software product, this is the value you should cite.

You can use the information presented in Table 13-7 as the basis for the calculation of cost risk. You recall (from Section 13.1) that you have been asked to determine the estimated cost for the software product development that corresponds to a 20 percent risk. This is defined as the value of cost that has a 0.20 probability of being exceeded. You go to Table 13-7 and interpolate between the two cost values that bracket the desired (cumulative) probability of 0.80 (= 1 − 0.20). They are: 687.23 LM (corresponding to a cumulative probability of 0.75) and 706.30 LM (corresponding to a cumulative probability of 0.8725). You thus determine the cost estimate for the 20 percent risk to be 694.86 LM. This means that there is a 20 percent risk (a probability of 0.20) that the actual cost of software development will be greater than 694.86 LM.

You plot the costs and the cumulative probabilities corresponding to them from Table 13-7 in the manner shown in Figure 13-1.

Cost (LM)	Probability (Percent)	Cumulative Probability (Percent)
266.41	8.00	8.00
273.80	10.00	18.00
410.70	2.00	20.00
501.19	20.00	40.00
515.10	25.00	65.00
687.23	10.00	75.00
706.30	12.50	87.50
772.65	5.00	92.50
973.00	2.00	94.50
1,000.00	2.50	97.00
1,059.45	2.50	99.50
1,500.00	0.50	100.00

Table 13-7. Example Linear Distribution of Costs

The figure also depicts the 20-percent-cost risk value just calculated.

Another risk type question could be asked of you that would be the complement of the one you just answered,"What is the cost corresponding to a 20 percent risk?" That other question would be, "What is the risk corresponding to a cost of ___LM?" The specific question could be, "What is the risk corresponding to a cost of 694.86 LM?" That type of question would be answered by determining the cost corresponding to the probability value stated in the question, using interpolation of the cost values instead of the probability values as was done in the example.

You might find it useful to plot the costs that you have estimated and their associated probabilities. That is, you plot the data "Cost" and the "Probability (Percent)" columns of Table 13-7. You thus produce the "probability density function" for the estimated possible costs of your software development project. This is done in Figure 13-2. You will observe that this plot looks roughly like a normal probability density function. This suggests that, in some instances, you might find it useful to approximate the density function of the costs for a software development project by a normal distribution.

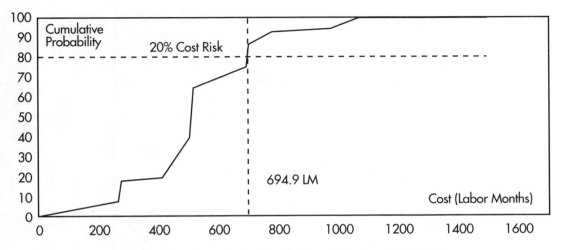

Figure 13-1. *Cumulative Distribution of Costs and Cost Risk*

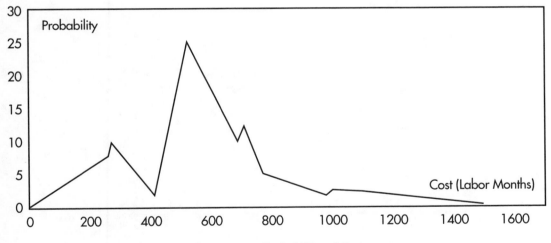

Figure 13-2. *Probability of Costs*

13.5 ESTIMATES OF POSSIBLE SCHEDULE VALUES AND RISK

Now, you develop an estimate of the amount of (calendar) time, or the schedule, required to perform the development that you have just costed. As you can recall from Section 8.3, there is a COCOMO schedule model that relates cost or effort in LM and schedule in months. The model equation is of the form:

$$T = aC^b$$

where T is the schedule in months, C is the cost in LM, and a and b are empirical constants.

Ideally, you have data about past projects in your database that you can use to calculate values for the constants a and b based on the experience of your organization. Assume, for the present example, that you do not have such data. Therefore, you will use the values in COCOMO. In Section 8.3, you will note a value of 2.5 for a and three alternative values for b: 0.32, 0.35, and 0.38. These values are quite close. Use a value of 0.33. It is a good engineering approximation and allows you to recognize that schedule essentially varies as the 1/3 power of cost, thus facilitating estimating the effect of cost changes on schedule. Thus, you decide to estimate the length of the development schedule, T (in months), as a function of the cost (in LM) using the equation:

$$T = 2.5 \cdot (LM)^{0.33}$$

Now, you calculate the values of schedule corresponding to the values of cost you have determined. The cost values, the corresponding schedule values, and their individual and cumulative probabilities are presented in Table 13-8. Note that this table contains the same values for cost as presented in Table 13-7.

Cost (LM)	Schedule (Months)	Probability (Percent)	Cumulative Probability (Percent)
266.41	15.79	8.00	8.00
273.80	15.93	10.00	18.00
410.70	18.21	2.00	20.00
501.19	19.45	20.00	40.00
515.10	19.63	25.00	65.00
687.23	21.59	10.00	75.00
706.30	21.78	12.50	87.50
772.65	22.44	5.00	92.50
973.00	24.21	2.00	94.50
1,000.00	24.43	2.50	97.00
1,059.45	24.90	2.50	99.50
1,500.00	27.93	0.50	100.00

Table 13-8. *Example Linear Distribution of Costs and Schedule*

You can combine the set of schedule estimates shown in Table 13-8 to produce a weighted average, or "expected value," of the schedule of your product in a manner similar to what was done for cost. The weighted average schedule is 19.9 months (= (15.79 × 0.08) + (15.93 × 0.10) + ...). If you are asked for *the* (one or your best) estimate of the schedule, or period of time, expected to be required to develop the new software product, this is the value you should cite.

Determine the estimated schedule corresponding to a 20 percent risk, using interpolation as in the case of cost risk estimation. Applying this method to the values in the table, you estimate the 20 percent schedule risk point to be 21.67 months. Because schedule varies only as the third power of cost, you would expect (and can observe from the table) that the schedule uncertainty range is considerably smaller than the cost values from Table 13-8. Similar to the situation with costs, this cumulative plot can be used to help you to answer questions such as, "What risk do I assume if I adopt a development schedule of 21.7 months?"

Figure 13-3 is a plot of the cumulative distribution of the possible schedule

Also, analogous to what was suggested that you do with cost data, you might find it useful to plot the schedule values that you have estimated and their associated probabilities. That is, you plot the data "Schedule" and the "Probability (Percent)" columns of Table 13-8. You thus produce the "probability density function" for the estimated possible values of schedule for your software development project. This is done in Figure 13-4. You will

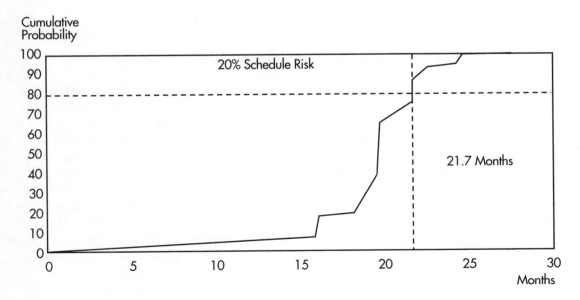

Figure 13-3. *Cumulative Distribution of Schedule and Schedule Risk*

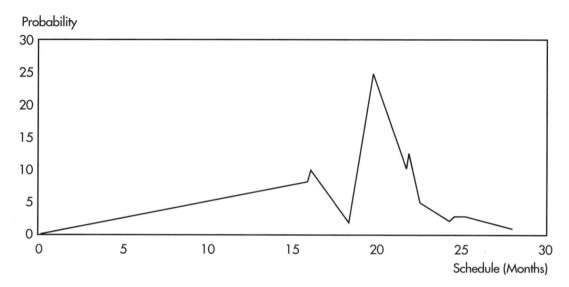

Figure 13-4. *Probability of Schedule*

observe that this plot looks roughly like a normal probability density function. This suggests that, in some instances, you might find it useful to approximate the probability density function of the estimated possible periods of time (schedule values) for a software development project as a normal distribution.

13.6 ESTIMATING PROJECT STAFFING PROFILE

Now, you develop a profile or spread of the effort you have estimated. You will estimate the number of full-time equivalent people that you believe is required per month to develop your prospective software product. You will use the Rayleigh curve model to initiate a staffing profile, using the techniques presented in Chapter 9. You should use a two-step process to develop a staffing profile. First, make an estimate based on the Rayleigh model. Next, look at the spread the Rayleigh model provides and decide if it looks reasonable, based on whatever experience your organization has. Your evaluation of the profile may lead you to modify it, perhaps adding more effort (i.e., a faster build-up) to the initial portion of the spread as well adding to the the staffing level in the later part of the development period. In addition, you will need to round off the numbers in your Rayleigh-based estimate. For example, Table 13-9 has entries carried to two decimal places (for the sake of showing a direct application of the formulas presented in Chapter 9 for labor resource spreading). However, practically, speaking, you would take this "theoretical" spread and probably round the monthly staffing figures to the nearest 0.5 staff month. In addition, of

Month Number	Full-Time Equivalent Staff Per Month, F(t)	Cumulative Number of Staff Months, Y(t)
1	11.70	11.70
2	33.94	45.64
3	48.79	94.43
4	70.68	165.11
5	74.71	239.82
6	76.85	316.67
7	73.85	390.52
8	66.97	457.49
9	57.63	515.12
10	47.24	562.36
11	37.00	599.36
12	27.74	627.10
13	19.96	647.06
14	13.76	660.82
15	9.13	669.95
16	5.83	675.78
17	3.57	679.35
18	2.11	681.46
19	1.19	682.65
20	0.67	683.32

Table 13-9. *Example Profile*

course, you would suitably adjust them, as mentioned above, to reflect your knowledge of the practicalities of the project that cannot be reflected in the output of the simple Rayleigh model that you have just applied. You may find that several modification cycles of your estimate may be required.

Now, you are going to develop an estimate of the profile or month-by-month spread of the staff required to develop the new software product for which you have already estimated the size, development labor, and duration of development (or schedule) required. You are going to do a spread of the number of full-time equivalent staff needed to apply the weighted average figure of 560.0 LM (see Section 13.4) that you have already estimated over a 20 month period (you estimated a weighted average of 19.9 months in Section 13.5). You might do the same for several other possible levels of the development staffing, such as that corresponding to the 20 percent risk level of 695 LM. You would use the technique presented here to do so.

Now, you need to determine the number of staff (or full-time equivalent) labor months that are (likely to be) required to yield the 560.0 LM you have estimated are needed to develop the new software product. You develop a ratio of full-time hours to billable (or applicable) hours. This is in recognition of the fact that people are not available to apply to a job 8 hours per day, 5 days per week, 52 weeks per year. They take vacation. Your company has holidays. People become ill. Also, you have to expect that your staff will attend meetings and might be used on proposals and/or at least briefly be applied to other projects for periods of time while they are nominally assigned full-time to your project. We are not going to consider the effect of overtime directly. Applying the software development staff on the basis of some planned overtime can be a fruitful business strategy, especially to enable your organization to respond to marketplace demands such as to meet some tight schedule.

Now, we develop an example value of the ratio of full-time hours to billable (or applicable) hours. Your particular organization's situation may be different from that reflected in the numbers now used. There are 2,080 (= 52 × 40 × 8) potential work hours available in one year. Suppose, furthermore, that the average software development staff member has an annual vacation of 80 hours, 80 hours of company-paid holidays, and, on average, 24 hours of company-paid sick leave. Thus, your hypothetical staff member could potentially bill or directly charge 1,896 hours (= 2,080 − (80 + 80 + 24)) = 2,080 − 184) per annum to the development effort. Further, our estimate should recognize the likelihood that this staff member will charge, say, 10 percent of his available time to such items as training, various meetings, proposal writing, etc. In the present case, this would be another 190 hours that are not available to the software project development manager. Thus, you estimate that 1,706 hours (= 1,896 − 190) are available per annum per staff member assigned to the software development project. Thus, you can estimate the ratio of full-time hours to billable (or applicable) hours as equal to 1.22 (= 2,080/1,706).

Therefore, in the present estimating situation, you should spread 683.2 LM (= 560 × 1.22) over the 20 month development period. To do this, you use the Rayleigh model presented in Chapter 9. This is:

$$Y(t) = \frac{k}{X} \cdot \left(1 - e^{-\frac{t^2}{t_p^2}}\right)$$

where Y(t) is the amount of effort (area under the curve) from time = 0 to time = t months; X is the ratio of the peak staffing level to the staffing level at the time of delivery, t_d (we use X = 0.999 here, which is the default value); K is the number of labor months to be spread over the development period, $0 - t_d$ (K = 683.2); and K/X = 683.9 (call it 684).

It is useful to recall that $E = K \times X$, where E is the area under the Rayleigh curve from 0 to infinity (we are interested only in the curve from 0 to $t_d = 20$, of course).

Before we can compute the values of K(t), the cumulative staffing curve, and of the monthly staffing curve, $F(t) = Y(t) - Y(t-1)$, we need the value of the parameter t_p, the (time) location of the peak of the monthly staffing curve. You should do this using the method illustrated in Section 9.6, by solving the following equation for t_p:

$$0.999 = 1 - e^{-\frac{20^2}{t_p^2}}$$

Solving this equation, you find that the $t_p = 5.38$ months. Therefore, $1/(2t_p^2) = 0.0173$. Thus, the equation for the cumulative value of the staff months from 0 to t months is:

$$k(t) = 684 \cdot (1 - e^{-0.0173 \cdot (t^2)})$$

This equation is now applied for $t = 0$ to $t = 20$, and the results are presented in Table 13-9. Also, the values of the full-time equivalent staff per month ($= Y(t) - Y(t-1)$ for each value to $t = 20$) are plotted in Figure 13-5.

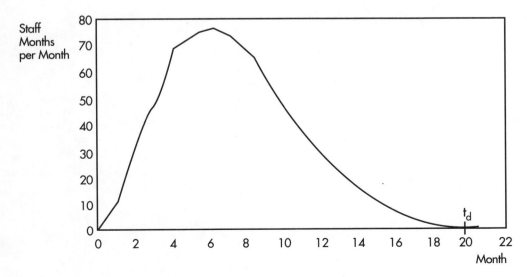

Figure 13-5. *Staff Months Per Month*

13.7 RECOMMENDATIONS FOR ESTIMATION

- Develop a range of estimates for size, unit cost, productivity, cost, and development schedule.

- Estimate the "expected values" for the size, cost, and development schedule. These are the values of each of the alternatives that you have identified for size, etc., weighted by its probability of occurrence. If you are asked for "your best estimate" for any or all of these parameters, respond with the "expected values."

- Estimate the size before you estimate the other parameters of interest.

- Use the ranges of size, unit costs, and schedule values that you have estimated, together with the management-determined objectives for cost and schedule, to determine the risk (or probability) of not attaining the cost and schedule objectives.

- Always keep in mind the basis for what you are doing when you are developing an estimate. You are trying to develop an estimate that uses all of the information available to you (which may be principally expert opinion and well-considered experience) and put it together in a rational manner.

- The objective of computing is insight, not numbers!

Abbreviations and Acronyms

AAF	Application adjustment factor		GFE	Government-furnished equipment
ADSI	Number of delivered source instructions		GQM	Goal-question-metric
CASE	Computer-aided software engineering		HIPO	Hierarchical input-process-output
CDR	Critical design review		HOL	Higher order language
CM	Configuration management		HW	Hardware
CMM	Capability maturity model		HWCI	Hardware configuration item
COCOMO	Constructive Cost Model		IDD	Interface design document
COPMO	Cooperative Programming Model		I/O	Input/output
COTS	Commercial off-the-shelf		IRS	Interface requirements specification
CPU	Central processing unit		ITD	Inception to date
CSC	Computer software component		KDSI	Thousand delivered source instructions
CSCI	Computer software configuration item		KESLOC	Thousand equivalent source lines of code
CSU	Computer software unit		KSLOC	Thousand source lines of code
DBMS	Database management system		LH	Labor hours
DM	Data management		LM	Labor months
EAC	Estimate at completion		LSS	Logical source statement
ECP	Engineering change proposal		MDSM	Measurement-driven software management
EDSI	Equivalent delivered source instructions		MFG	Manufacturing
ESLOC	(Cost) equivalent to new source lines of code		mips	Millions of instructions per second
ETC	Estimate to complete		MIS	Management information system
ETVX	Entry-task-verification-exit		MODP	Modern programming practices
EV	Earned value		MTBF	Mean time between failure
FQT	Final qualification test			

MTTR	Mean time to repair	SPC	Statistical process control
OPC	Overall proportion complete	SQA	Software quality assurance
PDL	Program design language	SQF	Software quality factors
PDR	Preliminary design review	SRR	Software requirements review
PSS	Physical source statement	SRS	Software requirements specification
PTR	Program trouble report		
QA	Quality assurance	SSS	System/segment specification
SAI	Software action item	STD	Software test description
SDD	Software design document	STP	Software test plan
SDP	Software development plan	SUM	Software users manual
SE	Systems engineering	SW	Software
SEI	Software Engineering Institute	TDEV	Development time in months
SEPG	Software engineering process group	TE	Test and evaluation
		TLH	Total labor hours
SLOC	Source line(s) of code (also known as source statement)	TLM	Total labor months
		VDD	Version description document
SLOD	Source line(s) of design	WBS	Work breakdown structure

REFERENCES

Air Force Systems Command, 1986: *Software Management Indicators.* AFSCP 800-43. Washington, D.C.: U.S. Air Force Systems Command.

Albrecht, A.J., 1979: Measuring Application Development Productivity. *Application Development Symposium Proceedings, GUIDE and SHARE International.* Monterey, California.

Albrecht, A.J., and J.E. Gaffney, Jr., 1983: Software Function, Source Lines of Code, Development Effort Prediction: A Software Science Validation. *IEEE Transactions on Software Engineering* SE-9.

Army Materiel Command, 1987: *Software Management Indicators,* AMC-P 70-13. Alexandria, Virginia: U.S. Army Materiel Command.

Bailey, E.K., 1984: *A Framework for Evaluating APSDE Usability.* Alexandria, Virginia: Institute for Defense Analysis.

Balda, D.M., and D.A. Gustafson, 1990: Cost Estimation Models for the Reuse and Prototype Software Development Life-Cycles. *ACM Sigsoft Software Engineering Notes* 15, 3:1-18.

Barker, T.B., 1990: *Engineering Quality by Design: Interpreting the Taguchi Method.* New York, New York: Marcel Dekker.

Basili, V.R., and D.M. Weiss, 1984: A Methodology for Collecting Valid Software Engineering Data. *IEEE Transactions on Software Engineering* SE-10, 6.

Baumert, J.H. andM.S. McWhinney, 1992: *Software Measures and the Capability Maturity Model,* CMU/SEI-92-TR-25. Pittsburgh, Pennsylvania: Software Engineering Institute.

Boehm, B.W., 1978: *Characteristics of Software Quality.* New York, New York: North Holland.

Boehm, B.W., 1981: Software Engineering Economics. Englewood Cliffs, New Jersey: Prentice-Hall.

Boehm, B.W., 1983: Software Cost Estimation: Outstanding Research Issues, Workshop on Software Cost Engineering. Bedford, Massachusetts: MITRE Corporation.

Boehm, B.W., 1987: Rapid Prototyping, Risk Management, 2167, and the Ada Process Model. *Proceedings of the Electronic Industries Association,* 1987 G-33/G-34 Workshop. Washington, D.C.

Boehm, B.W., 1988: A Spiral Model of Software Development and Enhancement. *IEEE Computer.*

Bowen, T.P., G.B. Wigle, and J.T. Tsai, 1985: *SPECIFICATION OF SOFTWARE QUALITY ATTRIBUTES: Software Quality Specification Guidebook,* RADC-TR-85-37. Rome, New York: Rome Air Development Center.

Britcher, R.N., and J.E. Gaffney, Jr., 1985: Reliable Size Estimates for Software Systems Decomposed as State Machines. *Proceedings of COMPSAC 1985,* IEEE Catalog No. 85CH2221-0. Chicago, Illinois.

Brown, D., 1990: Productivity Measurement Using Function Points. *Software Engineering.*

Campbell, G.H., S.R.Faulk,and D.M. Weiss, 1990: *Introduction to Synthesis.* Version 01.00.01 INTRO_SYNTHESIS_ PROCESS-90047-N. Herndon, Virginia: Software Productivity Consortium.

Carleton, A.D. et al., 1992: *Software Measurement For DoD Systems: Recommendations For Initial Core Measures,* CMU/SEI-92-TR-19. Pittsburgh, Pennsylvania: Software Engineering Institute.

Cherng, J.G., A. Fathy,and E. Lumsdaine, 1989: Improvement of Sound Measurement Procedures Using the Taguchi Method. *Proceedings of the Seventh Symposium on Taguchi Methods.* American Supplier Institute.

Cho, C.K., 1987: *Quality Programming: Developing and Testing Software With Statistical Quality Control.* New York, New York: Wiley.

Christensen, K., G.P. Fitsos,and C.P. Smith, 1981: A Perspective on Software Science. *IBM Systems Journal* 20, 4:372-387.

Chruscicki, A.J., 1992a: *Software Quality Technology Consortium Status Report.* Rome, New York: United States Air Force Rome Laboratory.

Chruscicki, A.J., 1992b: *Personal Communication.*

Conte, S.D., H.E. Dunsmore, and V.Y. Shen, 1986: *Software Engineering Metrics and Models.* Menlo Park, California: Benjamin/Cummings.

Crosby, P.B., 1979: *Quality Is Free.* New York, New York: Mentor.

Cruickshank, R.D., 1984: Cost Relationships in Simulator Software Development. *Summer Computer Simulation Conference.* Boston, Massachusetts.

Cruickshank, R.D., 1985: *Code Growth Factors for Software Development,* SSCE 85-0138. Manassas, Virginia: IBM Federal Systems Division.

Cruickshank, R.D., 1988: *A Course in System and Software Cost Engineering.* Manassas, Virginia: IBM Federal Systems Division.

Cruickshank, R.D., and J.E. Gaffney, Jr., 1980: *Software Design Coupling and Strength Metrics. NASA Annual Software Engineering Workshop.* Greenbelt, Maryland: National Aeronautics and Space Administration, Goddard Space Flight Center.

Cruickshank, R.D., and J.E. Gaffney, Jr., 1991a: *The Economics of Software Reuse,* SPC-91128-MC. Herndon, Virginia: Software Productivity Consortium.

Cruickshank, R.D., and J.E. Gaffney, Jr., 1991b: *An Economics Model of Software Reuse, Conference on Analytical Methods in Software Engineering Economics.* McLean, Virginia: MITRE Corp.

Cruickshank, R.D., and J.E. Gaffney, Jr., 1992: *A Software Cost Model of Reuse Within a Single System, Conference on Analytical Methods in Software Engineering Economics.* McLean, Virginia: MITRE Corp.

Cruickshank, R.D., and M. Lesser, 1982: An Approach to Estimating and Controlling Software Development Costs. *The Economics of Data Processing.* New York, New York: Wiley.

DeMarco, T., 1982: *Controlling Software Projects.* Englewood Cliffs, New Jersey: Yourdon Press.

Department of the Army Communications-Electronics Command, 1991: *Executive Management Software Metrics Guidebook,* SPS-EMSM-00391. Ft. Monmouth, New Jersey: U.S. Army Communications-Electronics Command.

Department of Defense, 1985: *Technical Reviews and Audits for Systems, Requirements, and Computer Programs,* DOD-STD-1521B. Washington, D.C.: Department of Defense.

Department of Defense, 1988: *Defense System Software Development,* DOD-STD-2167A. Washington, D.C.: Department of Defense.

Department of Defense, 1991a: *Department of Defense Instruction* 5000.2.Washington, D.C.: Department of Defense.

Department of Defense, 1991b: *Work Breakdown Structure for Software Elements,* MIL-HDBK-WBS.SW (1 October Draft). Washington, D.C.: Department of Defense.

Department of Defense, 1992: *Software Quality Program,* MIL-STD-2168A (Draft). Washington, D.C.: Department of Defense.

Department of Transportation Federal Aviation Administration, 1991: *Software Quality Metrics,* DOT/FAA/CT-91/1. Atlantic City, New Jersey: Department of Transportation, Federal Aviation Administration.

Deutsch, M.S. and R.R. Willis, 1988: *Software Quality Engineering.* Englewood Cliffs, New Jersey: Prentice-Hall.

Fenton, N.E., 1991: *Software Metrics, A Rigorous Approach.* London, England: Chapman and Hall.

Freiburger, K. and V.R. Basili, 1979: *The Software Engineering Laboratory Relationship Equation,* TR-769. College Park, Maryland: University of Maryland Computer Science Center.

Gaffney, J.E., Jr., 1981: Metrics in Software Quality Assurance. *Proceedings of the ACM '81 Conference.* Los Angeles, California.

Gaffney, J.E., Jr., 1982: A Macroanalysis Methodology for Assessment of Software Development Costs. *The Economics of Data Processing.* New York, New York: Wiley.

Gaffney, J.E., Jr., 1983: Approaches to Estimating and Controlling Software Costs. 1983 *International Conference of the Computer Measurement Group,* CMG XIV. Washington, D.C.

Gaffney, J.E., Jr., 1984a: On Predicting Software Related Performance of Large-Scale Systems. *1984 International Conference of the Computer Measurement Group,* CMG XV. San Francisco, California.

Gaffney, J.E., Jr., 1984b: Estimation of Software Code Size Based on Quantitative Aspects of Function (With Application of Expert System Technology), *Journal of Parametrics* 4, 3:23.

Gaffney, J.E., Jr., 1986: The Impact on Software Development Costs of Using HOLs. *IEEE Transactions on Software Engineering* 12, 3:496-499.

Gaffney, J.E., Jr., and R.D. Cruickshank, 1991a: *Code Counting Rules and Category Definitions/Relationships,* CODE_COUNT_RULES-90010-N. Herndon, Virginia: Software Productivity Consortium.

Gaffney, J.E., Jr., and R.D. Cruickshank, 1991b: The Measurement of Software Product Size: New and Reused Code. *Third Annual Oregon Workshop on Software Metrics.* Silver Falls, Oregon.

Gaffney, J.E., Jr., and R.D. Cruickshank, 1992: A General Economics Model of Software Reuse. *14th International Conference on Software Engineering.* Melbourne, Australia: IEEE.

Gaffney, J.E., Jr., and C.F. Davis, 1988: *An Approach to Estimating Software Errors and Availability,* SPC-TR-88-007. Herndon, Virginia: Software Productivity Consortium.

Gaffney, J.E., Jr., and T.A. Durek, 1991: Software Reuse—Key To Enhanced Productivity; Some Quantitative Models. *The Economics of Information Systems and Software.* Oxford, England: Butterworth Heineman.

Gaffney, J.E., Jr., and J. Pietrolewicz, 1990: An Automated Model for Software Early Error Prediction (SWEEP). *Thirteenth Minnowbrook Workshop on Software Engineering.* July 24-27, 1990. Blue Mountain Lake, New York.

Gaffney, J.E., Jr., and R. Werlin, 1990: *A Model for Analysis of Scale Economies and Software Productivity.* ANALYSIS_PROJECT_DATA-90018-N. Herndon, Virginia: Software Productivity Consortium.

Gaffney, J.E., Jr., and R. Werlin, 1991: *Estimating Software Size From Counts of Externals, A Generalization of Function Points,* SPC-91094-N. Herndon, Virginia: Software Productivity Consortium, and ISPA'91, New Orleans, Louisiana.

Gilb, T., 1988: *Principles of Software Engineering Management.* New York, New York: Addison-Wesley.

Goel, A.L., 1980: Software Error Detection Model With Applications. *IEEE Transactions on Software Engineering* 1, 243-249.

Goel, A.L., 1985: Software Reliability Models: Assumptions, Limitations, and Applicability. *IEEE Transactions on Software Engineering* 11, 12:1411.

Grady, R.B., and D.L. Caswell, 1987: Software Metrics: *Establishing a Company-Wide Program.* Englewood Cliffs, New Jersey: Prentice-Hall.

Grady, R.B., 1992: *Practical Software Metrics: For Project Management and Process Improvement.* Englewood Cliffs, New Jersey: Prentice-Hall.

Graybill, F.A., 1961: *An Introduction to Linear Statistical Models,* Volume I. New York, New York: McGraw-Hill.

Halstead, M.H., 1977: *Elements of Software Science.* New York, New York: Elsevier North Holland.

Hancock, W.C., 1982: Practical Application of Three Basic Algorithms in Estimating Software Systems Costs. *The Economics of Data Processing.* New York, New York: Wiley.

Humphrey, W.S., and W.L. Sweet, 1987: *A Method for Assessing the Software Engineering Capability of Contractors,* CMU/SEI-87-TR-23. Pittsburgh, Pennsylvania: Software Engineering Institute.

Humphrey, W.S., D.H. Kitson, and T.C. Kasse1989: *The State of Software Engineering Practice: A Preliminary Report,* CMU/SEI-89-TR-1. Pittsburgh, Pennsylvania: Software Engineering Institute.

IEEE, 1988: *Draft Guide for the Use of Standard Dictionary of Measures to Produce Reliable Software,* P982.2/D6. New York, New York: Institute of Electrical and Electronics Engineering.

IEEE, 1990: *Draft Glossary of Software Engineering Terminology,* P729/610.12/D8. New York, New York: Institute of Electrical and Electronics Engineering.

IEEE, 1992: *Standard for Software Productivity Metrics,* P1045. New York, New York: Institute of Electrical and Electronics Engineering.

Jones, C., 1986: *Programming Productivity.* New York, New York: McGraw-Hill.

Jones, C., 1990: *Cost Estimation for Software Development.* Wokingham, England: Addison-Wesley.

Jones, C., 1991: *Applied Software Measurement.* New York, New York: McGraw-Hill.

McCabe, T.J., 1976: A Complexity Measure. *IEEE Transactions on Software Engineering* 12, 4:308-320.

McCall, J.A., 1979: An Introduction to Software Quality Metrics. *Software Quality Management.* New York, New York: Petrocelli.

Musa, J.D., A. Iannino, and K. Okumoto, 1987: *Software Reliability Measurement, Prediction, Application.* New York, New York: McGraw-Hill.

Myers, G.J., 1975: *Reliable Software Through Composite Design.* New York, New York: Petrocelli/Charter.

National Aeronautics and Space Administration, 1990: *Managers Handbook for Software Development,* Revision 1, SEL-84-101. Greenbelt, Maryland: National Aeronautics and Space Administration, Goddard Space Flight Center.

Norden, P.V., 1970: Using Tools For Project Management. *The Management of Production.* Baltimore, Maryland: Penguin.

Norden, P.V., 1958: Curve Fitting for a Model of Applied Research and Development Scheduling. *IBM Systems Journal.*

Paulk, M.C., B. Curtis,M.B. Chrissis, 1991: *Capability Maturity Model for Software.* CMU/SEI-91-TR-24. Pittsburgh, Pennsylvania: Software Engineering Institute.

Putnam, L.H., 1978: A General Empirical Solution to the Macro Software Sizing and Estimating Problem. *IEEE Transactions on Software Sizing* 4, 4:345-361.

Putnam, L.H., 1990: Personal Communication.

Radice, R.A., and R.W. Phillips, 1988: *Software Engineering: An Industrial Approach,* Volume I. Englewood Cliffs, New Jersey: Prentice-Hall.

Rifkin, S. and C. Cox, 1991: *Measurement in Practice,* CMU/SEI-91-TR-16. Pittsburgh, Pennsylvania: Software Engineering Institute.

Rock, D. and D. Guerin, 1992: Applying AI to Statistical Process Control. *AI Expert* 7, 9:30-35.

Schultz, H.P., 1988: *Software Management Metrics,* ESD-TR-88-001/M88-1. Bedford, Massachusetts: MITRE Corporation.

Selby, R.W. andV.R. Basili, 1991: Analyzing Error-Prone System Structure. *IEEE Transactions on Software Engineering* 17, 2:141-152.

Shooman, M.L., 1983: *Software Engineering: Design, Reliability, and Management.* New York, New York: McGraw-Hill.

Tausworthe, R.C., 1982

Staffing Implications of Software Productivity Models, TDA Progress Report 42-72. Pasadena, California: Jet Propulsion Laboratory.

Walston, C.E. andC.P. Felix1977

A Method of Programming Estimation and Management. IBM Systems Journal 16, 1:54-73.

Weber, C.V., M.C. Paulk, C.J. Wise, and J.V. Withey1991

Key Practices of the Capability Maturity Model, CMU/SEI-91-TR-25. Pittsburgh, Pennsylvania: Software Engineering Institute.

Weiss, D.M., 1981

Evaluating Software Development by Analysis of Change Data, TR-1120. College Park, Maryland: University of Maryland Computer Science Center.

BIBLIOGRAPHY

Basili, V.R., and D.M. Weiss. "Evaluating Software Development by Analysis of Changes: Some Data From the Software Engineering Laboratory." *IEEE Transactions on Software Engineering* SE-11, 2 (1985).

Bratman, H., and T. Court. "The Software Factory." *IEEE Computer,* 1975.

Cruickshank, R.D., and J.E. Gaffney, Jr. *Progress in Software Sizing Methods,* SSCE 84-0141. Manassas, Virginia: IBM Federal Systems Division, 1984.

Cusumano, M.A. *Japan's Software Factories: A Challenge to U.S. Management.* New York: Oxford University Press, 1991.

Davenport, T.H., and J.E. Short. "The New Industrial Engineering: Information Technology and Business Process Redesign." *Sloan Management Review* 11-27 (1990).

Defense Science Board. *Report of the Defense Science Board Task Force on Military Software.* Office of the Under Secretary of Defense for Acquisition. Washington, D.C., 1987.

Dijkstra, E.W. "Notes on Structured Programming." In *Structured Programming.* Edited by O.J. Dahl, E.W. Dijkstra, and C.A.R. Hoare. New York, New York: Academic Press, 1972.

Fagan, M. *Design and Code Inspection and Process Control in the Development of Programs,* TR-21.572. IBM System Development Division, 1974.

Fagan, M. "Design and Code Inspections to Reduce Errors in Program Development." *IBM Systems Journal* 18, 3 (1976):182-207.

Fagan, M. "Advances in Software Inspections." *IEEE Transactions on Software Engineering* SE-12, 7 (1986):744-751.

Florac, W.A. *Software Quality Measurement: A Framework for Counting Problems and Defects,* CMU/SEI-92-TR-22. Pittsburgh, Pennsylvania: Software Engineering Institute, 1992.

Gaffney, J.E., Jr. "Software Metrics: A Key to Improved Software Development Management." *Proceedings, 13th Symposium on the Interface.* Pittsburgh, Pennsylvania (1981):211-220.

Gaffney, J.E., Jr. An Economics Foundation for Software Reuse, SW_REUSE_ECONOM-89040-N. Herndon, Virginia: *Software Productivity Consortium, and AIAA Computers in Aerospace Conference,* Monterey, California, 1989.

Gilb, T. Planguage. Working draft available from author, 1989.

Goethart, W.G., E.K. Bailey, and M.B. Busby. *Software Effort & Schedule Measurement: A Framework for Counting Staff-Hours and Reporting Schedule Information.* CMU/SEI-TR-92-21. Pittsburgh, Pennsylvania: Software Engineering Institute, 1992.

Grady, R.B. "Measuring and Managing Software Maintenance." *IEEE Software* (1987): 35-45.

Hon, S.E., III. "Assuring Software Quality Through Measurements: A Buyer's Perspective." *Journal of Systems and Software* 13 (1990):117-130.

Humphrey, W.S. Characterizing the Software Process: A Maturity Framework. *IEEE Software* 73-79 (1988).

Humphrey, W.S. *Managing the Software Process.* Reading, Massachusetts: Addison-Wesley, 1989.

Kuo, B.C., "Automatic Control Systems." Englewood Cliffs, New Jersey: Prentice-Hall.

Lanphar, R. "Quantitative Process Management in Software Engineering, A Reconciliation Between Process and Product Views." *Journal of Systems and Software* 12 (1990):243-248.

Mills, E.E. *Software Metrics. SEI Curriculum Module SEI-CM-12.-1.1.* Pittsburgh, Pennsylvania: Software Engineering Institute, 1988.

Parnas, D.L. "On the Design and Development of Program Families." *IEEE Transactions on Software Engineering* SE-2 (1976):1.

Pfleeger, S.L., and C. McGowan. "Software Metrics in the Process Maturity Framework." *Journal of Systems and Software* 12 (1990):255-261.

Poston, R.M. "Preventing Most-Probable Errors in Requirements." *IEEE Software* (1987):81-83.

Putnam, L.H., and A. Fitzsimmons. "Estimating Software Costs." *Datamation,* 1979.

Quenouille, M.H. *Associated Measurements.* London: Butterworth's Scientific Publications, 1952.

Robinson, W.N. "Negotiation Behavior During Requirement Specification." *Proceedings of 12th International Conference on Software Engineering.* Nice, 1990.

Schulmeyer, C.G., and J.I. McManus. *Handbook of Software Quality Assurance.* New York, New York: Van Nostrand Reinhold, 1987.

U.S. House of Representatives, Committee on Science, Space, and Technology. *Bugs in the Program: Problems in Federal Government Computer Software Development and Regulation.* Staff study by the Subcommittee on Investigations and Oversight. Washington, D.C.: U.S. Government Printing Office, 1989.

U.S. Secretary of Defense. Total Quality Management (TQM) Program. Letter from Secretary of Defense to Secretary of the Navy, 1987.

Werling, R. "Action-Oriented Information Systems." *Datamation,* 1967.

Werling, R. "Tailoring Information to Your Firm's Decision Models." *Proceedings, 1984 International Conference on Computer Capacity Management.* Sunnyvale, California: Institute for Information Management, 1984.

Werling, R. *Final Report: Data Collection System for Estimating Software Development Cost.* Prepared for USAF Business Research Management Center, AFBRMC/RDCB, Wright-Patterson AFB, Ohio, under Contract F33615-85-C-5123, 1986.

INDEX